JACKSONVILLE

"First Coast Enterprises" by
Judy Moore

Produced in Cooperation with the
Jacksonville Chamber of Commerce

Windsor Publications, Inc.
Northridge, California

To Lee and Char and Tim

CONTENTS

PROLOGUE

The place that is now called Jacksonville was once the farthest outpost of Western civilization, when a little band of French Huguenots arrived on the shores of the St. Johns River with a mission to establish New France in the New World. The Frenchmen failed in their mission, falling to Spanish swords in bloody battles up and down the east coast of La Florida, but they left a legacy of spirit that endures. It is a legacy that sees hardship as challenge, failure as opportunity. It is a spirit of adventure and daring, of risk-taking and enthusiasm, combined with a deep sense of pride in and appreciation for the astounding natural beauty of this place.

The Spanish and French saw La Florida as a sun-blessed Paradise, a Garden of Eden. For the Timucua, who had inhabited the land long before its European conquerors, the place was an enchanted land, where messages from the gods were received in the form of a blue jay's call, an owl's mournful cry, the sudden whiplash of a snake in the path. The land was holy—its herbs and flowers imbued with the sacred power of healing, and it was treated with great respect. This, too, is our heritage.

After 200 years of dominance by Spain, the English claimed the prize of East Florida as the spoils of the French and Indian War. The English built the King's Road from

The Atlantic Intracoastal Waterway passes through Nassau, Duval, and St. Johns counties, presenting countless photo opportunities as well as a protected way to travel by small boat between Florida and the Northeast. Photo by Judy K. Jacobsen

New Smyrna north to the Narrows of the St. Johns, where the river curved seaward. The Indians had called the Narrows *Wakka Pilatka,* meaning cow ferry, and the British translated the term into "the Cow Ford," though strictly speaking, the fording of the river by cows was impossible because of its depth at the Narrows. At the Cow Ford, they established a ferry crossing to the north bank, where the King's Road forked, one branch heading west toward the Apalachee region, the other extending northwest to the St. Marys River. Because it was so strategically located, the Cow Ford grew into a thriving trade center, a sturdy little frontier outpost.

When political unrest began to threaten British rule in the American colonies, the Cow Ford became the site of a historic meeting between British East Florida Governor Patrick Tonyn and Chief Long Warrior and Chief Pumpkin King of the Creek nation, during which the Creeks agreed to help defend the territory against American rebels in Georgia.

After the outbreak of the American Revolution, British loyalists streamed into East Florida, and effigies of John Hancock and Samuel Adams were hanged and burned in St. Augustine's public square. With the Tories came scores of colorful pirates, outlaws, and opportunists whose exploits have become the stuff of enduring local legends and whose names continue to be echoed in the place-names of modern Jacksonville.

The name of the most famous of these scoundrels has survived in McGirts Boulevard and McGirts Creek (now officially the Ortega River). Dan McGirtt (the second *t*

was dropped for the place-names) was a turncoat Revolutionary soldier who fled his regiment after an altercation with his commanding officer over a horse. He escaped to Florida, where he joined the British East Florida Rangers and led torch raids through the South Georgia countryside. When the war ended he established headquarters on the banks of a tributary of the St. Johns in what is now Ortega and became the leader of a band of outlaws who preyed upon the British, Americans, and Spanish alike. Captured by the British just before they ceded East Florida back to Spain in 1783, he was later sent to Havana for trial, but the Spanish released him on his promise to stay out of Florida. Of course he came back, and legend has it that he took up with the daughter of an Indian chief, who provided members of his tribe for McGirtt's Banditti. He was captured and imprisoned at the Castillo de San Marcos, but escaped with the help of his Indian princess and was brought, pale and emaciated, back to his beloved point to die in her arms. What actually happened is that McGirtt was packed off to the Bahamas, where he managed to ingratiate himself to the Governor, Lord Dunsmorel, and two years later he was back in Florida with an official passport from the royal governor, where he continued his famous exploits. (McGirtt did have a wife, and his son, Daniel McGirtt, Jr., later requested and was granted permission to open a dance school in St. Augustine!)

But Dan McGirtt was just one of the rugged individualists whose spirits imbue this place. Another was John Houston McIntosh, who entertained Aaron Burr at his plantation on Fort George Island, plotted with Thomas Jefferson and James Madison to seize East Florida for the United States, and led a Patriot army against the Spanish. Though he and his followers formed a government of the East Florida Republic and he got himself elected president, McIntosh's Patriot revolution was ultimately unsuccessful.

It was finally Andrew Jackson whose two invasions of Spanish Florida persuaded Spain to cede the Floridas to the United States in 1821. The following year Americans living at the Cow Ford laid out a town of 20 blocks and named it in honor of Major General Jackson. Later the General, as President of the United States, returned the favor, selecting his namesake town in Florida as an official port of entry.

But East Florida remained a relatively untamed territory of adventurous spirits, and detractors of the little frontier town were fond of quoting a favorite couplet: "Start a cow thief where you will, he'll bend his way to Jacksonville."

Reluctant to pay taxes, most Jacksonville residents opposed statehood, and only 31 voted for it in the statewide referendum, to 174 votes against. But statehood was approved by the rest of the territory's voters, and on March 3, 1845, Florida entered the Union, only to secede with the rest of the Southern Confederacy 16 years later. Jacksonville was occupied four different times by Union forces, but survived the war and Reconstruction to become "The Winter Capital" of the United States.

Jacksonville in the 1870s was *the* winter destination of sun-seekers from Northern climes, and a host of luxury hotels sprang up in the city to accommodate them—the Grand National, the St. James, the St. Marks, the Windsor. Most of these elegant hostelries opened around Thanksgiving and closed around Easter, and the winter season offered a nonstop glittering social whirl of dances and parties, excursions and picnics, and evenings at the Park Opera House, which presented entertainment almost every night—vaudeville shows, comic operas, band concerts—for, as a contemporary newspaper writer lavishly observed, "a city without a social side would be like champagne without the pop, the bubbles, the effervescence and the sparkle." Jacksonville's own brand of bubbly was made from wild oranges, and the tourists reportedly found it "palatable enough."

The poet Sidney Lanier, a frequent winter visitor, described a typical scene during the city's tourist season: *Bay Street, the main business street of the city, is a lively enough thoroughfare of a winter's morning. The curious visitors are trooping everywhere along the sidewalks—to the post office, to the fruit-stores, to the palmetto braiders, to the curiosity shops (where they may purchase such items as sea-beans, alligators' teeth, plumes of herons and curlews' feathers, cranes'-wings, angel-fish, mangrove and orange walking canes, coral branches, coquina figurines, etc.), to the wharf for a sailboat, to the fizzing steamboats for a trip up the St. Johns or the Oklawaha. The merchants and shop-keepers are all busy. Along with the noises of traffic comes the hum of the lumber-mills; fitly enough, for the latter are said to conduce no little to the prosperity of the former.*

Tourism, commerce, manufacturing—all were important components of turn-of-the-century Jacksonville—a flourishing little town gaining respectability and even fame as a prime destination in the fledgling southernmost state.

But even with its new respectability, Jacksonville retained vestiges of its wild reputation as the jumping-off place for filibustering vessels bound for Cuba with illegal arms and ammunition for the rebels in the months prior to the outbreak of the Spanish-American War. Among the famous filibusters was Napoleon Bonaparte Broward, later to become governor of Florida, and the writer Stephen Crane, who signed on as an "able seaman" for the voyage of the ill-fated *Commodore*, which sank off the coast of Daytona Beach. Crane's fictional account of his shipwreck ordeal, *The Open Boat*, has become a classic of American literature.

The Great Fire of 1901, begun when sparks from a family cookstove ignited moss fibers at the Cleveland Fibre Factory, left the grand hotels in ashes, along with most of downtown Jacksonville. (Miraculously, the town's "red-light district" along Ward Street was spared—some say because an army of firemen rushed to protect the popular "sporting houses.")

After the devastation, architects from the North poured into town to help rebuild the city. Among them was a young disciple of Louis Sullivan and Frank Lloyd Wright named Henry John Klutho, who modified his mentors' Prairie School style to fit the demands of the Florida environment and designed public buildings and residences that are still among the city's finest. Towering 10 stories high, his Bisbee Building on Forsyth Street was the state's tallest building, and his St. James Building, erected on the site of the St. James Hotel, was built with a "fast-track" method of construction more than half a century before it became a common practice in the building industry.

The city that rose from the ashes of the Great Fire was designed not as a winter playground, but as a year-round commercial center, and within a few years it had fulfilled its destiny, becoming The Gateway City to a burgeoning Florida.

Most of the tourists now stopped in Jacksonville just for overnight, then headed farther south to the playgrounds of the Gold Coast. But Jacksonville was developing as a transportation hub, a distribution center for the entire Southeast. Its trains carried people and freight, its highway system was praised by larger cities, and its port was always busy.

By the second half of the twentieth century Jacksonville was a leading financial and commercial center, but the same pioneer spirit that had energized its early settlers led civic leaders to attempt a daring experiment in municipal government—the combining of city and county governments into a new unitary system. Consolidation took effect in 1968, creating a strong mayor/council system, unified police and fire departments, and, at 841 square miles, the largest-in-

area city in the nation. Most civic leaders now see consolidation as one of the most significant events in Jacksonville's history. The city became known as the Bold New City of the South, and was charged with a new enthusiasm, a new spirit of adventure that has continued through two decades and sparked the growth of the entire region.

Today Jacksonville is the capital of Florida's First Coast, which comprises Baker, Clay, Duval, Nassau, and St. Johns counties. There have been many "firsts" in this region's colorful history. Undoubtedly, there will be many more.

—Peggy Friedmann

The Florida Theatre has been restored to its original Roaring 20s grandeur and is the site for major entertainment presentations, both inside the theater and out. Photo by Judy K. Jacobsen

Dawn spreads over Florida's First Coast and downtown Jacksonville. In the foreground is The Jacksonville Landing, and at center is the Main Street Bridge. Photo by Judy K. Jacobsen

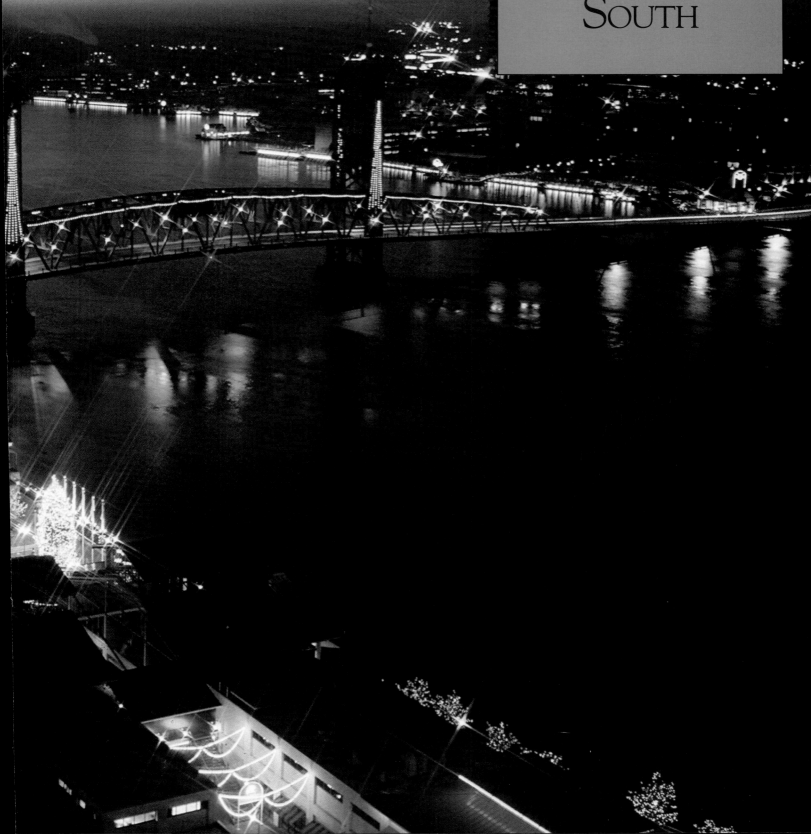

This is an artist's rendering of one of the British attacks on the Spanish at St. Augustine. Courtesy, Port of Jacksonville Authority

CHAPTER 1

UNDER MANY FLAGS

...

History

The Floridians have a kind of herb dried, who with a cane and earthen cup on the end, with fire—doe suck through the cane the smoke therof, which smoke satisfieth their hunger

JOHN HAWKINS

Above: Pedro Menéndez de Aviléz, the founder of St. Augustine and conqueror over René de Laudonnière at Fort Caroline in 1565. Courtesy, Port of Jacksonville Authority

Right: Jacques le Moyne was the official cartographer of the Laudonnière expedition and this is his map of the area the French called Florida. He visited only the lower St. Johns River (River of May) area and so only that part of the map is accurate, the rest being drawn from other maps and hearsay. Courtesy, Fort Caroline National Monument

That was how English sea captain John Hawkins described tobacco and the pipe the Timucua Indians used with that "kind of herb dried." He had seen a few Indians as well as French Huguenots in mid-summer 1565, when his four-ship flotilla called at the Fort Caroline settlement near the mouth of the St. Johns River to replenish its water supply. Hawkins' tale and the tobacco he took with him on his return to England was his countrymen's introduction to tobacco and pipe smoking.

Ironically, most of the French colonists, who came here with Rene de Laudonniere and Jean Ribault, were already dead by the time Hawkins was able to spread the word of this latest wonder of the New World. The French, who were undertaking the first serious attempt to colonize what is now the United States' Atlantic coast, had been wiped out by a Spanish force led by Pedro de Menendez de Aviles. Only days before the battle, Menendez had begun to establish an outpost at St. Augustine.

The Spanish triumph came about in part because of a bad turn in the weather. Ribault had just returned to Fort Caroline with a relief expedition from France. The colonists, having been dependent upon the Timucua Indians for food, were demoralized and near starvation because most of the Indians had abandoned them. They were making ready to abandon Fort Caroline and return to France.

Eight days after Ribault's return to Fort Caroline, Menendez and his ships appeared at the St. Johns. The Spanish commander ordered the French out as trespassers on Spanish territory. He cited Ponce de Leon's claim to Florida, made 52 years earlier (1513) when he landed at Mantanzas Bay. The next day, Menendez and his force returned to Matanzas Inlet and set up the permanent camp that became St. Augustine.

At Fort Caroline, Ribault told the ailing Laudonniere he would sail after Menendez and destroy the new settlement. Laudonniere

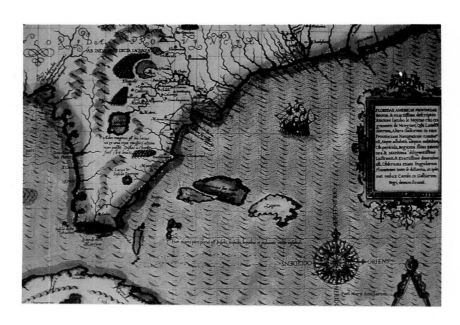

advised him to wait until after a storm that was brewing had passed by, but Ribault turned a deaf ear and set sail with virtually all the able-bodied men. A hurricane broke on Ribault's fleet, which was driven past Matanzas Inlet and wrecked somewhere on what is now the Daytona Beach-Ormond Beach shore.

Fort Caroline was defenseless. Menendez, who saw the French ships being blown past Matanzas Inlet, that night marched his 500 men through the storm to the fort and attacked at dawn on September 20. The battle was short and the Spanish won, losing no one. Laudonniere and a few of his men escaped to French ships and sailed to safety. The rest of the men were put to death. Some of the women and children were spared, but their ultimate fate is unknown.

Less than two weeks later, Menendez found some of Ribault's men on Anastasia Island and killed all but a handful. Finally, on October 12, 1565—Columbus Day—Ribault and the remaining French surrendered on Anastasia Island, but were massacred. France's efforts to hold sway in Florida ended and Spanish rule was assured.

Ribault had first set foot in Florida three years earlier and had erected a monument to his landing. He claimed the land for France and Charles IX. When Laudonniere returned with his colonists in 1564, he found the Timucuans worshiping at the monument, which was located on a bluff overlooking the St. Johns River.

The Indians prepared the land for cultivation by first making a hoe from fish bones and attaching them to wooden handles. After raking the light, sandy soil the women made small holes and planted seeds. Courtesy, Fort Caroline National Monument

The Timucuan Indians carried on a never-ending battle against alligators. Their lookout would call when he saw an alligator come ashore to find food. The hunters would ram a pole, small end first, down the alligator's gullet, then throw it over on its back to attack its soft underbelly. Courtesy, Fort Caroline National Monument

With Laudonniere was Jacques le Moyne, an artist whose watercolor portrayal of the French and Indians at the monument is one of the hallmark early paintings depicting America, its peoples, and their customs. Le Moyne was one of the few who was able to flee to safety with Laudonniere. Many of the artist's other works are of the Timucua Indians; they provide a vivid and detailed record of Indian life along the St. Johns River.

Shortly after Georgia was established in 1733, the Spanish attacked the British in the Brunswick-St. Simons Island area but were driven off. Several years later, the English attacked St. Augustine, but withdrew after the failure of a three-month siege. The St. Marys River became the de facto boundary between Spanish Florida and English Georgia when both sides were unable to extend their hegemony beyond the river.

The Spanish may have assured their rule over Florida, but they did little with it. Two years short of two centuries after the Fort Caroline massacre—when they lost Florida to England at the end of the French and Indian War in 1763—there were only two permanent settlements in East Florida: St. Augustine and St. Marks, the latter located almost due south of Tallahassee at Apalachee Bay. When Spain gave up Florida, virtually all the Spaniards abandoned their homes and holdings, and sailed to Havana, Cuba.

The English tried to settle Florida, but they had little success in advertising for settlers in East Florida. By 1771 the census showed only 288 whites and 900 blacks in all of East Florida, which lay east of the Apalachicola River. That contrasted sharply with increases in settlement in West Florida, stretching from Pensacola to Mobile, Alabama.

Finally, the English brought in 1,500 settlers from Greece, Italy, and Minorca (an English possession by virtue of the 1763 settlement) to found New Smyrna. They established the King's Road by improving and widening original Indian trails. The road went from New Smyrna to St. Augustine, on up to the Cow Ford at the St. Johns near where Liberty Street now meets the river in downtown Jacksonville. King's Road then split, one branch going northwest to the St. Marys River and Georgia, the other breaking off to the west around Hemming Plaza toward present-day Lake City.

Above: Indian villages were usually located near a stream so water could be diverted. The chief's dwelling was in the center, and, to ward off heat, was partly situated underground. The village was occupied nine months of the year and empty during the three winter months while the tribe went into the woods for warmth. Courtesy, Fort Caroline National Monument

Left: This is a contemporary artist's conception of one of the British attacks on St Augustine, and what the Castillo de San Marcos looked like in the early eighteenth century. Courtesy, Port of Jacksonville

At the end of the Revolutionary War, England lost more than her 13 colonies. She ceded East and West Florida back to Spain, which did little more in its 40 remaining years of control than it had done in its original 200. In its last years, Spain issued many land grants in northeastern Florida and unwittingly encouraged the growing Americanization of the area. Many Americans secured land grants; others simply ignored the international boundary and settled in northern Florida.

Fernandina, according to legend a pirates' outpost, was a Spanish port through which slaves were brought for illegal entry into the United States. Congress was outraged at the port's involvement in the slave trade. President Thomas Jefferson had halted the importation of slaves during his administration, and to cut off the trade, Congress in 1811 secretly authorized President John Madison to annex northeast Florida.

Madison sent General George Mathews, who was joined by John Houston McIntosh, a Fort George Island planter. McIntosh set up a short-lived East Florida republic and was elected its president. When Madison heard about that development and threats by Mathews and McIntosh against St. Augustine, he called off the adventure and apologized to Spain.

The United States acquired Florida from Spain in 1821 in settlement of claims and General Andrew Jackson was named territorial governor. When the two dozen residents of the Cow Ford, led by Isaiah D. Hart, decided to establish a town in 1822, they named it in the general's honor. Settlements in the vicinity of the new town—Ortega, St. Johns Bluff, San Nicholas, and Fort George—totaled around 200 people.

The first settler in what is now downtown Jacksonville had been Robert Pritchard in 1791. But Pritchard did not live long, and his heirs eventually abandoned the land grant before Florida became American territory.

The eighteenth-century Cow Ford had been that and little more for many years. In 1821, William G. Dawson and Stephen E. Buckles, who operated a log-house store on the north side of the ford, had a frame boardinghouse built. When Mrs. Sarah Waterman took charge with her six children, the settlement's population doubled.

During the Spanish-American War, Jacksonville Beach, then known as Pablo Beach, was an encampment area. Here, the Third Nebraska Volunteers drill at the beach. Courtesy, Beaches Area Historical Society

By 1830, the town's population was estimated at 100, and two years later Jacksonville was incorporated, becoming the ninth incorporated town in Florida. Both Fernandina Beach and St. Augustine were incorporated before Jacksonville.

By the mid-1840s, although Jacksonville was still smaller than St. Augustine, its docks had become the center of trade for East Florida. Cotton—the biggest cash crop in the area—and timber were brought to waiting ships at Jacksonville's port.

During the Civil War, Jacksonville was occupied four different times by Union forces between 1862 and the end of the war in 1865. The one major Civil War battle was fought in 1864 at Olustee (or Ocean Pond) in present-day Baker County, and was part of an effort to establish a loyalist state government and return Florida to the Union. Against orders, a Union general moved on the Confederates and his troops were routed.

After the battle, the Confederate forces mined the St. Johns, and three federal vessels were sunk in less than two months. Part of the wreckage of one ship, the *Maple Leaf*, still lies on the river bottom off Mandarin Point.

Early in the war, Union forces seized and fortified Fort Clinch at the mouth of the St. Marys River at Fernandina Beach. By the end of the war, Jacksonville was nearly devastated, having been sacked and burned by both sides.

The city undertook reconstruction, and by 1870, despite Reconstruction-style governments, it was recognized as a premier winter resort, with its eight hotels filled each season. The railroad had reached Jacksonville in 1860 from Lake City, then known as Alligator Town, but even before that Northerners had begun to winter here. Almost all arrived by ship, though some venturesome souls braved tortuous overland treks. By the end of the 1870s, the city's tourist trade quadrupled with each winter.

It wasn't until 1881 that Jacksonville and Savannah, Georgia, were linked by rail. Despite the connection, it still took three to four

During the 1864 Union occupation of Jacksonville, several gunboats operated on the St. Johns River. During one of its forays upstream, the gunboat Columbine *was attacked from the shore near Horse Landing by Confederate forces under Captain J.J. Dickison. The gunboat was eventually captured. Courtesy, Jacksonville Chamber of Commerce*

Above right: During the Civil War Jacksonville was occupied four times by Union troops. This photo, of buildings at Ocean and Bay streets, was taken circa 1862. Courtesy, Jacksonville Chamber of Commerce

Above left: Typical of sidewheelers which plied the St. John's River in the nineteenth century is the Darlington, launched at Charleston, S.C., in 1849. It was captured by Union forces in March of 1862 and returned to civilian service in 1866. It sailed until 1874. Courtesy, Jacksonville Chamber of Commerce

days to get from New York to Jacksonville by train. Southern railroads were not converted to standard gauge until just 100 years ago. By then, the time between Jersey City, New Jersey, and Jacksonville was cut to 29.5 hours.

Regular steamship lines were set up, and paddlewheelers plied the St. Johns River as far as Enterprise, 200 miles south of Jacksonville on Lake Monroe and on the other side of the river from Sanford. Resort hotels of various sizes and quality opened all along the St. Johns, and the river became an important artery for commercial traffic.

Resort hotels were expanded and new ones were built. In 1884-1885, an estimated 60,000 tourists wintered in Jacksonville. In 1885, Henry M. Flagler began building the plush Ponce de Leon Hotel in St. Augustine. To make the hotel accessible to tourists, he organized what eventually became the Florida East Coast Railway and began laying track along the roadbed of an old narrow-gauge line.

Henceforth, St. Augustine's role as a resort and tourist attraction was established. Jacksonville's businessmen did not realize it, but the St. Augustine hotels and especially the sun-seeking railroad would spell an end to the town's role as a winter resort.

In 1888 Jacksonville staged a Sub-Tropical Exposition, which celebrated the city's port status and its links with the Caribbean. The fair attracted many visitors, including President Grover Cleveland and his wife, Frances, and was repeated annually for several years.

Shortly after the first exposition closed, the dreaded yellow fever struck the city. This was not the first epidemic, but it was the most serious. The city was put under quarantine and virtually cut off from the country. Government all but ceased to function.

St. Augustine postal authorities refused to accept mail from Jacksonville, even though it had been fumigated. Waycross, Georgia, residents threatened to tear up the railroad tracks to keep Jacksonville residents away; steamship lines cut off service. It was not until a frost hit in late November, killing the disease-spreading mosquitoes, that the epidemic ended.

Just as Jacksonville's future seemed brightest, disaster struck again in 1901. The "Great Fire" wiped out most of the downtown district—

Left: Among the railroads that Henry M. Flagler bought to establish his Florida East Coast Railway Co. was the St. Johns Railway Co., which operated from 1858 until 1895. This is one of the Porter locomotives that was used on the St. Johns. Courtesy, Jacksonville Chamber of Commerce

almost 2,400 buildings on more than 400 acres—and left 10,000 people homeless. The bulk of city and county government records were destroyed, and for a while local government operated out of a tent.

By the time the city had completed rebuilding, the rest of the state had passed it by. Flagler's railroad had been extended to Palm Beach and eventually to Miami (ultimately, to Key West). Cold snaps convinced Northern snowbirds to travel farther south.

From the earliest days of Florida's statehood, Jacksonville's location marked it as a gateway city. Its harbor was better than St. Augustine's, and it was much closer by water to the industrial Northeast and Europe than was west coast Tampa on the Gulf. It was the closest Florida city to the North for those Northerners who first braved the long railroad ride in the winter months.

Thus, because of its location, Jacksonville became the first resort city in Florida, later a city for business, wholesaling, and transshipment. When travel became easier in the twentieth century and Jacksonville had lost all of its winter resort status, it still retained its role as a business and distribution center and developed in a unique fashion for a Florida city.

Jacksonville's role as a tourist center also suffered when many of its grand hotels destroyed in the 1901 fire were not rebuilt. The most noted of these was the St. James Hotel, on the north side of St. James

Below: The City of Jacksonville, seen here from a painting in 1905 by Antonio Jacobsen, was built in Wilmington, Delaware, in 1882 and remained in service until 1933. It was destroyed by fire in 1952 while it was serving as a restaurant moored at the Intracoastal Waterway and Atlantic Boulevard. Courtesy, Jacksonville Chamber of Commerce

Park, now Hemming Plaza. According to one Northern visitor in the 1870s, "the chances are strong that as one peeps through the drawing-room windows on the way to one's room, one will find so many New York faces and Boston faces and Chicago faces that one does not feel so very far from home." After the Great Fire the famous hotel was replaced by the St. James Building, which housed Cohen Brothers Department Store (later May Cohens). Another popular hotel, the Windsor Hotel, which also faced St. James Park, was rebuilt and enjoyed a long life, not closing until 1950.

In 1907, the city bought 300 acres at Black Point and gave the land to the state to build Camp Joseph E. Johnston, a troop training center. Other purchases utilized federal funds, and about 1,000 acres were secured. The first state troops used the camp in 1909, and during World War I the camp became a quartermaster training post. When the federal government complained about drunkenness among the troops, Duval County voters responded by making their county "dry." A generation later, the site of Camp Johnston became the nucleus for Naval Air Station Jacksonville.

In 1908, the fledgling film industry first moved into Jacksonville as crews from the North sought warmer weather for wintertime shooting. At that time, New York was the nation's film capital, and only Los Angeles had ever heard of Hollywood.

The heyday of Jacksonville's film industry was 1910 to 1916. During that time, moviemakers were establishing their basic techniques and learning how to plot and shoot a story. Comedy was the main film vehicle, and Oliver Hardy got his start in Jacksonville (joining up with Stan Laurel after the movies left town).

Some of the techniques of the early moviemakers caused concern among the local citizenry. Studios occasionally turned in false alarms so they could shoot scenes of fire equipment racing along the streets. A director saved the cost of hiring extras for a crowd scene by putting a bogus help-wanted ad in the paper.

The town fathers eventually became so disenchanted with the movie industry that they made life difficult for the studios, condoning

The Great Fire of May 3, 1901, filled the sky with smoke and ashes. This was taken from Springfield, probably in the vicinity of Phoenix Avenue. Courtesy, Port of Jacksonville Authority

the merchants' practice of raising prices on goods and refusing them credit. The industry even became a campaign issue in 1917, and Mayor J.E.T. Bowden, who had encouraged expansion of filmmaking in Jacksonville, was defeated. Two weeks later, construction was halted on a studio complex that would have rivaled Universal City in Los Angeles, and the moviemakers packed off for Hollywood. Jacksonville's film days were ended, except for a short renewal of work in 1919 and 1920.

But others were moving into Jacksonville, as new travel routes were being opened on land and on water. In 1910 the inland waterway, precursor of the Atlantic Intracoastal Waterway, was opened between St. Augustine and the St. Johns River. A few months later, Atlantic Boulevard was completed. It linked South Jacksonville with Mayport Road, eventually continuing on to Neptune Beach.

The Atlantic Boulevard project, considered to be the start of highway development in Florida, had been in the works since 1884 when a beach developer proposed a road to Pablo Beach (now Jacksonville Beach). Much of the grading was done in the 1890s by convicts, but the project stalled and was abandoned. It was revived in 1906 with the advent of auto races at Atlantic Beach. A partially completed road carried traffic after 1908.

World War I brought heavy work to Jacksonville shipyards, which were pressed into service to build vessels. The first ship was launched May 30, 1918, by Merrill-Stevens Shipbuilding Corporation. Other shipyards were J.M. Murdock Company, Morey & Thomas, St. Johns River Shipbuilding Company, and A. Bentley & Sons Company. In all, 25 ships were built under wartime contracts.

The 1920s brought the city unprecedented growth. Downtown construction, which had ceased during the Great War, was resumed, and residential development began anew in many parts of the city.

This major construction cycle had started in 1911 when the Florida Life Insurance Company built its 11-story building on Laura Street between Forsyth and Adams. It later became the Florida National Bank Building. The 15-story Heard Building opened in 1913 at the corner of Laura and Forsyth streets, and the 12-story Mason Hotel was completed the same year at Bay and Julia streets. The 11-story Rhodes-Futch-Collins Building went up on Main Street between Duval and Monroe streets. It opened in 1914, to complete an emerging pre-World War I skyline.

In the 1920s, downtown construction resumed with the construction of the Barnett National Bank, the Atlantic National Bank, the S.A. Lynch Building, and the George Washington Hotel. Downtown docks were full, and ships came and went with almost every tide. Plans were afoot to reclaim the empty shipbuilding yards on the south side of the St. Johns, opposite downtown.

But in 1928, prosperity began to falter in Jacksonville, although construction and shipments through the port continued to be strong into 1929. Nevertheless, there was growing distress among those at the

Pictured here is Forsyth Street, looking east from Hogan Street before the outbreak of World War I in 1914. At left is the Duval Hotel, the Post Office tower, and the Atlantic Bank building. Across the street is the Seminole Hotel, which was completed in 1910. Courtesy, Jacksonville Chamber of Commerce

lower end of the economic scale, and relief projects were instituted before the end of the decade.

With the start of the 1930s, Jacksonville slid into the Great Depression along with the rest of the country. The city's problems were multiplied by the fact that Florida was in the midst of its own depression, brought on by overspeculation in the mid-1920s land bubble. Still, the city would have been in worse condition but for the fact that the bubble was not as big as the boom farther south in the heart of the tourist country.

Local evidence of the 1920s bubble exists in neighborhoods such as San Jose, where both The Bolles School and San Jose Country Club began life as the posh San Jose Hotel complex and where Alfred I. du Pont built his Epping Forest estate. A few two-story stuccoed homes built in San Jose during that period are readily identifiable.

By the start of World War II, Jacksonville had developed into a distribution center and a working port with miles of docks. Its deepwater facilities and strategic location had attracted the attention of the U.S. Navy, which was looking for additional training facilities in the southeastern part of the country. In Duval County voters approved a $1.1 million bond issue to pay for a gift of land at Black Point, the old Camp Johnston, as the nucleus for what has become Naval Air Station Jacksonville. Some of the bond money also was used to buy land at Ribault Bay in Mayport for an anchorage and antisubmarine patrol base; Mayport Naval Station is the result. Cecil Field, 10 miles west of NAS Jacksonville, was established during World War II.

After the war, it was predicted by some that the Navy's installations would be mothballed, but instead Mayport's basin was dredged for capital ships and became the home base for two aircraft carriers, today the *Saratoga* and the USS *Forrestal*. Cecil Field was designated one of four Navy master jet bases, becoming a key airfield and home base for half of the Atlantic-based fleet aircraft. The Navy also added a

Forsyth Street is seen here from Laura Street in the years immediately following the Great Fire of 1901. The buildings seen in the background, at left, are the Duval Hotel, the Post Office, with its post-fire ornate tower, the Knights of Pythias' Castle Hall, and pillared National Bank of Jacksonville, predecessor of Barnett Bank. Courtesy, Jacksonville Chamber of Commerce

munitions depot at Yellow Water, northwest of the field. NAS Jacksonville became the base for regular antisubmarine patrols off the Southeast coast, as well as the site of an aircraft rehabilitation center—the Naval Air Rework Facility—now known as the Naval Aviation Depot. The city's enduring partnership with the U.S. Navy had been firmly established.

During the postwar years, Jacksonville blossomed into a leading financial center. Barnett Banks of Florida, the state's largest bank, was headquartered in Jacksonville, as was Florida National Banks of Florida and the Atlantic National Bank. At the same time, locally based life insurance companies began to grow, offering policies with reasonable weekly and monthly terms to area residents. Independent Life and Gulf Life were two of those prospering firms. American Heritage Life, the third-largest insurance firm based in the city today, was founded in 1956.

In the 1950s, Prudential Life of America decided to locate its Southeast regional home office in Jacksonville, a decision considered by many to have heralded the beginning of modern Jacksonville, establishing the city as the Insurance Capital of the South. The giant Prudential was the largest nationwide company ever to choose Jacksonville as the site of its major regional headquarters. Just as significant was the fact that Prudential decided to put its office building not downtown, but across the river, in the Southside, spurring the growth of that area of the city.

In spite of the growth of banking and insurance interests, Jacksonville's growth in the early postwar years lagged behind that of the rest of Florida. The port underwent significant changes as downtown piers and warehouses were closed and abandoned and the main port area

The Continental Hotel at Atlantic Beach was opened in 1901 as part of Henry M. Flagler's chain of Florida resort hotels. It burned down in 1919. Courtesy, Jacksonville Chamber of Commerce

Following the Great Fire of 1901, the Windsor Hotel at the west side of Hemming Park was rebuilt. This view was taken only a few years after the hotel reopened in 1902. It finally closed in 1950. Courtesy, Jacksonville Chamber of Commerce

moved downstream to the Talleyrand docks. The old docks were filled in and became parking lots, designed to meet the demand for downtown offstreet parking. The railroad tracks connecting Union Station to the downtown docks were pulled up, and that land eventually became the site of what is now the CSX building.

During the 1960s, Jacksonville was hit by the catastrophic hurricane Dora. Its citizens suffered an even more devastating blow when the county's public high schools were disaccredited by the Southern Association of Colleges and Schools.

Stung by the increasing evidence of governmental ineptitude, a group of citizens led by Claude J. Yates, president of the Jacksonville Chamber of Commerce, met in January 1965 to seek ways to remedy a situation that had become crucial to the well-being of their community. In a one-sentence proposal, they offered a solution: the consolidation of city and county governments. Known as the Yates Manifesto, the proposal read:

We, the undersigned, respectfully request the Duval County delegation of the Florida Legislature to prepare an enabling act calling for the citizens of Duval County to vote on the consolidation of government within Duval County to secure more efficient and effective government under one governmental body.

It was two more years before the requisite bargaining and politicking produced the plan for consolidation and finally the vote, which took place August 8, 1967. The proposal carried almost two to one.

County government has all but disappeared into city offices. The city has a strong mayor-council form of government. There is one fire department, one police department under an elected sheriff, and one health department. Officials of the new government were elected in November 1967 and took office on March 1, 1968.

Residents of Baldwin, to the west, and the three Beaches municipalities voted to remain independent of consolidated government, though they voted in favor of allowing Jacksonville and the rest of the county to consolidate.

At the same time, the school system worked to regain accreditation. Four high schools were reaccredited at the end of 1968, five more in 1969, and two in 1970. By 1977, all the county's schools, both elementary and secondary, had been accredited. From the disgrace and shame of disaccreditation, Duval County's public school system became and remains the largest fully accredited program in the nation.

Between the end of World War II and consolidation, government buildings made up a large measure of the downtown construction. hey included the county Courthouse and the City Hall next door, the Civic Auditorium, the Veterans Memorial Coliseum, and the Federal Office Building on West Bay Street, built in 1967. The late Haydon Burns, who served five terms as pre-consolidation mayor of Jacksonville, was elected governor of Florida in 1963. His campaign relied heavily on "The Jacksonville Story" and the slogan, "Burns Builds."

After the first Prudential building went up, private sector construction included the Atlantic Coast Line Building (now CSX) in 1960, Florida National Bank in 1961, and Barnett National Bank of Jacksonville in 1962. The first of the modernistic office towers, Gulf Life on the Southbank, was completed at the end of 1967.

Above: This photo shows Bay Street circa 1880, with the St. Johns River and wharves in the background. Courtesy, Jacksonville Chamber of Commerce

Left: Jacksonville and the St. Johns River in 1892 are seen here shortly after Henry M. Flagler's single-track railroad swing bridge, in center background, was completed. Courtesy, Jacksonville Chamber of Commerce

Automobile parking was allowed right on the beach at Jacksonville until the 1970s. The tower at right marks the Red Cross lifeguard station. This photo dates from the mid-1960s. Courtesy, Beaches Area Historical Society

Consolidation produced a new outlook for Jacksonville, and in a few years, the city experienced unprecedented growth. The political climate had changed markedly. Before consolidation, there was constant conflict between City Hall and the business interests represented by the Chamber of Commerce, but that atmosphere of hostility began to change into a partnership for the common good.

In 1979, Jake M. Godbold was elected mayor. His candidacy had been opposed by much of the business community, and many of the city's leaders feared the worst. But Albert Ernest, Jr., president of the Chamber of Commerce, led a delegation that pledged to support Godbold. If the mayor would lead, then the business community would follow, Ernest said. Godbold led, and the business comunity lived up to its word.

Huge glass-sheathed towers began to be built downtown: Independent Life and Atlantic Bank in 1975; later came buildings for Southern Bell, Florida National Banks of Florida, SunBank, and Southeast Bank. Prudential built a new three-building complex near its original Southbank headquarters.

Other areas of the city blossomed. At Southpoint, once a dairy farm along Butler Boulevard at Interstate 95, eight miles from downtown, contemporary office buildings appeared. A mile to the south, Baymeadows Road shopping strips and light industrial parks opened, seemingly overnight.

The city discovered that the St. Johns River and its banks were great places for recreation. Metropolitan Park was created out of abandoned docks near the Gator Bowl. By the mid-1980s the Southbank Riverwalk opened. A year later, The Jacksonville Landing, a festival marketplace, opened on the Northbank.

The city grew because of its quality of life. Businesses liked Jacksonville and moved in; new neighborhoods flourished, both in older parts of the city and in new areas; golf courses and tennis courts were built; THE PLAYERS Championship and the PGA TOUR moved to Sawgrass, built its own golf course, and the Sawgrass-Ponte Vedra area exploded with upscale housing. Even more people moved in, attracted by quiet neighborhoods, pleasant living, and affordable housing throughout the city.

The University of North Florida, which had opened in the 1960s, expanded its academic scope from two to four years. Florida Community College at Jacksonville completed construction of four major campuses and opened additional instructional centers throughout the city. Jacksonville University constructed a new business school building, with grants from Davis family foundation gifts. Edward Waters College, founded in 1866, continued to operate as a liberal arts institution with a predominantly black student enrollment.

The Navy added to its Mayport-based fleet and expanded NAS Jacksonville operations. Mayo Clinic opened in 1986; Joslin Diabetes Clinic in 1987; Nemours Foundation began construction of a major children's clinic; and University Hospital became a teaching hospital.

The old railroad station was converted into a convention center, and Omni Hotels opened a 300-room hotel downtown. Construction of an Automated Skyway Express began, linking the convention center to downtown. Proposals were made to redevelop another portion of the downtown waterfront where the courthouse, jail, and parking lots stand.

Construction began on a new downtown tower for American Heritage Life, and there was talk of plans to convert the old building into luxury apartments. Ground was broken for a Barnett Bank building downtown that would become the tallest building in the city. Construction of golf courses and housing developments continued.

When Jake Godbold took office in 1979, it was as though all that had passed in the 415 years since Jean Ribault's landing at the mouth of the St. Johns River was merely a prologue.

Jacksonville's time in the sun had come.

This is Downtown Jacksonville and its waterfront circa 1935. Construction had not yet begun on the Main Street Bridge, which opened in 1941. Courtesy, Jacksonville Chamber of Commerce

The St. Johns River reflects the afternoon sun. In the foreground is the Fuller Warren Bridge, at right center the highrises at Winter Point. Photo by Richard Kevern

CHAPTER 2

THE RIVER AND THE CITY

...

Downtown Redevelopment

The train comes to a stop on the wharf: as one steps from the car, one hears a pleasant plash among the lily-pads underneath the platform, and, lifting the eyes at this suggestion of waters, perceives the great placid expanses of the St. Johns stretching far away to the south and east.

SIDNEY LANIER
1875

33

The re-creation of Fort Caroline along the banks of the St. Johns River is under the care and jurisdiction of the National Park Service of the U.S. Department of the Interior. It is on the south bank of the St Johns River, near the reproduction of the French monument claiming the land for King Charles IX and France. The actual site of the fort is believed to have been washed away by the river a century ago. Photo by Richard Kevern

The short-lived sixteenth-century French Huguenot colony at Fort Caroline was located on the St. Johns River because the river was deep and the anchorage was protected from rough seas. This same rationale is also serving as the catalyst for today's renaissance in the city's downtown.

The Timucua Indians used the narrows of the river in the present downtown as their crossing point. Early white settlers set up a ferry there and called the crossing Cow Ford, though they actually ferried their cattle across because the river is far deeper than a true ford.

As the city grew, the St. Johns River continued its domination, providing the means for oceangoing ships to sail into the heart of the city and make Jacksonville a major Atlantic seaport.

Today the city rises from the banks of the river as an impressive cluster of skyscrapers and a latticework of bridges, its skyline mirrored in the waters. Jacksonville is here because of the river. Since the beginning, the St. Johns River and the settlement that was to become Jacksonville have been locked in a symbiotic relationship. The river has provided sustenance and recreation, and has been a busy thoroughfare and a quiet retreat.

There was a time when respect for the river was low, when acres of its downtown banks were bulkheaded, filled, and asphalted over for parking lots. Its waters were polluted with sewage and chemical waste.

Today the city knows the river as a thing of beauty, and as the poet John Keats wrote,

> *A thing of beauty is a joy forever*
> *Its loveliness increases.*

In fact, a new appreciation of the St. Johns River as a source of pleasure is the driving force behind downtown redevelopment.

Metropolitan Park, a mile east of downtown and next to the Gator Bowl complex, was the first recreational site to be developed along the river. Carved from a tangle of weeds and abandoned docks, it was an immediate success when it opened in 1984, and its popularity has continued to increase. It is the site of the annual Jacksonville Jazz Festival, which is sponsored by the public television and radio stations WJCT-Channel 7 and Stereo 90, whose state-of-the-art studios are next to the park.

The St. Johns River City Band, a local brass and woodwind ensemble, offers free Sunday concerts from April through October under the Florida National Pavilion, recalling a century-old tradition of brass band concerts in the city park.

The Southbank Riverwalk, a wide-plank boardwalk completed in 1986, meanders 1.2 miles along the riverbank from the Duval County Board of Education Building to Friendship Park. The result of efforts to clean up the river's Southbank, the Riverwalk makes the river accessible to the public.

Hydroplane races were inaugurated on the St. Johns River downtown in 1987. Photo by Richard Kevern

Right: The Riverwalk along the Southbank at the Jacksonville Hotel in downtown Jacksonville is seen here. Photo by Richard Kevern

Below: Light clouds and a bright sky are reflected in a Southpoint office building. Recently planted palm trees are silhouetted in front of the building. Photo by Richard Kevern

The Riverwalk furnishes many places for yachts and small craft to tie up. It offers riverside restaurants, parks, shops, and a marina, as well as brightly painted pavilions suitable for picnicking.

The Jacksonville Landing, opened in mid-1987, has given a new dimension to urban living in Jacksonville. Developed and operated by the Rouse Company, which has similar successful marketplaces in other major cities, The Landing offers a mix of upscale retail and gift shops, food shops, restaurants, and walk-up food stands. Entertainment is offered regularly in the central courtyard, open to the river, and The Landing has its own dock.

The opening of The Landing, coupled with heavy use of the Riverwalk on the opposite bank, has spawned river taxi services linking the banks. The water taxis are especially popular with patrons going back and forth between The Landing, the Omni Hotel, Metropolitan Park on the Northbank, and the several restaurants and two hotels (Sheraton at St. Johns Place and the Jacksonville Hotel) on the Southbank.

There already exists a riverwalk of sorts along most of the downtown Northbank. It is a concrete sidewalk along the river's edge, protected from the river by a heavy concrete railing. The railing is sturdy enough to allow ships to tie up, especially along the two-block stretch across Coast Line Drive from the Courthouse and City Hall parking lots. Both the Navy and U.S. allies occasionally send vessels up the St. Johns River to tie up at the downtown quay so that residents can tour the ships. The sidewalk extends from the Jacksonville Shipyards west to the CSX building, which occupies the site of the old railroad docks.

Jacksonville has always set precedents in skyscraper design for Florida, a state whose shifting sand and high water tables provide slippery footing for such giants. Young Henry John Klutho attracted considerable attention in 1912 with his Florida Life Tower, which soared 11 stories to dominate the Jacksonville skyline. It is still stand-

Above: Country singer Charlie Daniels is seen here in concert at the Florida Pavilion in Metropolitan Park. Photo by Judy K. Jacobsen

Left: Clowns and other entertainers are part of the regular fare at the Jacksonville Landing. Photo by Judy K. Jacobsen

Presenting a study in horizontals are the Florida National Bank Building, the Omni Hotel, at left, and the Southern Bell Building in the background. Photo by Kelly LaDuke

ing as part of the NCNB National Bank Building, with its broad "Chicago" windows and elaborate ornamentation in the pier capitals.

In 1913 the 15-story Heard Building was the state's tallest; in 1955 it was the Prudential Insurance Company's regional office tower, a true skyscraper at 22 stories. When the 27-story Gulf Life Tower opened in 1967, it was not only the tallest building in Florida but the tallest pre-cast post-tensioned concrete structure in the world.

The disastrous Great Fire of 1901, which wiped out more than 400 acres of the city including most of downtown, marked the beginning of modern Jacksonville. There have been five distinct periods of development in the central city since then. First was immediate rebuilding from the fire's ashes and rubble, a major effort lasting through about 1905. Then came 10 years of new growth, which produced the beginnings of the modern skyline, including several buildings of 10 or more stories.

Construction stopped during World War I, but resumed in the 1920s, resulting in several 15- to 20-story buildings. The Depression halted growth once more, beginning a hiatus that was to last until the end of World War II.

The 1950s were marked by the addition of public buildings, including the present City Hall and Courthouse, the Veterans Memorial Coliseum, and the Civic Auditorium.

Construction of the original Prudential Insurance Company Building (now called One Prudential Plaza) in 1955 signaled the coming of the modern business age in Jacksonville. The Seaboard Coastline Building (now CSX) was completed in 1960; the Gulf Life Tower in 1967.

The latest period of downtown development is the "Billion Dollar Decade" of the 1980s, with new towers dominating the skyline. Paragon Group is building a 42-story downtown Barnett Center, which will serve as headquarters for Barnett Banks. Rouse and Associates expects its second Jacksonville Center skyscraper to be about the same height. (The first, which will be anchored by American Heritage Life Insurance Company, is now under construction.)

Additions of the 1980s include the 30-story Southern Bell tower, the largest office building in the city; the Jacksonville Landing; Sun Bank Building; the Jacksonville Chamber of Commerce; and the first

Below: Red plumes of water at Friendship Fountain frame the Gulf Life Tower on the Southbank. Photo by Bill Hennefrund

Bottom: Friendship Fountain at the west end of the Southbank's Riverwalk, with Prudential Plaza Two in the background are seen here. Photo by Richard Kevern

A fountain in front of 111 River-side Plaza completes its geometric forms with its water jets. Photo by Richard Kevern

two buildings in Faison Associates' Enterprise Center—the Florida National Bank tower and the Omni Hotel.

Independent Square, the city's landmark and tallest building to date, was completed in 1975, as was the First Union building. At the western edge of downtown in the beginnings of the Riverside district, The Haskell Company opened its riverfront headquarters building in 1986. The building is the first of three planned for the site.

Wilma Southeast, an Atlanta-based development firm, is negotiating with the city concerning the largest single project ever proposed in Jacksonville—the $500-million Renaissance Place, which would be located on the site of the present Duval County Courthouse and jail.

Wilma is proposing to build both high- and low-rise office buildings, retail space in an enclosed mall, a hotel, a performing arts center, and parking facilities. The company has already begun development of a separate industrial/warehouse/office project, the $350-million Jacksonville International Tradeport located on 100 acres next to Jacksonville International Airport. It, too, has a 10-year completion date.

Jacksonville was founded on the north side of the St. Johns River, and until the 1950s most of the growth was on the north and west sides. Southside growth was inhibited because of the lack of a vehicular bridge. Only the Florida East Coast Railway bridge and ferries crossed the river prior to construction of the Acosta Bridge in 1921.

The construction of the Acosta Bridge set the stage for serious development of the Southside. The addition of the Main Street Bridge in 1941 increased accessibility and ended the ferries' operation.

Today there are five bridges crossing the river from the downtown area. The Fuller Warren Bridge is several hundred yards south of the Acosta Bridge and carries Interstate 95 through traffic. Two high-level toll bridges are the Hart Bridge, which links the Gator Bowl area to the Southside at Atlantic and Beach boulevards, and the Mathews Bridge, which links the Gator Bowl to Arlington at Arlington Expressway.

The Main Street and Acosta bridges are toll free and both are lift bridges. The Fuller Warren Bridge is a toll bascule span. The State of Florida is completing plans to replace the Acosta Bridge with a fixed span. Designed to carry at least six lanes of traffic, it also has a reserved width for the possible extension of the Automated Skyway Express

This American Airlines worker checks to see all is in order before flight. Photo by Richard Kevern

Below: Angles, patterns and light distinguish the downtown bridges. They are the Florida East Coast railroad bridge in lower foreground, St. Elmo Acosta Bridge, upper foreground, and Main Street Bridge, lower background. Photo by Richard Kevern

Facing page, top: Prehistoric skeletons are among the exhibits at Jacksonville's Museum of Science and History at the west end of the Southbank Riverwalk. Photo by Richard Kevern

Facing page, bottom: A mime shows off her craft at Hemming Plaza. Photo by Judy K. Jacobsen

mass transit system. Contracts for the new Acosta Bridge are expected to be awarded in 1989 and 1990, with completion expected by 1994.

Development parallels the river along both banks. Property values have increased dramatically near the river, especially since the opening of The Landing, demonstrating the commercial potential of the downtown waterfront.

Joining the Southbank skyline in recent decades were the Sheraton at St. Johns Place, the Jacksonville Hotel, the IBM Building, the 1300 Building, the Southeast Bank Building, and the stunning Prudential Plaza Two.

The Museum of Science and History, next to Friendship Park, opened a major new addition in the fall of 1988; Florida East Coast Industries is constructing DuPont Center, a set of four-story office buildings between St. Johns Place and I-95; and Baptist Medical Center continues to expand. It soon will be joined by the Nemours Foundation, which will build a children's clinic on the other side of Interstate 95. It will be linked to Baptist by monorail.

Among the most controversial of recent projects is the Automated Skyway Express, the first .7-mile phase of which is nearing completion. It is sponsored and funded mainly by the U.S. Department of Transportation, in conjunction with the Jacksonville Transportation Authority, the City of Jacksonville, and the Florida Department of

Transportation. It will run between the Prime F. Osborn III Convention Center and Enterprise Center, three-quarters of a mile away, its cars moving on an elevated concrete guideway.

The original line will cost $30 million, of which the federal government is paying $23 million. Proposed additions would cost another $100 million. There is no firm source of funding yet, though Washington has authorized funds for some planning of extensions.

The Wilma Southeast proposal to redevelop the present government center area has set off relocation proposals for the Courthouse, jail, and City Hall.

A group of downtown merchants and developers has proposed moving City Hall to the St. James Building on the north side of Hemming Plaza. The building, constructed after the 1901 fire, replaced the famed St. James Hotel with Cohen Brothers department store, later renamed May Cohens. May Florida closed its Hemming Plaza location in 1987 after about 85 years there and moved all of its retail operations to suburban malls. It was the last major department store in the old retail heart of the city. In mid-1988 Maison Blanche, Incorporated, based in Baton Rouge, Louisiana, bought May Florida.

At Christmastime in 1987, the first year The Landing was open and the downtown May Florida was closed, The Landing was heavily patronized and Hemming Plaza shops saw a serious downturn in trade.

Jacksonville City Hall. Photo by Richard Kevern

Facing page: Huddled low along the Northbank downtown is the Civic Auditorium, with the fly loft standing high above its roof. At right is the distinctive Florida National Bank Building. Photo by Richard Kevern

The proposal to move city offices to Hemming Plaza has the two-fold purpose of freeing the present site for redevelopment and adding it to the tax rolls, and of bringing potential customers to the Hemming Plaza area—city employees and persons who have business to conduct at City Hall.

Several proposals exist for use of the riverfront Daniel Building if state offices now located there are moved. They include conversion to use as the Jacksonville Art Museum and/or the downtown campus of the University of North Florida.

Three major theaters are presently located downtown, two of them in the Civic Auditorium, which opened in 1962. A highlight of the 1980s was the restoration of the third theater, the Florida Theater, a 1,900-seat 1920s Mediterranean style vaudeville and movie house.

Another triumph of recent years was the conversion of the abandoned 1919 Union Terminal into the handsome Prime F. Osborn III

Top: Jacksonville's Union Station, once in danger of being torn down, has been restored, renovated, and recycled to become the Prime F. Osborn III Convention Center. Photo by Richard Kevern

Above: The former waiting room of Union Station is now one of the many meeting rooms in the Prime Osborn Convention Center. Photo by Kelly LaDuke

Convention Center. It was cited by Omni Corporation officers as one of the main reasons they decided to locate an Omni Hotel in downtown Jacksonville. The facility opened in 1986 with the exhibit of the Ramses II artifacts and jewelry from Egypt's Cairo Museum. The hotel has been operating near capacity since it opened in the fall of 1987.

Recent studies have demonstrated the feasibility of downtown housing. One proposal calls for the present American Heritage Life Building at Main and East Forsyth streets to be converted into condominium units after American Heritage moves into its new building at Jacksonville Center, probably in 1989.

KBJ Architects, in a general study of the downtown area, recently proposed the creation of residential "superblocks" at the northern fringes of downtown where several highrises for the elderly already exist. The plan calls for closing some streets; townhouse and multistory buildings would ring the perimeter of the superblocks, allowing for the creation of a park within.

Another proposal for providing housing close to downtown involves rehabilitation of the LaVilla and Brooklyn neighborhoods adjoining downtown on the west, to take advantage of the Victorian styling of many of the homes. Linked with that proposal is a plan to restore and redevelop the Ritz Theater and the surrounding district on Davis Street into an art, restaurant, and entertainment district.

In 1984, an initiative known as Florida's First Coast 2005—a Regional Vision, developed overall objectives for the entire First Coast area. In 1987, those objectives were updated in a First Coast planning conference report, which urged further downtown revitalization efforts so that "continuing private sector investment in downtown Jacksonville will create a lively, around the clock atmosphere, including additional quality hotels, commercial/professional offices, expanded retail shopping, day/night dining, movie theaters and live entertainment as well as middle- and upper-income residential development."

Jacksonville's downtown district is moving in that direction. But even as new towers are changing the face of Jacksonville's skyline, some of their older neighbors are being restored to recapture the flavor and charm of the city's past. Henry Klutho's Dyal-Upchurch Building, built just after the Great Fire, was renovated in 1981 and stands at the corner of Main and Bay streets among the towering giants. Klutho's Carnegie Library Building at Adams and Ocean Street now serves as law offices for the firm of Bedell, Dittman, DeVault and Pillans, and KBJ Architects makes its home in the old Porter Mansion, one of the most impressive local survivors of the Victorian era.

Jacksonville has come to appreciate not only the natural treasure of the river, but also the man-made treasures of its past—and both will continue to be valued as the city grows.

At sunset, lights shine along the Riverwalk, while across the St. Johns River downtown's towers march across the landscape, led by Independent Square at right. Photo by Richard Kevern

Cranes walk stiff-legged across the skyline at Jacksonville Shipyards. Photo by Richard Kevern

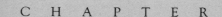

CHAPTER 3

FLORIDA'S WORKING CITY
. . .
Business and Industry

I happen to think if a man doesn't
work he's not happy. I know I'm not.
I try to keep busy.

J.E. DAVIS
FOUNDER, WINN DIXIE STORES, INC.

Low and sleek, the American Transtech building stretches along a lagoon. Photo by Richard Kevern

Jacksonville has not been a typical Florida city in the twentieth century. It has been neither a tourist mecca nor a retirement haven, though tourists come to Jacksonville and there is a significant retirement community in the city. Instead, the city has developed as a business and financial center, its citizens always busy, always working. Its location as the gateway to the Florida peninsula led Jacksonville into wholesaling and distribution, then into banking and insurance. Today, because of its location, it is becoming a regional medical center. Long a city with many small manufacturing plants, Jacksonville is also becoming a Southern playground with the opening of lavish seaside resorts, where beach activities share the spotlight with golf and tennis.

Wholesaling and distribution have taken on new meaning and direction in the city. Companies like American Transtech and Humana Health Care Plus, which use 800-number telemarketing, are emerging as economic leaders. One of Jacksonville's newest corporate citizens is American Express Travel Related Services Company, Incorporated, which, in the spring of 1988, announced plans to build a credit card operations center that will employ 1,500 people by 1990.

Jacksonville is becoming a leader in health care in the Southeast with the opening of the Mayo Clinic, the Joslin Diabetes Clinic, and the construction by Nemours Foundation of its Nemours Clinic to fight children's diseases. Nemours will operate in conjunction with

Baptist Medical Center and Wolfson Children's Hospital, and will be a teaching clinic for the University of Florida College of Medicine.

Traditional businesses and industries remain, and, in most cases, are expanding. The continuing base of civilian employment in Jacksonville and the First Coast area continues to be a diverse mixture of paper and forest products, chemicals, shipyard work, transshipping, banking, insurance, and retail and wholesale trade.

Jacksonville's unemployment rate is consistently below that of the rest of the state and the nation. In June 1988, the latest date for which figures are available, the Florida Department of Labor and Employ-ment Security reported an employed civilian labor force of 474,700, up more than 27,800, or 6.2 percent, from the June 1987 figure of 446,900. There were 24,200 unemployed, a rate of 5.1 percent of the work force. In June 1988 the state jobless rate was 4.8 percent; the national rate was 5.5 percent.

The largest private sector employer in the First Coast is Winn-Dixie Stores, Incorporated, with 5,500 employees. Founded by the Davis family, who opened their first grocery store in Miami in 1925, the Jacksonville-based company is a home-grown success story, having blossomed into the largest supermarket company in the South. South-ern Bell is next with 4,026. Other major employers include Sears, Roebuck & Company, which employs approximately 2,300; Publix

A pond and plaza in the foreground mark the entrance to Mayo Clinic-Jacksonville. Photo by Richard Kevern

The tug Ann Moran *nudges a container ship against the dock at the Port of Jacksonville. Photo by Richard Kevern*

Supermarkets with 2,513; AT&T/American Transtech with 1,200; Maison Blanche, about 1,069; Cybernetics & Systems, Incorporated, a subsidiary of CSX, 950; Revlon Professional Products, 597; J.C. Penney, 500-600; P-I-E Nationwide, 500-600; and Tompkins-Beckwith, Incorporated, Construction, 350.

The Jacksonville Chamber of Commerce lists 97 manufacturers with 100 or more employees. They range from Aetna Steel with 195 employees, to Xomed, Incorporated, with 250, to Jacksonville Shipyards with 2,000. Baroody-Spence Furniture Industries, makers of plastic furniture, employs about 80; Florida Rock & Tank Lines, Incorporated, in mining, concrete, and trucking, 70; Montgomery Industries International, makers of shredding equipment, air pollution control devices, and blow pipe systems, 50; and Moore Pipe & Sprinkler Company, makers of automatic fire sprinkler systems, 20.

After Jacksonville Shipyards, the next largest industrial employer on Florida's First Coast is also St. Johns County's largest non-governmental employer, Grumman St. Augustine with 1,290 workers. In third place is Paramount Poultry with 1,200.

Grumman St. Augustine rebuilds, refurbishes, and modifies military aircraft for the Navy, Air Force, and friendly foreign nations. Paramount Poultry, a subsidiary of the huge grain, foodstuffs, and agricultural products company Cargill, processes poultry.

Other major manufacturing employers and their work force are Florida Publishing Company, with 975; Anheuser-Busch, 850; Vistakon Incorporated, 700; Engine Products Division of Allied Bendix Corporation, 505; Container Corporation/Mill Division at Fernandina Beach, 592; Maxwell House Division of General Foods Corporation, 540; and Anchor Glass Container, 483.

There are 3,300 railroad workers in the city, including 3,000 at CSX Rail Transport, as well as 10,700 trucking and warehousing employees; 29,100 are employed in wholesale trade.

The Jacksonville Chamber of Commerce lists 188 companies that employ 100 or more persons in the First Coast area. They include such diverse enterprises as A-B Distributors in Jacksonville, whose 109 workers distribute Anheuser-Busch products; ITT Rayonier, Incorporated, which employs 430 in Fernandina Beach in cellulose and paper processing; and Taylor Concrete & Supply, Incorporated, which

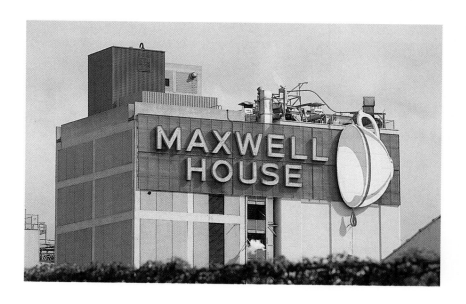

Above: Florida Publishing Company publishes Jacksonville's two major daily newspapers, The Florida Times-Union *and the* Jacksonville Journal. *Photo by KBJ Architects, Inc.*

Left: One of the largest coffee processing plants in the world is located just east of downtown Jacksonville. Photo by Richard Kevern

employs 160 in Green Cove Springs in the making and delivering of pre-mixed concrete.

The list also includes such Jacksonville business firms as Alliance Mortgage Company, which employs 461 in the preparing and servicing of mortgage loans; Koger Properties, Incorporated, (Koger Company merged with Koger Properties) which employ 550 in the development and management of suburban office parks; and Wells-Fargo Service, which employs 350 in its security service and investigations.

There are other major employers such as Amelia Island Company, which has approximately 975 at work full- and part-time operating resort and residential properties on Amelia Island; Gilman Paper Company, with 140 employees making paper products in Maxville; and Tree of Life, Incorporated, with 220 employees distributing health foods in St. Augustine.

The diversity of business and industry is one of the hallmarks of the First Coast region of Florida. It is also one of the key factors in the economic health of the region. If one segment of the economy suffers a downturn, others remain strong. Despite high employment in banking, insurance, and health care, the First Coast still has a broad base of business and industry on which to rely.

One of the most interesting manufacturing companies is Sally Industries, Incorporated, a builder of robotic characters and shows. The company creates talking figures with movable arms, heads, and bodies. There are fewer than 50 employees, but Sally Industries products are used by business, industry, and entertainment enterprises throughout the world.

Service employment is one of the fastest-growing economic segments in Jacksonville. At the end of the second quarter of 1988, the state reported 39,400 people at work in finance, insurance, and real estate, and 5,500 in banking, 15,000 in the insurance industry, 28,400

Seen here are some of the robotic characters manufactured by Sally Industries, Incorporated. Courtesy, Sally Industries, Incorporated.

The mirrored walls of Prudential Plaza Two create optical illusions. Photo by Kelly LaDuke

in health services, and 8,200 working in hotels and other lodging places.

Growth of the service industries is directly attributable to one of Jacksonville's strongest assets—a highly productive white-collar work force. Prudential Insurance Company doubled the size of its Jacksonville operations while closing offices elsewhere because of Jacksonville workers' productivity and low absenteeism. AT&T American Transtech located in Jacksonville for many of the same reasons.

Government employment, excluding the 40,000 men and women in uniform who form the largest single group of employees in the city, accounts for 58,600 positions, of which 17,600 are federal, 7,500 are state, and 33,500 are in local government, including schools and municipalities.

There are an estimated 500 black-owned businesses in the city, most of them of comparatively small size. Efforts are being made to increase the influence and strength of black businesses.

The First Coast Black Business Investment Corporation is one of six such groups in the state, funded in part by the Florida Legislature. Its lending capacity is $2.1 million. Private funds are matched by state money, which is put into a revolving loan fund. The group's purpose is to provide loans to black entrepreneurs who are unable to raise money through traditional channels.

Another venture is the Enterprise Club, which was formed in 1987. The club helps foster a working relationship between black busi-

nesses and the general business community. It is also designed to help black business owners improve their business skills and provide a networking vehicle for small-business entrepreneurs.

Because of its size, location, and the resulting diversity of its retail stores, Jacksonville is a main retail shopping city for a large section of northeast Florida and southern Georgia. In years gone by, the draw was to downtown Jacksonville, but in the modern era of superhighways and automobiles, suburban shopping malls have come to dominate retailing, as they have across the country.

The largest mall is Regency Square, with 1.1 million square feet and 173 stores at Arlington Expressway and Atlantic and Southside

With more than one million square feet under its roof, Regency Square Mall is the First Coast's biggest shopping mall. Photo by Richard Kevern

Gateway Center is one of the major malls in the Jacksonville area. Photo by Kelly LaDuke

boulevards. It is anchored by four department stores: J.C. Penney, Maison Blanche, Ivey's, and Sears, Roebuck & Company.

Next in size is the Orange Park Mall, anchored by the same four department stores. The mall has 980,000 square feet and 132 stores. It is located on Blanding Boulevard, just south of Interstate 295. Argyle Village Square Shopping Center is located near the Orange Park Mall, with 300,000 square feet and 45 stores.

Other major malls are Gateway Center with 680,000 square feet and 100 stores on the Northside at Norwood Avenue, east of I-95; Roosevelt Mall with 240,000 square feet and 50 stores on Roosevelt Boulevard on the Westside; and Market Square with 430,000 square feet and 36 stores at Phillips Highway and Emerson Avenue on the Southside.

Gateway Center is anchored by J.C. Penney and Maison Blanche. Roosevelt Mall is anchored by Maison Blanche and Steinmart. Market Square is an off-price mall anchored by Direct Furniture Factory Outlet.

Normandy Mall, at 5200 Normandy Boulevard on the Westside, is anchored by Sam's Wholesale Club, a Wal-Mart store. The mall has 416,000 square feet and 60 stores. Grande Boulevarde Mall on Baymeadows Road is anchored by Jacobson's.

In addition to the malls, there are many shopping plazas and strips throughout the First Coast area. Regency Square has attracted more than its share of plazas and strips. The bigger ones are Regency Park Shopping Center (300,000 square feet, 40 stores), Regency Court (200,000 square feet, 38 stores), and Regency Plaza Shopping Center (175,000 square feet, 21 stores). The opening of the Broward Bridge at Dames Point is expected to increase the flow of traffic into the Regency area because of the easier access from the Northside. That should mean more trade for Regency retail outlets.

Two additional malls are planned for areas near I-95 on the Southside, but it is doubtful that both will be built. May Florida, now

Maison Blanche, has agreed to anchor a regional mall known as The Avenues at Phillips Highway, I-95, and Southside Boulevard. Jordan Marsh and Burdines are planning to sign leases with Clear Lake Mall, less than five miles away at Southside and J. Turner Butler boulevards.

Retailers and real estate developers are agreed that, with metropolitan Jacksonville having less than one million residents, both malls will not be built now.

Jacksonville's communications industry includes newspapers, television and radio facilities, advertising and public relations agencies, video production firms, and printing firms. The main employer in this sector, and the most influential on the First Coast by virtue of being publisher of the area's major daily newspaper, is Florida Publishing Company, a wholly owned subsidiary of Morris Communications of Augusta, Georgia. Its newspaper, the *Florida Times-Union*, published in the morning, had a fall 1988 circulation of 159,000 on weekdays. The 101-year-old *Jacksonville Journal* closed in late October 1988.

Morris Communications also owns the *St. Augustine Record* (circ. 10,500), which is published daily except Sunday. Other daily newspapers published on the First Coast are *Clay Today*, based in Orange Park, and *Financial News and Daily Record*, which carries the bulk of the Duval County legal advertising.

There are several weekly publications. These include the *Jacksonville Business Journal*, which reports area business news; the *Beaches Leader* and its companion the *Sun Times*, which concentrate on news of the beaches, and their sister weekly, the *Mandarin News*, which covers another old but rapidly growing area of Jacksonville; the *Florida Star*, which concentrates on covering the black community as does the *Jacksonville Advocate*; *Folio Weekly* and *Southeast Entertainer*, both of which report on the entertainment scene; the *Jacksonville Register*, dedicated to Jacksonville society; and the *Ponte Vedra Recorder*, which covers Ponte Vedra, the beaches, and northern St. Johns County. There are a few others that publish intermittently or to limited audiences. All three major naval stations also publish weeklies.

Gateway Center is supported by JC Penney and Maison Blanche. Photo by Kelly LaDuke

The three network television affiliates are owned by major national communications companies. The CBS affiliate, WJXT-Channel 4, is a subsidiary of The Washington Post Company. WTLV-Channel 12, the NBC outlet, was purchased by the Gannett Company at the end of 1987 from Harte-Hanks Communications. WJKS-Channel 17, the ABC affiliate, is owned and operated by Media General, Incorporated.

Independent television stations are WAWS-TV-Channel 30, and WNFT-TV-Channel 47. WJCT-Channel 7 is the public television station.

There are more than 20 radio stations in Jacksonville; most are commercial stations. Based on 1987 reports, the leader was WAPE-FM, which airs contemporary Top-40 music. It is owned by H&G Communications.

Other stations with strong shares of the listening audience are WQIK-FM (contemporary country music), WAIV-FM (adult contemporary), WFYV-FM (album-oriented rock), WKTZ-FM (easy-listening), WCGL-AM (gospel), WIVY-FM (adult contemporary), WZAZ-AM (black urban), and WPDQ-FM (urban contemporary).

WKTZ is one of three non-commercial stations in the area. The others are WJCT-FM, public radio, and WNCM-FM, Christian contemporary.

Two magazines are published in Jacksonville: *Jacksonville Magazine,* which recently celebrated its first quarter-century of publication, is published by the Jacksonville Chamber of Commerce; and *Jacksonville Today Magazine,* which offers upbeat articles on the First Coast lifestyle.

Jacksonville's advertising and public relations field is dominated by William Cook Advertising, Incorporated, which reported 1986 capitalized billings of $56.5 million and has a local staff of 147.

Caraway Kemp Communications, Incorporated, is another major advertising and public relations firm. Its 43 local employees generated $32.5 million in 1986 capitalized billings. The third-largest firm is West & Company Marketing & Advertising, with $18.1 million in billings and 32 employees.

The audio-visual, film, and videotape production firms in the area are led by two firms: Florida Production Center with 36 employees, and Images Incorporated, with 25.

In the printing field, Miller Graphics and Financial Printing, Incorporated, are the oldest of the major firms, both founded in 1912. The two firms employ 70 and 28 people, respectively.

The largest employer in the printing field is Bill Kight's Copy Center, with 102 employees in eight offices. Other major employers are Drummond Press, Incorporated, and Stan Murphy Company, both with 70 workers.

In 1987 Jacksonville had 18 law firms with 10 or more attorneys. An important factor in the legal community is continuity of service within a community. Mahoney Adams Milam Surface & Grimsley goes back to 1854. With 40 attorneys, Mahoney Adams is the second-largest law firm in the city. Rogers, Towers, Bailey, Jones & Gay, founded in 1906, is the largest with 41 attorneys. Second-oldest among the large legal firms in the city is Bedell, Dittmar, DeVault & Pillans, which was founded in 1865 and had 11 attorneys in 1987.

Other major law firms more than 50 years old are Smith & Hulsey with 39 attorneys (founded 1936); Ulmer Murchison Ashby Taylor & Corrigan with 20 (1927); Marks, Gray, Conroy & Gibbs with 20 attorneys (1910); and Taylor, Mosley & Joyner with 10 attorneys (1906).

All of the Big Eight accounting firms are represented in Jacksonville. They are, in fact, all included among the 10 largest accounting firms in the *Jacksonville Business Journal's* 1988 *Book of Lists.* The largest is Peat Marwick, with 52 accountants.

The largest, and oldest, local accounting firm is Smoak, Davis & Nixon, with 24 accountants. Smoak Davis was founded in 1924. Other large local accounting firms are LaFaye, Hannon & Brock, with 14 accountants, and two firms with nine each, Garrard & Carter and Masters, Smith & Wisby.

The city's largest architectural firms are KBJ Architects, Incorporated, Reynolds, Smith & Hills, Incorporated, and Saxelbye, Powell, Roberts & Ponder, Incorporated.

Recent major projects of KBJ in the First Coast area include design of the Ramses II exhibit in 1986-1987; the Jacksonville Center, the first building of which is under construction for American Heritage Life Insurance Company; and the Jewish Community Alliance center in Southside.

Another major project for KBJ is a proposal for revitalizing all of downtown Jacksonville. The project calls for, among other things, establishing residential superblocks in the northeast portion of the downtown, moving City Hall to the St. James Building in Hemming Plaza, and developing a pedestrian spine and retail attractions between The Jacksonville Landing and Hemming Plaza.

RS&H projects undertaken recently include the Prime F. Osborn III Convention Center and the Paragon Group office building in the Southpoint area. Saxelbye, Powell's recent projects include the Florida National Bank Building and the Ponte Vedra Surf Club.

Other major architectural firms include the design division of The Haskell Company and Clements/Rumpel/Goodwin/d'Avi Architects Planners, Incorporated. Recent Haskell projects include Bellemeade 95 Corporate Center, The Riverside Center in St. Augustine, and the Haskell Building in Riverside in Jacksonville.

Clements/Rumpel has recently completed the renovation of the Alcazar Hotel building in St. Augustine and the Ocala Performing Arts Theater.

Among the city's engineering firms, Reynolds, Smith & Hills (RS&H) and The Haskell Company are ranked among the largest, just as they are among the architectural firms. Also among the major engineering firms are Flood Engineers Architects Planners, Incorporated,

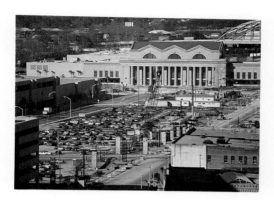

Pillars to support the Automated Skyway Express march from the Prime Osborn Convention Center in the background toward downtown, three-quarters of a mile away. Photo by Kelly LaDuke

Smith and Gillespie Engineers, Incorporated, and the Sverdrup Company.

RS&H and Sverdrup did engineering work for the new Broward Bridge; RS&H also did work for the Automated Skyway Express downtown and the Jacksonville International Tradeport. Other Sverdrup jobs include the CSX Dispatch Facility, work for the Jacksonville Port Authority, and the Navy's Kings Bay project management.

Flood Engineers projects include Southwest sewerage plants and Interstate-95 reconstruction in Duval County. Haskell projects include

the Haskell Building and Mazda Corporate Office Park Center in Southpoint. A major recent Smith and Gillespie project has been expansion of the Buckman Street sewerage treatment plant.

The leading commercial building contractors include The Haskell Company, Blosam Contractors, Incorporated, The Auchter Company, Patterson Enterprises, Incorporated, and Kimmins Corporation.

Haskell's recent projects include Office Building I at 95 Corporate Center at Southpoint, the General Foods Building, and the Holiday Inn at Commonwealth Avenue and I-295.

Beach estates line the shore in Ponte Vedra. In the background is the Ponte Vedra Golf Course. Photo by Richard Kevern

Flying panels in the three-story lobby of the 111 Riverside Plaza building, home of The Haskell Company, provide a focal point for the dramatic interior. Photo by Richard Kevern

Blosam's recent First Coast projects include Hillman Square, Lake Pointe Business Park, and Cedar Creek Landing. The jewel in The Auchter Company's crown is The Jacksonville Landing downtown. Other recent projects include the DePaul Building for St. Vincent's Hospital and Stockton Plaza.

There are 20 publicly held corporations based on Florida's First Coast, many of them banking and insurance companies. The largest is Winn-Dixie Stores, Incorporated, the supermarket chain, with a total of 80,000 employees and annual revenues of more than $8 billion. Winn-Dixie's revenues are greater than the combined revenues of all other First Coast-based publicly held companies. Banks and insurance companies on the list are Barnett Banks of Florida, Incorporated, Florida National Banks of Florida, Incorporated, Independent Insurance Group, Incorporated, American Heritage Life Investment Corporation, and George Washington Corporation.

The Charter Company, which went through bankruptcy and reorganization early in the decade, has emerged as a new company that deals mainly in petroleum products, convenience stores, and insurance.

The St. Joe Paper Company is a sugar grower and a manufacturer of paper and corrugated containers. It is also a major Florida land and forest owner and is involved in communications and transportation. St. Joe owns much of Florida East Coast Industries, Incorporated, which is based in St. Augustine and is the parent company of Florida East Coast Railroad. The bulk of the St. Joe properties were put together by the late Edward Ball, brother-in-law of Alfred du Pont and later trustee of du Pont's estate.

Closely held St. Joe Paper Company stock, very difficult to price, is even more difficult to buy, commanding a price of about $9,000 a share. It is traded over the counter.

Above left: A welder undertakes repairs on a ship in drydock at Jacksonville Shipyards. Photo by Bob Milnes

Above right: The CSX Transportation building is framed by trees and yachts at Harbormasters Marina across the St. Johns River. Photo by Kelly LaDuke

An atrium links the Florida National Bank Building and the Omni Hotel (background) in Enterprise Center. Photo by Richard Kevern

Florida Rock Industries, with revenues of $270 million, is involved in concrete and construction aggregates. The firm has 340 employees in Jacksonville.

The driving power behind Koger Properties, Incorporated, is founder Ira Koger. Koger Properties develops and builds the suburban office parks that are Koger's hallmark. Koger Company, a subsidiary, owns and operates the completed buildings. Combined, the two companies have $90 million in annual revenues.

Other publicly held real estate companies in Jacksonville are Sunstates Corporation, which deals in real estate development, sales, and management; Riverside Group, Incorporated, which deals in real

estate construction and development; and Riverside Properties, a real estate trust holding company.

One of the newest publicly held companies is Family Steak Houses of Florida, Incorporated, based in Neptune Beach and operator of several Ryan's Family Steak Houses in Jacksonville and elsewhere in Florida. Another relatively new publicly held company is Insituform Southeast, a pipeline repair company.

Mobile America Company deals in mobile office leasing and sales, insurance, and finance. Its revenues are more than $9 million annually. Jacksonville's Daylight Industries is a holding company, and Growth Fund of Florida, Incorporated, is an investment company.

A drive through Jacksonville reveals an abundance of fast-food and chain restaurants as well as convenience store outlets. They provide employment, both full- and part-time, for a large number of people. They include: Gate Petroleum Company, 2,000 employees; Southern Industrial Corporation/Burger King, 900; Huntley Jiffy Stores, Incorporated, 825; Wendcoast of Florida/Wendy's, 730; Lil' Champ Food Stores, Incorporated, 611; Famous Amos Restaurants, Incorporated, 600; Pizza Hut, 600; Popeye's Famous Fried Chicken, 500; Taco Bell, 400; Shoney's, 355; Hardee's, 350; Domino's Pizza, 300; Dairy Queen, 255; Kentucky Fried Chicken, 250; Captain D's, 250; Ponderosa Steak House, 225; Rax Restaurants, 208; R.T. Fast Food Enterprises, Incorporated/Rally's, 200. Figures were not available for McDonald's or 7-Eleven stores.

The diversity in business, industry, and employment opportunities that marks Florida's modern First Coast is so great that the economic indicators regularly register stronger than the rest of the state and the rest of the country. Jacksonville is truly Florida's Working City.

The Prudential towers stand as a
leader in insurance. Photo by
Steven Brooke

C H A P T E R   4

THE LEADERS
...
Insurance and Banking

With the favorable business climate
here and a strong work ethic,
Jacksonville appeals especially to the
quality employees we have brought
here from other places.

W. ASHLEY VERLANDER
CHAIRMAN OF THE BOARD AND
CHIEF EXECUTIVE OFFICER
AMERICAN HERITAGE LIFE
INVESTMENT CORPORATION

69

A study in lines, colors and masses is formed by the old Barnett Bank Building rising above the newer one in the foreground. Photo by Kelly LaDuke

Long a financial center, and, since 1982, headquarters for Florida's largest bank holding company, Jacksonville is also a major insurance center, The Hartford of the South. Seven of the 10 largest office buildings are bank or insurance buildings, and more than 15,000 persons are employed in the financial and insurance industries on the First Coast. (Some think that, when insurance agents are included, the figure is closer to 20,000.)

Jacksonville-based Barnett Banks of Florida is the state's largest bank holding company. Barnett rose from Florida's fifth-largest in 1965 to No. 2 by the mid-1970s, behind Miami-based Southeast Banking Corporation, and to No. 1 in deposits in 1982, and then in total assets. It has been widening its lead since then.

The Paragon Group is building Barnett Center, the $90-million Barnett corporate headquarters downtown that, at 42 stories and 593 feet, will be the tallest building in Jacksonville. It will replace the 535-

Independent Square has been Jacksonville's signature structure and its tallest building for more than a dozen years. Photo by KBJ Architects, Inc.

foot, 37-story Independent Square building, home of Independent Insurance Group, Incorporated, as the city's tallest structure. Independent Square has held this distinction since it opened in 1975. (For a while, it was also the tallest building in Florida.) Barnett employs more than 3,450 in all its First Coast and headquarters operations.

The other major Florida bank based in the city is Florida National Banks of Florida, Incorporated, which moved into its $45 million, 23-story building in Enterprise Center in 1986. Second to Barnett in size among bank holding companies based in Jacksonville, it employs 1,600. Florida National Bank has an agreement to merge with Chemical Bank of New York when federal banking laws are changed to permit such a merger.

First Union Bank of Florida, a subsidiary of First Union Corporation of Charlotte, North Carolina, is based in Jacksonville. The bank was known as Atlantic Bancorporation and was among the largest Florida-based bank holding companies when it merged in 1985 with First Union. There are nearly 1,845 employed in First Coast operations.

Other major banks include Southeast Bank N.A. with 250-275 employees, American Banks of Florida, Incorporated, with 375, and Sun Bank/North Florida N.A. with 244. Though Southeast is No. 2 in the state, it ranks fourth in Jacksonville and Duval County, behind First Union, Barnett, and Florida National Bank.

Among savings and loans, First Federal Savings & Loan Association of Jacksonville had $971 million in deposits, which comprised nearly half of all First Coast thrift deposits on December 31, 1987. First Federal provides employment for 470 people. Duval Federal Savings & Loan Association of Jacksonville, a statewide thrift based in Jacksonville, had $366 million, or about half its deposits, in Duval County, and they equal about 25 percent of all area thrift deposits. It has 550

Four light stripes and its sign quickly identify the First Union National Bank of Florida building, standing above The Jacksonville Landing in the foreground. Photo by Kelly LaDuke

employees. CalFed, Incorporated, a Los Angeles-based savings and loan holding company, made a proposal in the spring of 1988 to acquire Duval Federal.

Other thrifts with deposits of $100 million or more include Anchor Savings Bank F.S.B., Jacksonville Federal Savings & Loan Association of Jacksonville, American Federal Savings & Loan Association of Duval County, and Florida Federal Savings & Loan Association.

Among life insurance firms, the regional home office of Prudential Life Insurance Company of America dwarfs the others, with 3,200 employees, assets of $8.7 billion, and $32.5 billion worth of life insurance in force. (These are 1986 year-end figures as supplied by Prudential. All figures originated from the respective insurance companies.) Prudential expanded into its Prudential Plaza Two complex in 1986.

Gulf Life Insurance Company, which is based in Jacksonville, lists $1.2 billion in total assets, $8.9 billion in life insurance in force, $363 million in premium income, and 1,060 employees. It is a wholly owned subsidiary of American General Corporation, the fourth-largest shareholder-owned insurance firm in the nation based on assets and premium income.

Independent Life and Accident Insurance Company reports assets of $869 million, $5.6 billion of life insurance in force, premium

Friendship Fountain on the Southbank of the St. Johns River marks the western end of the Riverwalk, at left. Photo by Kelly LaDuke

income of $270 million, and 1,175 employees. The company completed its building in 1975.

The Bryan and Lyon families, who hold controlling interest in the company, specified that they wanted an outstanding building architecturally, one that would be a credit to both the company and the city. Independent Square has become both a city landmark and the signature building of Jacksonville.

American Heritage Life Insurance Company, founded in 1956 in Jacksonville, has $280 million in assets with $8.8 billion of life insurance in force, premium income of $123 million, and 435 employees.

Above: The Gulf Life Tower, at one time the tallest building in Florida at 433 feet, dominates its Southbank neighbor, the Jacksonville Hotel. Photo by Kelly LaDuke

The Deerwood Business Park is one of the many modern Jacksonville business parks which have been built in a campus-like setting in the '80s. Photo by Richard Kevern

Rouse & Associates is building a corporate headquarters tower downtown for the company; it will be across the street from both Independent Square and The Jacksonville Landing.

The regional office of State Farm Insurance Company reports $4.3 billion of life insurance in force and $47.7 million in premium income. Unlike the other insurance companies that have located downtown, State Farm has put its regional office in the Deerwood-Baymeadows area. The firm has 937 employees.

Blue Cross and Blue Shield of Florida, based in Jacksonville, is one of the city's major employers, with 3,500 employees at the head-

A corner of one of the Quadrant office buildings at Southpoint displays a modern interpretation of art deco. Photo by Kelly LaDuke

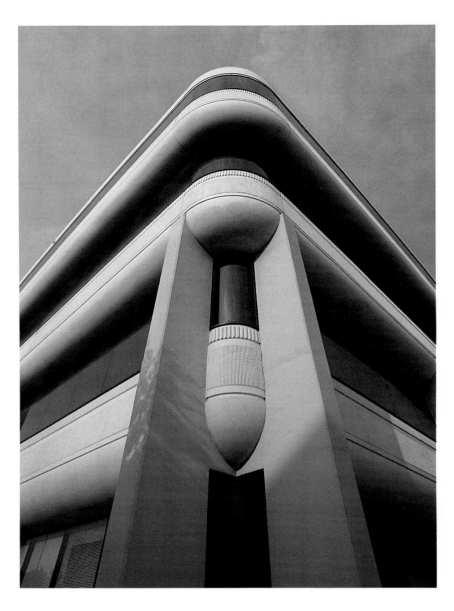

quarters building in Riverside and Deerwood-Baymeadows. As health care has changed in the 1980s, so has Blue Cross and Blue Shield. In addition to the traditional group health insurance, it now provides coverage through preferred provider organizations (PPOs), health maintenance organizations (HMOs), and similar programs, which have developed both in Jacksonville and around the country.

Barnett Banks of Florida, Incorporated, ranked No. 5 in the state at the end of 1965 when it embarked on an expansion program, has become the largest bank holding company in Florida. At that time, banking in Florida was governed by Depression-era legislation that banned any form of branch banking, in the belief that big banks were bad. Without intending to, the law hindered community growth by effectively denying local banks the ability to finance major projects.

No bank could finance a multimillion-dollar project by itself. Instead, a bank had to try to finance a project by persuading other banks to join it in the venture. The time involved in setting up such deals, along with the varying priorities of the potential participants, tended to restrict the size and number of big financial deals that Florida banks put together. This resulted in increasing numbers of businesses turning to banks and financial institutions outside of Florida for the big deals. Bankers saw this business leaving the state and began utilizing bank holding companies as the path around the unit law.

Barnett already had a holding company in Barnett National Securities Corporation, which owned six banks, including three in Jacksonville and one in St. Augustine. Other banks embarked on a similar course, including Atlantic, Florida National Banks of Florida, Incorporated, Southeast in Miami, and Sun Bank in Orlando.

Barnett embarked on an aggressive acquisition campaign. In *Barnett Action*, the bank's house organ, Charles E. Rice, Barnett chairman and chief executive officer, said in 1986, "What Barnett did was to simply use the holding company to purchase small, mostly independent banks in attractive economic markets."

That policy gave Barnett the opportunity to "consolidate assets and capital for greater lending capacity," Rice said. Barnett banks could take on loans bigger than any one could handle singly, with other Barnett banks picking up a portion of the loan.

State banking laws were changed in 1977 to allow banks to consolidate their operations within counties. That meant that in each county, banks that were affiliated with one another through a bank holding company could be brought together into one bank with several branches or offices. Statewide consolidation was legalized in 1981, which allowed banks to have branches throughout the state without use of the bank holding company vehicle. Other expansion-minded banks like Atlantic, Southeast Bank N.A., Florida National, and Sun Bank used the new law to consolidate statewide, but Barnett did not.

Barnett's Rice notes that of the 15 largest Florida bank holding companies in 1980, only four still operate as independent Florida-based holding companies, or without agreements to merge with money-center banks. Two of those four, Barnett and Southeast, are major banks in Jacksonville, and only Barnett is based in the city.

In reviewing the expansion years and the direction Barnett has taken, Rice said of the other bank holding companies, "They all had the same opportunity we did. How you use opportunity makes all the difference."

In addition to its headquarters building downtown, Barnett is constructing an office park to consolidate all of its non-banking operations as well as some banking operations. The new facility will be part of The Avenues, a 200-acre office and shopping mall development at the junction of Interstate-95, Phillips Highway, and Southside Boulevard. Barnett's share of the project is more than $120 million. The first phase, scheduled for completion in 1989, includes a 10-story office building and two five-story buildings, a conference center, and a cafeteria and bank operations building, as well as a parking garage. When

Glass wall of Florida National Bank's atrium creates a dramatic base for the FNB glass tower. Photo by Bill Hennefrund

the project is completed in 1991, Rice expects that 3,700 bank employees will work there. The project will encompass 1.2 million square feet.

Southeast, itself in existence only since 1967, found the new banking laws to be especially advantageous. Until consolidation in 1981, the largest loan that Southeast's affiliates could make in Jacksonville without calling in another affiliate to participate was $1 million or less. The consolidation of Southeast Bank in 1981 boosted its legal lending limit to $35 million; its present legal lending limit is around $50 million.

What happened to Southeast's lending limit also happened to lending limits at the other major Florida banks that consolidated. Barnett, which chose not to consolidate, has a similar lending limit, but it is arrived at differently, since it is the sum of the individual lending limits of its affiliated banks.

Southeast, which grew out of the First National Bank of Miami, came to Jacksonville in the early 1970s when it purchased the First Bank and Trust Company located in the old Duval County Courthouse. Other purchases by Southeast were the First National Beach Bank in Jacksonville Beach, the Bank of Orange Park, and the Bank of Edgewood.

Taking advantage of the 1977 law, Southeast merged its affiliate banks in each county so that by 1980 it had 19 affiliate banks with 120 to 125 branches. When the branching laws were changed again, Southeast merged its entire branch network into one Southeast Bank N.A. in late 1981, creating a centralized statewide branch bank.

That was especially helpful to Southeast in Jacksonville. Until then, each bank had only a small market share and there was very little Southeast could do about it. The bank could serve local markets and neighborhoods well, but not the larger business and real estate markets.

Decentralized lending authority gave Southeast the ability to undertake much larger types of credit without having to go through the loan participation process. Southeast started a corporate banking division in 1981 to take advantage of the larger lending authority.

Southeast also added branches. In 1981 it opened facilities in Deerwood and on Blanding Boulevard, in late 1983 in Regency, and in early 1984 in Mandarin and Ponte Vedra. With 10 branches, Southeast does not rival other big banks in the city, but its lending capacity makes it a major player in town, financing larger deals and associating with many of the larger and more prestigious companies in Jacksonville.

Jacksonville is the northern regional headquarters of Southeast Bank. The northern region includes 30 branches from Jacksonville to Pensacola. The central region is based in Tampa and the southern region in Miami. In 1985 the 10-story Southeast Bank Building, a Rouse & Associates development, opened at Gulf Life Drive and South Main Street, bringing together in one building operations that had been scattered.

Florida National Banks of Florida marked its centennial year in 1988. The bank holding company traces its roots to Southern Savings and Trust Company, which started at 26 Pine Street with S.B. Hubbard as president. It went through several changes before becoming Florida National Bank of Jacksonville in 1907.

In 1926, Alfred I. du Pont began buying Florida National stock, and in 1927 his brother-in-law Edward Ball joined the board of directors. An effort was made in 1929 to merge Barnett and Florida National Banks, but the required legislation was not adopted and the merger failed. Du Pont became bank president in 1930 but died in 1935. In 1937 Ball became president of Florida National, and in 1943 coordinator of Florida National Group of Banks. He resigned as president, chairman, and director of Florida National Banks in 1971.

Ball is credited by national political writers with major responsibility for the present tax structure in Florida, which relies heavily on property taxes and the sales tax. The state constitution bans a personal income tax. There is a small corporate income tax, which was adopted in Ball's waning years. The effort by Governor Bob Martinez in 1987 to secure a tax on services represented the first concerted effort to break away from the tax system that Ball championed. After five months the services tax was repealed and replaced with an additional one-cent sales tax.

Florida National Bank and Alliance Corporation, a mortgage company, merged in 1982. Jack Uible, former chairman of the board and chief executive officer of Alliance, was named chairman of Florida

An urban garden flanks the entrance to the Florida National Bank Building. Photo by Richard Kevern

National Banks of Florida, Incorporated, in 1983. Two years later, Florida National sold Alliance Mortgage Company to Owens-Illinois, Incorporated.

The largest bank in Jacksonville is First Union National Bank of Florida. Until 1985, it was Atlantic National Bank of Florida, a wholly owned subsidiary of Atlantic Bancorporation, a bank holding company based in Jacksonville with 114 offices statewide.

At the end of 1987, First Union reported 208 branches in Florida, including 26 in the Jacksonville area. That included 23 in Duval County, one in Ponte Vedra, and two in Orange Park. Barnett, the state's largest bank holding company but second to First Union in the Jacksonville area, reported 23 offices areawide, including 19 in Duval County, one in Ponte Vedra, two in Orange Park, and one in Green Cove Springs.

Atlantic Bank was founded in Georgia by Savannah financiers who looked south of the state line in 1903 and saw what they felt was fertile banking soil in Jacksonville. From the start, it was named Atlantic National Bank and used a clipper ship as its trademark. Edward W. Lane, Sr., of Valdosta, Georgia, was president.

The first steps toward building a banking group were taken in 1925 and 1926 with the establishment of affiliate banks in the Fairfield, Riverside, and Springfield sections of Jacksonville. In 1928, Atlantic Bank reached out to Sanford and Palatka, and in 1929 to

West Palm Beach. Banks in Daytona Beach and Gainesville were added in 1930 and 1931.

Growth resumed after World War II, and by 1974 Atlantic consisted of a statewide group of 31 banks. When Florida's banking laws permitted consolidation, Atlantic took advantage. By the time of the merger with First Union, Atlantic was one bank, sixth in size in the state with assets of more than $3.8 billion.

Atlantic President B.J. Walker said the bank consolidated in each of its counties in 1977 and then statewide in 1981 because of what the bank viewed as the eventual coming of interstate banking and the need to compete with money-center banks.

Regional interstate banking laws were adopted in 1984 in Florida and other southern states. In mid-1985, regional interstate banking was upheld by the U.S. Supreme Court.

The merger of Atlantic Bancorporation into First Union, which is based in Charlotte, North Carolina, was conceived in early 1984 when Edward E. Crutchfield, Jr., then president and now chairman and chief executive officer of First Union, scouted Florida to see what opportunities might lie ahead if interstate banking were to come about. Crutchfield met with executives from several other banks, including Barnett, as well as with Walker. In the year that followed, each man investigated the other's bank and banking practices—unbeknownst to the other. Each liked what he saw.

In May 1985, Crutchfield came to Jacksonville to meet again with Walker, and they are reported to have spent the meeting discussing how they ran their banks. A few days after the U.S. Supreme Court ruling, Crutchfield returned to Jacksonville to complete the merger, and learned he was buying a $496-million bank.

At the end of the third quarter of 1987, the latest period for which figures are available, First Union National Bank of Florida reported assets of $7.4 billion. First Union Corporation, the parent company, reported assets of $25.1 billion. It is among the 25 largest bank holding companies in the nation.

In addition to Atlantic Bancorporation, First Union's Florida purchases include First Bankers Corporation of Florida, with assets of $1.3 billion; Sarasota Bank & Trust Company N.A., assets of $23.6 million; Collier Bank and Edison Banks, Incorporated, combined assets of $89.3 million; and Miami-based Florida Commercial Banks, assets of $1 billion.

Sun Bank/North Florida N.A. is a subsidiary of Orlando-based Sun Banks, Incorporated, which, in turn, is a subsidiary of Atlanta-based bank holding company SunTrust Banks, Incorporated. Sun Banks is the first bank in Florida to be owned by a Georgia bank holding company. In fact, the SunTrust deal was the first to cross state lines under the regional interstate banking laws adopted in 1984 by Florida and other southern states.

Sun Bank/North Florida N.A. came to Jacksonville when Sun Banks bought the St. Johns River Bank in 1973. St. Johns River Bank had opened in 1968 in the Gulf Life Tower, and its first annual report listed profits almost double its projections.

By 1984, Sun Banks had six offices in the Jacksonville area. In that year it acquired Flagship State Banks, Incorporated, statewide. Flagship had six offices in the Jacksonville area and they were added to the Sun Banks system.

Rather than concentrate its strength in Florida, Sun Banks looked at the advantages it saw in interstate banking, and in midyear agreed to combine with Atlanta-based Trust Company of Georgia to create SunTrust Banks, Incorporated. At the time of the merger, the two bank holding companies had assets totaling $15.6 billion. By the end of 1986, with growth and additional acquisitions, SunTrust assets had grown to $26.2 billion, and SunTrust ranked second only to Barnett in the state, with deposits of $9 billion to Barnett's $13 billion. Southeast was third at $7.4 billion, Florida National sixth at $4.54 billion, and First Union of Florida seventh at $4.51 billion.

Among the smaller Jacksonville-based banks, American Banks of Florida, Incorporated, has grown to 23 offices in four counties with assets of $401 million. It is bigger in Jacksonville than Sun Banks, but ironically, it came within a whisker of never being established. Approval for the bank, as Southside Bank, was granted December 8, 1941, the day after the attack on Pearl Harbor. Frank Sherman, the bank's founder, said his charter was the last the state granted until after the war in 1945. By then, changing conditions might well have resulted in the bank not being founded.

Southside Bank opened on January 2, 1942, and it was the end of 1959 before it opened a second office in Mayport. By 1983, the bank had grown to nine offices. In 1984, three offices were acquired in Gainesville. Two more were acquired in Orlando in 1986. The remainder of the offices are the result of internal expansion.

Before Southside Bank opened, several of the bigger banks downtown had investigated the possibility of opening a Southside affiliate, but they always pulled back because they didn't see enough business there.

Two independent banks had tried such an expansion and had failed. Sherman worked for Barnett and had turned in a negative report himself. But when banks began charging small accounts for banking services, he felt that a Southside bank had become financially feasible.

Southside Bank might not have survived if Barnett Bank had not assisted. Sherman explains:

Harry Fannin of Panama City was first chairman and owned controlling stock. After a little over a year he decided to get out and came to me and asked if I wanted to buy him out. I told him I would be glad to, but I would like the directors to take equal shares. I talked to B.H. Barnett at Barnett Bank, telling him that Fannin wanted to sell and I would like to arrange for financing. He loaned us the money and we bought out Fannin.

Once we opened, the downtown banks quit soliciting in our territory. About a year later Ed Ball wanted to buy the bank. Brown L. Whatley had become chairman when Fannin sold, and then left the board to go on Ball's board at Florida National.

Ball had big plans, but I... went back to Barnett to borrow the money to buy the bank. It was touch-and-go as to who got it, but I got it and Barnett again loaned money to buy the controlling stock.

In 1978, controlling interest in the bank was bought by Raymond K. Mason, Sr., who continues to hold that interest and is chairman of the board. Raymond K. Mason, Jr., is president as well as chairman and chief executive officer of American National Bank of Florida.

The Guaranty Bank, with two offices (at King Street and May Street in Riverside-Avondale), has roots extending back to the American Bank. Julian Fant, Sr., founder of Riverside Bank in 1947, had been associated with Sherman in the founding of the Southside Bank.

When the war ended and Fant returned from the Navy, they began thinking of expanding and decided to go to Riverside. Fant and Frank Sherman decided that only one of them should try Riverside, and after some discussion, Fant made the move.

In 1967 the name became First Guaranty Bank and Trust Company to reflect the newly acquired trust power and services being offered countywide. In 1969 First Guaranty opened its affiliate bank, the Five Points Guaranty Bank.

Other local banks include NCNB National Bank of Florida, a subsidiary of NCNB Corporation of Charlotte, North Carolina; Ocean State Bank in Neptune Beach; Keystone State Bank in Keystone Heights; Citizens Bank of Macclenny; Marine National Bank; Tucker State Bank; SouthTrust Bank of Jacksonville N.A.; Prosperity Bank of St. Augustine; Beneficial Savings Bank of Jacksonville; and Enterprise National Bank of Jacksonville.

• • •

Local bank NCNB National Bank of Florida is a subsidiary of NCNB Corporation of Charlotte, North Carolina. Photo by Kelly LaDuke

First National Bank is one of the smaller community banks in Jacksonville. Photo by Kelly LaDuke

Savings and loan associations in Jacksonville and the First Coast are evenly divided between stock companies and mutual companies. The scales are tipping toward stock companies as the thrifts convert.

The latest savings and loan to convert to a stock company is American Federal Savings and Loan Association of Duval County, which completed its conversion in early 1987. It is ranked fourth-largest in the county. The three larger thrifts are all mutual companies.

Savings and loan associations are children of the Depression. Franklin D. Roosevelt's New Deal created the Federal Home Loan Bank System in June 1933, and that authorized the thrifts.

The oldest thrift in Jacksonville is Anchor Savings, which began as Sun Federal Savings in 1933. First Federal, the giant among First Coast thrifts with nearly 50 percent of all deposits, was founded next, in 1934. It has $970 million in deposits.

First Federal originally occupied a desk in the offices of Tucker Brothers, a mortgage company that is now part of Tucker Holding Company, Incorporated. In 1940 it moved to a new building. In 1956, First Federal again moved, to the Hildebrandt Building at Adams and Julia streets. In 1982, First Federal and Fidelity Federal Savings and Loan Association of Jacksonville merged to create the present thrift.

Jacksonville Federal Savings & Loan, ranked third in size with $172 million in deposits, was founded in 1945. Duval Federal (second-

largest, with $403 million) and Florida Federal (fifth-largest, with $104 million) were both founded in 1954. No. 6 Citizens Federal ($65 million) opened in 1955, and No. 4 American Federal ($135 million) opened in 1962.

Other thrifts (and their deposits) in the First Coast area are Community Savings Bank ($61 million), Security First Federal Savings & Loan Association in St. Augustine ($76 million), Great Western Bank in Jacksonville Beach ($16 million), First Trust Savings Bank ($7 million), and Coast Federal ($1 million). Coast Federal is part of a statewide thrift with $932 million in deposits at 33 offices.

In addition to dominating the thrift deposits on the First Coast, First Federal also has the largest number of branches, with 19 in this area. No. 2 Duval Federal has 12 branches, though it has a total of 27 statewide. American Federal and Florida Federal have seven branches each; Jacksonville Federal has six.

Florida Federal, though it has a small profile in this area with only six offices and $104 million in deposits, is part of a statewide thrift that has $3.4 billion of deposits in 86 offices.

Of the other smaller thrifts, Citizens Federal has four offices, Community Savings Bank three, Security First Federal, First Trust Savings Bank, and Anchor Savings Bank two each, and Great Western Bank one. Great Western has 27 offices statewide and is a subsidiary of a California-based thrift.

* * *

The first insurance company to set up shop in Jacksonville was formed in 1900; it was founded as Florida Mutual Benefit Association, now known as Peninsular Life Insurance Company. The second firm established was Afro-American Industrial and Benevolent Association, which later became Afro-American Life Insurance Company, founded in 1901. After 86 years of providing insurance, mainly funeral expenses to blacks in Florida and two other states, Afro-American closed its doors in 1987.

The life insurance business in Jacksonville is dominated by Prudential, Gulf Life, Independent Life, and American Heritage Life. The four companies have written $53 billion of the $66 billion worth of life insurance written by all Jacksonville-based firms. Prudential alone wrote $32 billion of the $66 billion.

Gulf Life was founded in 1911 by T.T. Phillips in Pensacola. It moved to Jacksonville in 1916, where T.T. Phillips' brother, E.L. Phillips, had been selling policies since shortly after the company was founded. The influenza epidemic of 1918-1919 wiped out the company's surplus funds and part of its capital, but the company was able to pay all claims. In 1923, Gulf Life began writing industrial life policies, and in 1924 it began providing ordinary life insurance.

Gulf Life merged with Victory National Insurance Company of Tampa in 1928. During the early years of the Depression, Gulf Life showed a decrease, but became the largest life insurance company in Florida, based on in-force business.

Community Savings Bank has three offices in the Jacksonville area. Photo by Kelly LaDuke

The company went public in 1951 after the death of T.T. Phillips, and before mid-decade the company had $500 million of insurance in force. In 1952, an addition was built at the Church Street offices, which gave Gulf Life the largest office building in Jacksonville.

The Gulf Life Holding Company was formed in 1968 and began investing in industries other than insurance. In the 1970s, insurance in force increased from $2.5 billion to more than $5.3 billion.

The largest merger in the life insurance industry took place in 1980 when Gulf United bought Interstate Life and Accident Insurance Company and merged it with Gulf Life. In 1984, Gulf Life merged into American General Corporation. President and chief executive officer of Gulf Life is Robert James R. Tuerff; vice chairman is Robert O. Purcifull.

Independent Life and Accident Insurance Company was founded in 1920 by seven men: George C. Cobourn, Jacob F. Bryan II, Henry Gooding, Claybourne G. Snead, J. Arthur Howard, Harry H. Lyon, Sr., and John S. Young. Their policies carried death benefits of $75, but by the end of the first year, the company had more than $700,000 of insurance in force.

Cobourn headed the company until his death in 1932. By then, the company had $3.8 million of insurance in force. Bryan was named interim president until Gooding was elected president. Gooding led the company for 10 years. In 1938, the company moved into the Jenks Building, Jacksonville's first fully air-conditioned office space.

Snead became president in 1942, and the company expanded into Georgia the following year. It was the world's largest insurance company selling weekly premiums only, with policies amounting to $18 million.

By 1956, Tennessee became the company's fifth state of operations, and it reached $1 million in weekly premiums. Jacob F. Bryan III became chairman and president in 1957 and introduced ordinary life insurance. Mississippi and Oklahoma were added to operations in 1959.

Independent bought Southeast Life Insurance in 1960 and changed its name to Herald Life. That allowed the company to conduct business in places where Independent could not operate because of name similarities. The company made its public offering of stock in 1965, and in the following year entered the remaining field of life insurance: group business.

Independent bought two fire insurance companies in 1968, merged them, and renamed them Independent Fire Insurance Company. A subsidiary, Herald Fire, was organized in 1970, again to overcome the name problem.

By 1975, Independent ranked in the top 6 percent in assets, life insurance in force, and total premium income, of the 1,790 companies qualified to sell insurance in the country.

Descendants of the founding families are still running Independent Life. At the parent Independent Insurance Group Incorporated, Wilford C. Lyon, Jr., is chairman of the board and chief executive officer; Jacob F. Bryan IV is president; Wilford C. Lyon, Sr., is first vice president; G. Howard Bryan is second vice president; J. Alex Howard is vice president-secretary; Boyd E. Lyon, Sr., is vice president and treasurer, chief financial officer; Kendall G. Bryan is vice president and chief operating officer.

American Heritage Life Insurance Company (AHL) was formed in 1956 by W. Ashley Verlander, James E. Davis, and Claude R. Kirk, Jr. Davis was chairman and remains chairman of American Heritage Life Investment Corporation. Kirk, later to become Florida's first twentieth-century Republican governor, was president, and Verlander was executive vice president. Kirk succeded Haydon Burns as governor of Florida, giving Jacksonville claim to two successive chief executives in Tallahassee.

In its first sales campaign, in January 1957, it sold $1.1 million in life insurance. American Heritage began expanding immediately, buying Blue Grass Life Insurance Company, and by the end of its first year it had $85.1 million of life insurance in force. The key to that success lay in the formation of the group life insurance department, which sold life insurance through payroll deduction.

AHL entered the fire and casualty business in 1959 with the purchase of Reliable Insurance Company of Dayton, Ohio, and turned its first profit of $348,000. In 1960, Acme United Life of Atlanta was acquired. In 1963, deciding to concentrate on life insurance, AHL sold Reliable. The following year, the company bought the Lynch Building and declared its first dividend of five cents.

The company reached $1 billion of insurance in force in 1968, only 11 years after it began operations. That same year, American

Heritage Life Investment Corporation was formed as a holding company to own the insurance company and Florida Associated Services.

By 1972, AHL topped $2 billion of insurance in force, achieving that goal in slightly more than 15 years, a record for the insurance industry. American Heritage Life has continued to grow through the years, establishing new standards for its segment of the industry. Verlander was named chairman and chief executive officer in 1986 and T. O'Neal Douglas was named president.

George Washington Life Insurance Company, formed in 1906, is among the older insurance firms in the city. It has $180 million in

The glass-sided Prudential Plaza Two lights up the Southbank. At far right, with its sign atop the building, is the original Prudential Plaza One. Photo by Richard Kevern

insurance in force. Professional Insurance Corporation was formed in 1936 and has $1 billion in insurance in force.

By the early postwar years Jacksonville already had laid claim to being an important regional insurance center. In 1955, Prudential Life Insurance Company of America decided to locate its south-central regional home office in Jacksonville. That action transformed the city into the Hartford of the South. But it did more than that. By deciding to locate its offices in a new building on the south side of the St. Johns River, rather than in downtown Jacksonville on the Northbank, Prudential defined a new area for major development. A transformation began in the general wasteland that had developed between the San Marco neighborhood and downtown following the closing of the World War I shipyards and warehouses.

At that time, only Baptist Medical Center was located in the area, at the north side of San Marco. The Southbank has since developed into a commercial area with its own personality—part of downtown, distinct from the Northbank yet accessible by foot as well as car across the Main Street and Acosta bridges.

With the development of the Southbank area, Prudential chose the area between the Main Street and Acosta bridges to build its Plaza Two center. That added a striking mirrored complex that extends over several acres and is marked at its peak with the Prudential logo, representing the Rock of Gibraltar.

One of the newest insurance companies in the city is becoming one of the largest. It is Guarantee Security Life Insurance Company, a

privately held company specializing in annuity and single-premium business. It was formed in Miami in 1969 and moved to Jacksonville in 1982.

Guarantee Security has about $800 million in assets and an annual premium volume of $158 million. When Guarantee Security moved to Jacksonville, it had $39 million in assets.

Other, smaller life insurance companies in Jacksonville and the value of life insurance in force are Dependable Life Insurance Company, founded 1975, $892 milion in force; Southern Protective Life Insurance Company, $57 million in force; and Voyager Life Insurance Company, founded in 1965, $1.1 billion in force (one of Voyager's founders was former Florida Governor Farris Bryant of Ocala, who chose to reside in Jacksonville after his term was over). The regional office of a Chicago firm, United Insurance Company of America, has $361 million in force.

Jacksonville's leading banks and insurance companies grace the city skyline. Photo by Steven Brooke

Mayo Clinic Jacksonville is a multi-specialty, outpatient clinic providing adult medical care. Photo by Richard Kevern

CHAPTER 5

"A TOWN LEARNING TO SAVE LIVES"

...

Health Care

To the citizens and visitors nothing has become more apparent than the need of a hospital in our city.

FIRST ANNUAL REPORT
ST. LUKE'S HOSPITAL
APRIL 1874

It's not unusual to find ducks inhabiting the many lagoons in Jacksonville. These are at St. Luke's Hospital at Southpoint. Photo by Kelly LaDuke

Among the thousands of winter visitors to Jacksonville in the 1870s were "invalids" seeking the health benefits of Florida's sunshine and sea air. They came hoping for miraculous cures, but often found themselves drained of resources, homeless, destitute and dying far from friends and family.

Jacksonville was not insensitive to these unfortunate travelers, and several charitable organizations were formed by the wives of the town's leading merchants and professional men to provide the transient and homeless with food, shelter, and medical care. One of these groups, the Relief Association of Jacksonville, led by three courageous women—Mrs. Susan Hartridge, Mrs. Myra H. Mitchell, and Mrs. Anna Doggett—determined to establish a hospital, and set about raising funds for that purpose.

On February 25, 1873, the ladies staged a fair for the benefit of St. Luke's Hospital, shrewdly timed to coincide with the opening of the 150-room Grand National Hotel. The fair was a great success, and two weeks later St. Luke's Hospital was opened in "a somewhat dilapidated building" on Hogan's Creek, a few blocks east of Main Street.

St. Luke's ministered to the victims of the yellow fever epidemic in 1888 and the typhoid fever epidemic 10 years later, and narrowly escaped the Great Fire of 1901. The hospital building was protected from the flames by the marshy banks of Hogan's Creek.

Today St. Luke's Hospital is an impressive complex of contemporary buildings on J. Turner Butler Boulevard, near the Mayo Clinic. But the old Palmetto Street building still stands, restored to its former dignity by a group of concerned citizens, as a monument to the city's early concern for the health of its people.

During the 1970s Jacksonville attracted nationwide attention with a pioneering CPR education program, and the city became the prototype for such community efforts. In an article titled "The Story of a Town Learning to Save Lives," the March 1972 issue of *Today's Health* magazine reported:

Officials in Jacksonville, Florida, estimate they have saved 100 lives a year since they began training their citizens and firemen in the latest techniques for rescuing heart attack victims. Now nearly 200,000 people in Jacksonville have been taught to perform emergency cardiac pulmonary resuscitation, and other cities are starting similar programs.

Today Jacksonville is recognized as one of the Southeast's major medical centers. A measure of the strength, importance, and vitality of the city's medical profession lies in the fact that Jacksonville advanced from ninth among major cities in the state in physicians per 100,000 population to fourth by 1985, the latest year for which figures are available. There were 142 physicians per 100,000 population in 1981, and that number rose to 181 per 100,000 by 1985. This compares favorably with cities ranked among the top 20 health care leaders in the nation, as listed in a 1985 report. For example, Detroit, ranked seventh, reported 182 physicians per 100,000 population; No. 20 Dallas reported 185; No. 15 Atlanta reported 195.

The increase in Jacksonville's physician-to-population ratio in the early 1980s took place before the influence of the latest factors fueling growth in the medical community had begun to be felt. One of these was the presence of Baptist Medical Center, which recruited physicians during the first half of the decade to fill its new medical office building. "We did that," said William Mason, chief executive officer at Baptist, "and we now find that all our beds are occupied." He reports that Baptist is running at about 90 percent of capacity, which he feels is close to optimum use.

Other factors responsible for the growth of the medical community in the late 1980s include:

—In 1986, the Mayo Clinic opened in Jacksonville its first satellite clinic outside of Rochester, Minnesota. The clinic is located near the

Mayo Clinic's first satellite clinic opened in Jacksonville in the fall of 1987. Photo by Richard Kevern

Above: The videocommunications system and sharing of medical resources are important parts of the Mayo Clinic in Jacksonville, serving patients at locations in Rochester, Minnesota, and Scottsdale, Arizona. Courtesy, Mayo Clinic Jacksonville

Facing page, bottom: Physicist Stephen Givens adjusts the parameters of the Linear Accelerator used for Radiation Oncology. The accelerator is capable of directing measured doses of radiation therapy to any part of the body, thus treating the affected area while not disturbing the surrounding tissue. Courtesy, Mayo Clinic Jacksonville

Intracoastal Waterway and J. Turner Butler Boulevard.

—In a shift from Rochester practice, the Mayo Clinic took over St. Luke's Hospital in order to provide its own facility for clinic patients requiring hospitalization.

—The Joslin Diabetes Clinic opened its first satellite clinic outside Boston, locating in 1987 at Memorial Medical Center.

—University Hospital on the Northside was designated a teaching hospital affiliated with University of Florida Medical School at Gainesville.

—Construction was begun in 1987 on a new Methodist Hospital medical center on the site of the old St. Luke's Hospital in Northside.

—Expansion continued at Salisbury Lakes Medical Parke in the Southpoint area. It is a complex of five buildings already in use with various types of outpatient medical treatment, including one-day surgery. Additional buildings are planned.

—Charter Hospital of Jacksonville opened a 64-bed child and adolescent psychiatric care facility in 1987. The hospital is near the Salisbury Lakes Medical Parke.

But the major development in the medical field in 1988 is the construction of the Nemours Foundation's children's clinic, which is being established to treat "crippled children" (any child who is incapacitated because of an illness), under the terms of the Alfred I. du

Pont will. It is affiliated with the University of Florida Medical School as a teaching clinic, and in Jacksonville with Baptist Medical Center and its Wolfson Children's Hospital. The clinic will serve the southeastern region of the country and Latin America. For years, the foundation had operated Hope Haven Hospital here for children.

The Nemours clinic will include research facilities, and observers of the health care industry expect it to reach a level of importance in pediatric medicine equal to that of the Mayo Clinic in its fields.

A new campus for the Nemours clinic is being created just south of Interstate-95, near Baptist Medical Center. The freeway will be spanned by a monorail that will permit patients and staff to move back and forth quickly between Baptist facilities and the clinic.

The Nemours Foundation will have as much as $20 million a year available to spend on clinic operations. The foundation, with an estimated worth of $2 billion or more, is under court order to spend a portion of its money yearly or lose its tax-exempt status.

Although construction of its buildings has just begun, Nemours has already brought in more than 20 physicians and researchers and is operating temporarily from space in the Baptist Medical Center. The Foundation gave up its pediatric beds at its old location because it saw no need for two pediatric hospitals in Jacksonville.

The Mayo Clinic has the latest in Diagnostic Radiology equipment, including MRI (Magnetic Resonance Imaging), seen here in use by technician Lonnie Foster. Courtesy, Mayo Clinic Jacksonville

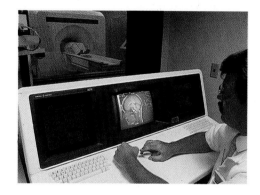

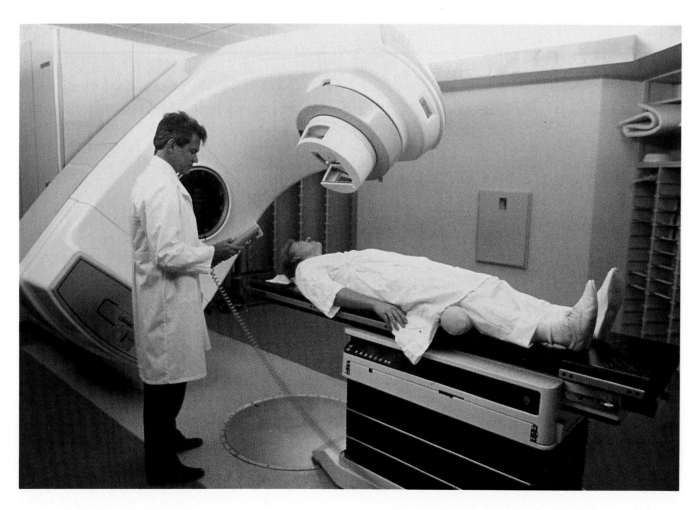

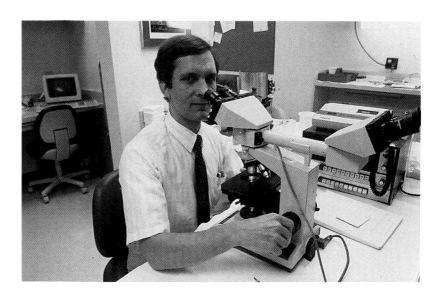

Above: Clinic pathologist Dr. Art Jones examines a specimen for a Mayo Clinic surgeon operating from St. Luke's Hospital, a Mayo-affiliated hospital. Courtesy, Mayo Clinic Jacksonville

Below: The Nemours Magnetic Resonance Imaging (MRI) center provides state-of-the-art technology without harmful radiation. Courtesy, The Nemours Childrens Clinic

Facing page, top: Nemours medical staff is comprised of pediatric subspecialists who work closely with primary care pediatricians and family physicians. Courtesy, The Nemours Childrens Clinic

Facing page, bottom: These children receive one-on-one care in the Physical Therapy/Occupation Therapy Department. Courtesy, The Nemours Childrens Clinic

William Mason foresees a reordering of hospital beds at the Baptist complex, with the number of pediatric beds being increased while the number of beds for adult care is reduced. Plans are being made to replace the original Wolfson Children's Hospital with a new building to accommodate the increased emphasis on pediatrics at Baptist.

Baptist, with its Wolfson Children's Hospital and link with Nemours Clinic, is increasing its emphasis on pediatrics and neonatal care as well as OB/GYN services. While still maintaining a general medicine posture, Baptist is also increasing its presence in the fields of heart, cancer, and pulmonary diseases as well as older-adult services, including an Alzheimer's disease center. It employs 2,400.

First Coast hospitals include Baptist with 579 beds; Beaches Hospital with 82 beds; Charter Hospital, 64 beds; Ed Fraser Hospital in Baker County, 25 beds; St. Augustine General Hospital, 155 beds; Humana Hospital-Orange Park, 196; Jacksonville Medical Center,

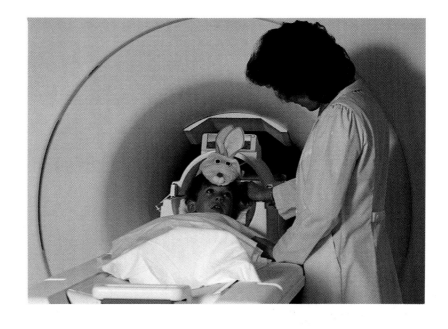

107; Methodist Hospital, 226; Riverside Hospital, 183; St. Luke's Hospital, 289; St. Johns River Hospital, 99; St. Vincent's Medical Center, 518; University Hospital, 485.

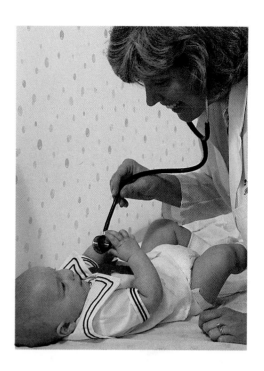

The Beaches Hospital, an acute care facility, is designed to serve the population in the oceanfront communities. It employs 177 and is now replacing its existing building with a $12-million facility that will be about twice the size of the present building. Included in the new hospital, which is being built next to the existing one, will be a CAT scan unit. The new complex will be known as First Coast Medical Center.

Charter Hospital is a child and adolescent psychiatric hospital that treats psychological and psychiatric problems, including alcohol and drug addiction as well as learning disabilities.

Clay Memorial Hospital in Green Cove Springs was founded in 1958. It is an acute care, general services hospital, serving mainly the southern part of Clay County. It has 60 beds and employs 56 persons.

Ed Fraser Hospital, an acute care, general services facility, is operated by the Baker County Hospital Authority in Macclenny. In addi-

tion to Baker County, it also serves some of the western part of Duval County.

Flagler Hospital was founded by Henry M. Flagler to provide medical care for winter visitors to St. Augustine. Today, the hospital is an acute care, general services hospital with 131 beds. It has 321 employees.

St. Augustine General Hospital, affiliated with Hospital Corporation of America, is an acute care, general services hospital in St. Augustine, serving much of St. Johns County. It employs 250.

Humana Hospital in Orange Park is a subsidiary of Humana, Incorporated, based in Louisville, Kentucky. The hospital, which serves Clay County and southern Duval County, is beginning construction of a cardiac catheterization laboratory, a center designed to provide diagnostic data on cardiovascular problems. The cost is estimated at $3 million. Expansion valued at $6.3 million is also underway in the obstetrics unit and nursery, as well as the outpatient surgery unit. Humana Hospital employs 706.

Jacksonville Medical Center has developed the Southeastern Pain Clinic to treat chronic pain, and an industrial medicine department designed both to treat industrial injuries and to seek ways to prevent those injuries. It also offers a 24-hour family care center, and employs 350.

Memorial Medical Center has grown from its founding in 1968 to become a significant health care provider. In addition to the hospital, it also operates the Memorial Regional Rehabilitation Center, a 128-bed facility devoted to physical and vocational rehabilitation. The rehabilitation center is the largest institution of its kind in the southeastern United States. In addition to its inpatients, the rehabilitation center can care for 200 outpatients each day. It employs 1,500.

The Joslin Diabetes Clinic occupies one floor in the Memorial Medical Center office building. It draws patients from throughout the

A Trauma One air rescue helicopter is preparing to leave its landing pad. Photo by Richard Kevern

Memorial Medical Center, one of the newer hospitals in Jacksonville, is the site of the Jacksonville offices of the Joslyn Diabetes Clinic. Photo by Judy K. Jacobsen

Southeast. Joslin's parent clinic in Boston is affiliated with Harvard University's medical school.

Methodist Hospital is in the midst of a $39.75-million renovation and construction program that began in 1984 with the purchase of the old St. Luke's Hospital building. The program includes renovation of the old St. Luke's building into the Methodist Pavilion, and construction of the Methodist Surgical Center. Methodist also has a level II trauma center, which includes a special-care facility for burn and chemical spill victims. Now nearing completion is a six-story medical center. Methodist Hospital employs 1,165.

Nassau General Hospital in Fernandina Beach is an acute care, general services hospital with 54 beds. The hospital employs 130 persons.

Riverside Hospital is an acute care, general services hospital that also offers pain management, women's services, senior services, psychiatric care, and coronary care. It employs 450.

St. Johns River Hospital specializes in acute psychiatric and substance-abuse care for both adults and adolescents.

St. Luke's Hospital, founded in 1873, was the first private hospital in Florida. It is also one of the newest hospital buildings in Jacksonville, having been completed in 1984 after moving from the Northside to Southpoint. It employs 1,152. St. Luke's has been taken over by Mayo Clinic and acts as the Mayo hospital, but it is also open to non-Mayo patients. Specialties include cardiology and orthopedics, including microsurgery, arthroscopy, and total joint replacement.

St. Vincent's Medical Center developed from the DeSoto Sanitorium, which had been established in Springfield in 1906. In response to a request from the Most Reverend Michael J. Curley, Roman Catholic Bishop of St. Augustine, the Daughters of Charity looked over the health situation in Jacksonville in 1916 and took over the sanitorium, which became St. Vincent's Hospital a few months later.

Memorial Medical Center has grown from its founding in 1968 to become a significant health care provider in Jacksonville. It also operates the Memorial Regional Rehabilitation Center, which is the largest institution of its kind in the southeastern United States. Courtesy, Memorial Medical Center

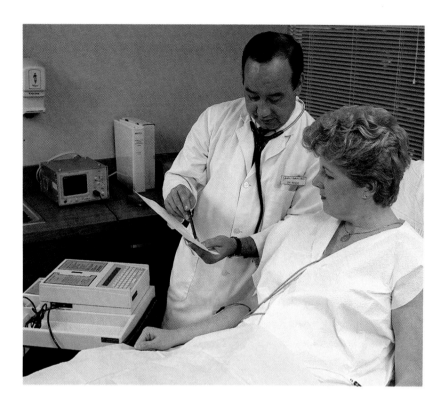

In the mid-1920s, a capital campaign was successfully completed, and a new hospital at the present Riverside site was opened in 1927. An addition was completed in 1955. There were many renovations and additions to facilities during the next 30 years, resulting in today's campus, which is centered around the 518-bed hospital.

St. Vincent's has developed a cancer research unit, which among other projects is investigating the high incidence of lung cancer in Jacksonville. Some medical observers suspect the problem can be traced to Jacksonville's shipyards, which used asbestos in large quantities during World War II. In addition to cancer research, St. Vincent's has departments dealing with eating disorders and heart and pulmonary disease, and the hospital has the First Coast's only poison control center. The medical center employs 2,182.

University Hospital is the city's lone teaching hospital, being affiliated with the University of Florida College of Medicine in Gainesville, 90 miles away, and acting as the medical school's urban hospital campus. The hospital also operates one of only 20 level I trauma centers in the nation. All 150 of its attending physicians are University of Florida medical professors, which makes the hospital a major affiliate of the university's J. Hillis Miller Medical Center. In addition to the trauma center, other unique services offered at University Hospital include pediatric cardiovascular surgery, pediatric dialysis, a children's crisis stabilization unit, and a neonatal intensive care unit. It employs 2,500.

The newest development in health care in Jacksonville is the more businesslike approach pressed on the entire industry by Medicare, which called for shaking off old traditions. Most visible of the new approach to health care is the emergence of neighborhood health and treatment clinics, familiarly called Doc-in-a-box. St. Vincent's Medical Center operates 14 such clinics, the most of any health care provider in the First Coast area.

Jacksonville's rise as a transportation, distribution, and warehousing center, which has been responsible for much of the city's growth since 1821, has been manifested in the health care field. Jacksonville's favorable transportation location has given rise to a healthy medical supply distribution industry. Four medical supply houses serve wide areas of the Southeast: Durr-Fillauer Medical, Incorporated; Physician Sales & Service, which is based in Jacksonville; Owens & Minor, Incorporated; and General Medical Corporation. There are two pharmaceutical houses: Johnson Drug Company and Lawrence Pharmaceuticals, Incorporated. A third pharmaceutical house, Southeastern Laboratories, serves veterinarians.

Several manufacturing companies in Jacksonville produce medical supplies and health aids. The largest of these is Xomed, Incorporated, a subsidiary of Bristol-Myers Company, which employs more than 250 workers. The firm specializes in products for ear, nose, and throat ailments.

In the summer of 1987, Xomed officials announced production of a new hearing aid, which would be implanted into the skull behind the ear. The hearing aid is designed to send sound waves through the skull to the inner ear. Xomed President Patrick Cusick estimates the new aid will be able to help 25,000 to 50,000 people in the country.

Vistakon, Incorporated, a wholly owned subsidiary of Johnson & Johnson, currently employs about 150 in the manufacture of contact lenses. Vistakon will produce a new type of throw-away contact lens, which can be worn for an extended period and then be discarded and replaced with new contacts. If Vistakon projections hold firm, local employment will reach 300 shortly and it will become the largest manufacturer of medical goods in the city.

Two other major employers in the medical products field are Hudson Oxygen Therapy Sales Company in Orange Park and Cuda Products Corporation in Southside. Hudson employs 50 in making disposable molded plastic breathing masks. Cuda sells 75 percent of its fiber-optics products to the medical field. Cuda, which is 10 years old, employs 60 people.

In all, there are 10 manufacturers in the city that devote all or a majority of their work to making products for the medical field. Eight more manufacturers devote less than half of their business to the medical field.

Health insurance is a major business in Jacksonville. Leading the way is Blue Cross-Blue Shield of Florida, which was founded in the city in 1944 and is based in Jacksonville. Health insurance premiums of all kinds that are paid to Jacksonville-based companies total $1.4 billion annually. That includes all Blue Cross-Blue Shield money, which eventually funnels through the Jacksonville headquarters. The corporation

Throughout Florida's First Coast, neighborhood medical clinics are bringing comprehensive medical care to the people. Photo by KBJ Architects, Inc.

employs 3,500 in Jacksonville in three locations: the three-building headquarters complex in Riverside, offices in Broadmoor Executive Center not far from the headquarters, and in Deerwood Center off Baymeadows Road.

In 1986, Humana Health Care Plus established a regional claims office that employs 400. Eventually all Humana claims from a large section of the Southeast will be handled through the Jacksonville office.

Health care spending in 1984 (the last year for which figures are available), broken down by category, list hospitals as accounting for

University Hospital on Jacksonville's Northside is the city's public hospital. It also serves as a teaching hospital affiliated with the University of Florida Medical School in Gainesville. Photo by Judy K. Jacobsen

$404 million; physicians, $187 million; long-term care, $187 million; medications, $78 million; dental and other personal care, $69 million; and equipment and other expenses, $59 million.

In total, Jacksonville's health care industry, encompassing hospitals, physicians, health insurance, and other health-related businesses and industries, employs more than 92,000 people.

The health care field is among the most important economic elements of the First Coast community. Indeed, on the basis of the $2.5 billion in annual expenditures, there are many who contend that the health industry is Jacksonville's primary economic force.

Fog shrouds the Main Street
Bridge, blotting out the opposite
bank of the St. Johns River downtown. Photo by Richard Kevern

CHAPTER 6

THE GATEWAY CITY

...

The Port of Jacksonville and Transportation

The Port of Jacksonville is unique. It is a transportation crossroads, a center of transportation, the center of the compass. It is a mixing point, a node.

RON KOPICKI
CSX CORPORATION
ASSISTANT VICE-PRESIDENT
INTERMODAL MARKETING

107

The Dames Point Bridge, under construction for nearly three years, has just been completed and opened. It links the Northside and Arlington. Photo by Judy K. Jacobsen

The Port of Jacksonville, which stretches 15 miles along the St. Johns River from Blount Island to the Talleyrand Docks, is one of the major ports in the Southeast and the leading Atlantic Coast port of entry for foreign automobiles. The port is crucial to Jacksonville's economic prosperity as the basis for much of its wholesaling and transshipment trade.

In 1984, the latest year for which figures are available, the U.S. Army Corps of Engineers reported that 11,849,955 tons of domestic and foreign cargo moved through the Jacksonville Port Authority and private terminals.

Jacksonville has always been the gateway to Florida. The Charleston-built *George Washington* arrived in Jacksonville in May 1831, initiating East Coast steam transportation. Regular packet service was established on the St. Johns in 1834 between Savannah and Picolata with stops in Darien, St. Marys, Jacksonville, and Mandarin. In 1861 the first cross-state railroad line was completed, from Fernandina to Cedar Key, primarily because of the efforts of U.S. Senator David L. Yulee, president of the Florida Railway Company, who received aid from both the state and federal governments.

Today, with aircraft, interstate highways, and railroads, Jacksonville shares its passenger gateway status with Florida's main tourist destination cities, but still remains the principal Florida point of entry for all kinds of freight and commerce. The city lies only 30 miles from the Georgia state line and 35 miles from St. Augustine. Daytona Beach is 91 miles distant, Cape Canaveral 160, and Disney World at Orlando 140 miles away. Tampa is a 194-mile drive or flight, Miami 348, Key West 509, and Pensacola, at the western end of Florida's Panhandle, 360. Two rail lines head north from Jacksonville, two stretch southward, and one runs west and southwest. Four Amtrak trains serve the city daily. All major international shipping lines call at the Port of Jacksonville.

Two interstate highways link the city with the national system. They are Interstate 95, which is the East Coast interstate between Maine and Miami, and Interstate 10, which begins in Jacksonville, skirts the Gulf of Mexico to Houston, and ends in Los Angeles.

The Florida Department of Transportation reports that in 1986, I-95 just below the Georgia state line carried an average of 28,360 vehicles daily both ways. Virtually all of them go through Jacksonville or around the city on I-295, the bypass route. On I-75, 100 miles west of Jacksonville and serving Florida's Gulf Coast, the average daily traffic count just south of the state line is 23,750 vehicles. A significant portion of the I-75 traffic turns east onto I-10, either bound for Jacksonville or passing through the city on its way south.

Three railroads serve the city. They are CSX Corporation, which absorbed the old Seaboard Coastline; Southern Railway, an operating subsidiary of Norfolk Southern Corporation; and Florida East Coast Railway Company. Each railroad has major facilities in the city, including classification yards and intermodal yards. All three lines serve the Port of Jacksonville as well as other businesses and industries in the city.

The Florida East Coast line operates the only railroad bridge across the St. Johns River in northern Florida, and its tracks serve all of Florida's Atlantic coast. CSX and Norfolk Southern lines link Jacksonville with the rest of the country.

Of the 20 largest motor freight companies serving the city, 12 operate throughout the 48 contiguous states and six also serve Hawaii and Alaska. Seven of the lines offer international service, including service to Canada, Mexico, and the Caribbean, including Puerto Rico. Virtually all of the trucking companies have their terminals in the northwest quadrant of the city where their proximity to I-10 and I-295 provides a bypass west of the main portion of the city. Since the opening of I-295, trucking and warehousing facilities have increased rapidly

CSX, one of the three railroads serving the city, absorbed the old Seaboard Coastline railroad. Photo by Kelly LaDuke

CSX employs nearly 3,000 persons in Jacksonville and has influenced the expansion of other transportation industry companies in the city. Photo by Kelly LaDuke

in the northwest quadrant, joining rail facilities that have long been in operation there.

The natural paths of travel have led to and through the area for more years than the city has been in existence. Before the white man entered northeastern Florida in the late sixteenth century, Indians had already blazed trails across Florida. One route crossed the St. Johns River at what came to be known as the Cow Ford, not for its shallowness, but for its narrowness. The original town of Jacksonville was laid out on the north bank of the St. Johns River, and the Cow Ford was in what is now downtown Jacksonville.

The combination of the easy navigability of the St. Johns and its tributaries, combined with the problems of tracking through Florida's swamps, discouraged early road construction. During their 20 years of control of Florida (between 1763 and 1783), the English improved the Indian trails into what they called King's roads, and began to link Northeastern Florida with Georgia and West Florida.

All those early trails are paralleled today by modern railroads and highways. Because of its location, Jacksonville is second only to Atlanta in the Southeast for rail and highway connections.

It has not always been so easy to get around in Jacksonville. The first vehicular bridge across the river, the Acosta Bridge, was opened in 1921. The second, the Main Street Bridge, was completed in 1941.

Today there are five bridges downtown, two of them high-level, as well as the twin-span three-mile-long Buckman Bridge linking Mandarin and Orange Park and carrying I-295 south of the city.

Just opened is the spectacular Broward Bridge, first known as the Dames Point Bridge. It links Arlington and the Northside and will form part of the I-295 eastern loop bypass.

Thirty miles to the north, at the north end of Amelia Island, is the Port of Fernandina in Nassau County. The deepwater port, with 1,000 feet of marginal wharf and a 36-foot draft at low water, opened for business in 1987. Its main purpose is to handle cargo from two paper plants: Container Corporation of America, which makes corrugated paper and board; and ITT Rayonier, which makes chemical cellulose. However, the port also can handle containers and other general cargo. There is a stack area for up to 2,500 20-foot equivalent containers.

The wharf is about two miles from the ocean, and the main entrance channel has a minimum 49-foot depth. Access to the pier and the turning basin is 34 feet, mean low water. The port is served by CSX and is 14 miles from I-95.

Nearby Fernandina Beach was the site of the birth of Florida's shrimping fleet. The fleet later expanded to Mayport and Jacksonville and now counts as its base the port at St. Augustine. The sizable fleet of shrimp boats at St. Augustine is in large part built and maintained by the St. Augustine shipyards.

Answering a call, a tug moves up the St. Johns River under the Matthews Bridge. In the background is the Hart Bridge. Commodore Point terminal is at right. Photo by Richard Kevern

Seen here are the Talleyrand docks at the Port of Jacksonville. In the background is the Matthews Bridge, linking Arlington to downtown. Photo by Richard Kevern

At Jacksonville International Airport, which is owned and operated by the Jacksonville Port Authority, travel is not circumscribed by the dictates of terrain or tradition. Built in 1968, the airport is beginning a $90-million expansion program that will add loading gates, baggage handling facilities, and a parking garage. Reynolds, Smith, and Hills, Incorporated, expects to complete construction in 1990, and the new terminal will be able to handle twice as many flights daily.

The airport handles more than 100 regularly scheduled passenger flights daily. Passenger use of the airport increased from 2.3 million in 1984 to 2.4 million in 1985, 2.8 million in 1986, and 2.95 million in 1987. That increased passenger load, as well as forecasts of continued growth through the end of the century, have prompted the expansion work.

There is an international arrivals building of 32,000 square feet, which can process 350 passengers an hour through U.S. Customs. The air cargo facility has 23 bays with 66,000 square feet of storage.

Today, Jacksonville International Airport offers non-stop service to all major cities in Florida as well as to New York (via Newark), Atlanta, Memphis, Washington, D.C., Baltimore, Pittsburgh, Philadelphia, Chicago, St. Louis, Houston, Dallas-Fort Worth, Charlotte, N.C., and Raleigh-Durham, N.C. Connections at those cities provide one-stop service from Jacksonville to almost every city in the nation served by a scheduled airline.

Jacksonville International Airport has two runways, one 10,000 feet long and the other 7,700 feet. It is classified as a medium hub, category II airport. It is served by 11 major carriers, five commuter airlines, and 10 airfreight forwarders. The airport is near the intersection of I-95 and I-295, 18 miles north of downtown.

Delta Airlines is the dominant air carrier in Jacksonville, with 382 employees, not including its marketing and reservations office in the Gulf Life Tower. Next largest is Piedmont Airlines with 152 workers. Eastern Airlines has 96, and Continental and Henson airlines have 50 each.

The airport encompasses 7,000 acres and is surrounded by special zoning so that incompatible uses can be kept to a minimum.

Top: Piedmont ground crews at Jacksonville International Airport load baggage for a departing flight. Photo by Richard Kevern

Above: Delta Airlines is the dominant air carrier in Jacksonville with close to 400 employees working at the airport alone. Photo by Richard Kevern

Right: Ships undergo repairs and refitting in both the wet and dry slips at the Jacksonville Shipyards. Photo by Richard Kevern

Below: Located seven miles from the sea, Blount Island Terminal has 4,700 feet of berthing space, and is a general cargo, auto, and container terminal that covers 866 acres of land. Photo by Richard Kevern

The Port of Jacksonville's maritime facilities stretch for 22 miles along the St. Johns River, from the Atlantic Ocean to downtown Jacksonville. The facilities include nine oil terminals, including the U.S. Navy fuel depot; several single business piers, like that of the U.S. Gypsum Company; and industry terminals, like the Jacksonville Bulk Terminals as well as four general cargo terminals owned by Jaxport, the logo name of the Jacksonville Port Authority. Two of the general cargo terminals are operated by the port and two by private operators. They include:

—Talleyrand Docks and Terminals, a general cargo terminal 18 miles from the ocean. Owned and operated by Jaxport, it was first developed in 1913, handling steel, lumber, autos, containers, coffee, paper, and frozen goods. The facility has 2,900 feet of usable berthing space, an 80-foot wide apron, and 91 acres of paved, lighted, and secured space.

—Blount Island Terminal, a general cargo, auto, and container terminal owned and operated by Jaxport. Its 866 acres are seven miles from the ocean. It has 4,700 feet of usable berthing space, an 80-foot-wide apron at transit sheds, 245 paved, lighted, and secured acres, two Ro/Ro (Roll on, Roll off) berths for side or stern ramps, 153-foot apron, and 367 acres of open storage.

—Sea-Land Terminal, owned by Jaxport, operated by Sea-Land Service, Incorporated. This general cargo terminal handles Sea-Land's container vessels. It is 20 miles from the ocean, with 1,200 feet of usable berthing space, open apron width, and a 23-acre paved marshaling yard.

—Eighth Street Terminal, owned by J.M. Family Enterprises, Incorporated-Jaxport, and operated by J.M. Family Enterprises, Incorporated. This terminal is leased to Joyserv Company for docking and handling Toyotas. Situated 20 miles from the ocean, the two wharves have 707 feet of usable space each, open apron width, and 54 acres of paved storage.

A yacht heads north in the Atlantic Intracoastal Waterway. Is its destination Jacksonville, or perhaps Annapolis, New York or Bar Harbor? Photo by Kelly LaDuke

The harbor depth is 38 feet past Talleyrand and then 34 feet to Jacksonville Shipyards, Incorporated (JSI), located on the Northbank at the east end of downtown.

Jacksonville Shipyards' commercial division consists of three floating drydocks, the biggest of which will handle a 33,000-ton lift and nine wet berths, one of which is 750 feet long. The shipyard provides repairs, new installations, and conversions to all types of commercial vessels up to 900 feet in length, as well as construction of all types of commercial vessels up to 500 feet. In addition, the shipyards repair Naval vessels. The yards have been owned by the Freuhauf Corporation since 1969.

The Bellinger Division of JSI is on the Intracoastal Waterway at Atlantic Boulevard. The yard has shops and services for the repair of all types of vessels up to 400 feet in length. There are three floating drydocks, the largest of which can handle 2,800 tons. There is a 400-foot side-launching building way and a 250-foot panel line. Bellinger can build vessels with beams of up to 100 feet.

The North Florida Shipyards uses space of the Commodores Point Terminal, the largest privately owned terminal in the Jacksonville

port. The shipyard has a 6,500-ton, 500-foot drydock. It also has nearly 5,000 feet of marginal wharf for wet berthing. It is equipped for complete ship repair. Commodores Point has 800 feet of general cargo wharf available.

Atlantic Marine and Atlantic Dry Dock are affiliated companies on Fort George Island, opposite Mayport. Atlantic Dry Dock can handle vessels up to 450 feet in length; pierside facilities can handle 650-foot vessels. Atlantic Dry Dock has marine railways with a capacity of 1,000 and 4,000 tons. Atlantic Marine has two launchways for vessels of up to 250 feet.

Moody Bros. of Jacksonville, Incorporated, has a 42-acre yard on the St. Johns River at Green Cove Springs. It has a 1,000-ton synchrolift dry dock.

St. Augustine Trawlers/Shipbuilding, Incorporated, builds wood and fiberglass fishing boats and trawlers as well as steel-hulled vessels. The company can build floating dry docks up to 400 feet long and 74 feet wide. It also builds barges. The company occupies 27 acres along the San Sebastian River in St. Augustine.

Foreign Trade Zone No. 64 is linked to the Port of Jacksonville. The zone is in the northwest quadrant of the city, where most of the trucking terminals and other transportation facilities are located. The operator of the zone is Unit Assembly Support, a wholly owned subsid-

Jacksonville Shipyards, Incorporated, is located on the North-bank at the east end of downtown. Photo by Richard Kevern

iary of Unit Distribution, Incorporated, a privately held transportation service company based in Jacksonville.

CSX is expanding its Jacksonville operations, with plans to control train movements of its entire system from the city. A new $12.5-million train dispatch center will control the 15,000 miles of track that CSX expects will remain after it completes disposition of 7,000 miles of little-used track.

The control system will replace 33 dispatch sites in the District of Columbia, Ontario, and the 20 states that CSX Transportation serves. Some of the more than 500 dispatchers, supervisors, and aides will be transferred to Jacksonville.

The dispatch center, which goes into full use in early 1989, resembles a space-age amphitheater. Dispatchers work at the more than 75 individual screens surrounding the room interior that will depict track segments and the trains moving on them. Assistant directors and traffic controllers will be at supervisory stations on higher levels in the amphitheater.

CSX employs nearly 3,000 persons in Jacksonville, including more than 1,000 housed in the 16-story CSX building along the banks of the St. Johns River.

About 12 miles west of Jaxport's Talleyrand Docks, a state-of-the-art railroad yard is adding a new economic dimension to the Port of

In addition to repairing and constructing commercial vessels, Jacksonville Shipyards, Incorporated, also repairs naval vessels. Photo by Richard Kevern

Jaxport's Talleyrand Docks is a state-of-the-art railroad yard which handles containers and truck trailers. The yard is CSX's $19.3 million intermodal facility and adds a new dimension to the Port of Jacksonville. Photo by Richard Kevern

Jacksonville. The yard is CSX's $19.3-million intermodal facility, which opened in the summer of 1986. An intermodal railroad yard handles containers and truck trailers only, all shipped on flatcars.

The yard makes it possible for containers to be moved directly from flatcars to trucks, which haul the containers to dockside. There they are loaded onto vessels for overseas shipment. The process works in reverse as well.

The intermodal yard allowed CSX to consolidate its two other classification yards in Jacksonville at the new facility. Each day, the yard handles an average of 600 containers and trailers of up to 50 feet in length. (The greatest volume-day of the week normally is Tuesday, when 700 units are handled.) The yard is in operation 24 hours a day, seven days a week, and handles as many as 20 trains a day. It is already operating at capacity and expansion has begun.

The CSX intermodal yard has spurred the expansion of other transportation industry companies in Jacksonville. United Parcel Service has opened a terminal near I-295 and the CSX yard, consolidating and expanding its Jacksonville operations to serve major portions of Florida and Georgia. UPS officials said the intermodal yard was the key factor in determining the move.

Crowley Maritime Corporation consolidated its South American shipping operations at Jacksonville, in part because of the intermodal yard. Its American Transport Line handles 400 to 600 containers per sailing on the Talleyrand Docks. Also influencing Crowley was the establishment by CSX of the Gulf Wind Express, an all-container and trailer train that runs from Charleston, South Carolina, and Savannah, Georgia, through Jacksonville to Mobile, Alabama, New Orleans, Houston, San Antonio, El Paso, Phoenix, Los Angeles-Long Beach, and Oakland, California. The train and yard permit shippers to cut up to six days off shipping time between the two coasts—and time amounts to money and profits.

Within a month of the start of Gulf Wind Express train operations, Florida East Coast Railway joined the service to provide daily pickup and deliveries along the Atlantic Coast to Miami.

CSX is not the only operator of an intermodal yard in the city. Both Norfolk Southern and Florida East Coast Railway also have intermodal yards, and both railroads also serve the port. The FEC yard parallels Phillips Highway (U.S. Highway 1) and serves primarily to move freight between the railroad and trucks heading both north and south.

The builder of the Florida East Coast Railway was Henry M. Flagler, who made a fortune as one of John D. Rockefeller's partners before coming to Florida. Flagler became interested in Florida as a resort locale while he was wintering in St. Augustine in 1883-1884. He decided he could create an American Riviera and began building the Ponce de Leon Hotel in St. Augustine in 1885.

Flagler had not gone very far in the hotel-building business when he realized there needed to be a better way for tourists and vacationers to get to his hotel. He bought the Jacksonville, St. Augustine and Halifax River Railway at the end of 1885 and began rebuilding it with standard-gauge track. In the next few years, he added other lines until his railroad holdings had reached Daytona Beach. By 1889, the roadbed was improved to Daytona Beach.

In January 1888, the elegant Ponce de Leon Hotel opened its doors. At the same time, the first all-Pullman train with enclosed vestibules left New York—actually, Jersey City—and arrived in Jacksonville 29 hours and 50 minutes later. The train offered speed and comfort previously unknown. Tourist and snowbird travel finally had been made easy. But not completely.

Travelers still had to ferry the St. Johns River at Jacksonville to pick up the line to St. Augustine and beyond, so Flagler had a railroad bridge built in 1890, and through travel was assured.

Loading vessels is a common sight at the Port of Jacksonville. Photo by Richard Kevern

Jacksonville's interstate highways link the city with the national highway system. Photo by Richard Kevern

Flagler extended the railroad to Palm Beach and created that resort in 1894 with the opening of the Royal Poinciana Hotel. The resort was an immediate success, and in 1895 Flagler began construction of the Palm Beach Inn, later renamed the Breakers.

That same year, Flagler began extending the railroad still farther south toward Miami, and the railroad's name was changed to Florida East Coast Railway (FEC), still its name today.

As much as anyone, Flagler, by extending the railroad beyond Jacksonville and building his bridge over the St. Johns, assured Jacksonville's end as a premier tourist resort through most of the twentieth century, and at the same time reinforced the city's growing importance as a transfer and wholesaling point. The FEC operates 16 trains daily between Jacksonville and Miami.

The Southern Railway Company is one of two wholly owned railroad subsidiaries of Norfolk Southern. The other is the Norfolk and Western Railway. Norfolk Southern operates 18,000 miles of track in 20 Eastern, Southern, and Midwestern states as well as Ontario, Canada.

The Jacksonville Norfolk Southern intermodal terminal handles both trailers and containers. It is the third-busiest intermodal yard in the system, ranking behind Atlanta and Chicago.

Five trains operate southbound into Jacksonville and four northbound; three are dedicated piggyback trains. Norfolk Southern connects with Florida East Coast Railway to operate dedicated intermodal trains to FEC destinations south of Jacksonville.

In Jacksonville, Norfolk Southern has a car repair facility at its terminal, and both a classification yard and an adjoining intermodal yard, which underwent a major expansion in 1982. The work more than tripled Norfolk Southern's capacity for moving piggyback freight traffic through Jacksonville and resulted in greatly improved service to shippers.

Of the three railroads, Norfolk Southern Railway Company has the smallest presence in Jacksonville and the First Coast area. Its 137 employees in the five-county area are paid a total of $3.9 million, and the railway spends about $7.9 million in making local purchases. The rail line has 209 miles of track in Florida, with 261 employees on the payroll, including the First Coast workers.

Norfolk Southern owns a 5,300-acre tract at Westlake, just east of the Navy's Whitehouse training airfield, five miles west of I-295, and three miles north of I-10. Industrial and mixed-use tracts are included in the acreage. The Norfolk Southern industrial development department in Atlanta has worked closely with Jacksonville officials in designing potential development plans for the property.

Jacksonville is the leading Atlantic Coast port of entry for foreign cars. Automobile preparation centers employ more than 2,000 persons

Pillars for the Automated Skyway Express mark the south side of West Bay Street in downtown Jacksonville. Photo by Kelly LaDuke

in readying imported cars for delivery throughout the Southeast. Most car unloading facilities are leased by the port to car preparation companies, principally to Joyserv Company Ltd., the largest handler of all makes of imported cars.

Construction is underway on additional car docks and storage space on Blount Island. Many of the arriving cars are already unloaded at the Blount terminal. When the new facilities are ready, plans are to move all the car unloading facilities except Toyota to Blount Island. Toyota is expected to stay at Talleyrand because it owns its facilities there.

Several factors have prompted the transfer of the car import facilities to Blount Island. Blount is close to the mouth of the St. Johns River, and sailing time to its docks is much shorter than to the Talleyrand area. It is next to I-295 and the Broward Bridge across the St. Johns River. The bridge, opened in 1988, allows shippers to move their cars directly onto the interstate system without having to contend with urban traffic.

The Blount Island location will keep imported cars separated from much of the general cargo port to prevent the possibility of stored cars being dirtied, and to prevent damage to finishes. This reflects Jaxport's efforts to segregate vessels and cargo so that incompatible activities are kept apart.

In mid-1987, employment in the trucking and warehousing industry in Jacksonville totaled 9,700, an increase of 800, or 9 percent, from the year-earlier figures. The Florida Department of Labor and Employment Security reported in its July 1986 employment summary that growth in the trucking field in Jacksonville exceeded the statewide average.

Some of the largest trucking companies in the nation have terminals in Jacksonville. Among those companies are Yellow Freight Systems, Incorporated; Roadway Express, Incorporated; Consolidated

Above: The Port of Jacksonville is the biggest car importer on the East Coast. Here, recently unloaded Toyotas are lined up awaiting inspection and then shipment to dealers throughout the Southeast. Photo by David Dobbs

Right: The Jacksonville rapid transit system makes it easier for residents to get around. Photo by Kelly LaDuke

The St. Elmo W. Acosta Bridge, the first vehicular bridge to span the St. Johns River in Jacksonville, is all angles, girders, and traffic signs. At left is the raised railroad bridge. Photo by Kelly LaDuke

Freightways Corporation; and P-I-E Nationwide, Incorporated, which is based in Jacksonville.

There are many regional trucking companies serving Jacksonville, as well as two Florida-based lines: Alterman Transport Lines, Incorporated, and Watkins Motor Lines.

In ancient times, villages grew up along the main caravan routes and at sheltered bays and river mouths, where goods could be transferred to and from sailing ships. In modern times, virtually all of the world' greatest cities are seaports and transportation hubs. Jacksonville's role as a transportation hub is growing, and the city is meeting the challenges and taking the opportunities that are open to it. The city and its deepwater port are within 24-hour reach of all the major commercial centers of the Southeast and within 48 hours of the Great Lakes. Situated as it is, Jacksonville continues to be the transportation hub of the Southeast and the heart of the Sun Belt.

Submarine-hunting helicopters on the line. Photo by Richard Kevern

CHAPTER 7

THE NAVY PARTNERSHIP

. . .

The Navy in Jacksonville

Jacksonville is known throughout the Naval establishment as the 'Best Navy Town in the U.S.A.' Both the Navy and Jacksonville are proud of this distinction.

CAPTAIN JAMES R. COMPTON
UNITED STATES NAVY

125

Navy F-18s on the line at Cecil Field NAS, one of the Navy's four master jet bases. Photo by Richard Kevern

In May 1987 the nation was shocked and angered by the attack in the Persian Gulf on the guided missile frigate USS *Stark,* and saddened by the loss of 37 of the ship's crewmen.

In Jacksonville, news of the attack tightened chests and sent thousands to their television screens, radios, and telephones. The loss was a personal one, because the *Stark* is based at the Mayport Naval Station, at the mouth of the St. Johns River. Among those killed and injured, the city knew, would be friends, neighbors, and relatives.

As it has done in past wars and emergencies, Jacksonville rallied to aid and comfort the families and took to its heart the widows and children whose husbands and fathers had been killed.

With about 40,000 men and women in uniform, plus a quarter as many civilian employees, the U.S. Navy is an integral part of the community as well as Jacksonville's largest employer. The figures are impressive: At the Jacksonville Naval Air Station (NAS Jacksonville) there are 10,750 military and 7,000 civilian employees. At the Cecil Field Naval Air Station (NAS Cecil Field), there are 11,200 military and 1,100 civilian employees. At NAVSTA Mayport, as it is referred to in the Navy, there are 18,000 military and 3,000 civilians in the work force. That adds up to 51,050 full-time military and civilian employees at the three installations.

Jacksonville is the Navy's third-largest complex, behind Norfolk, Virginia, which is headquarters for the Atlantic fleet, and San Diego, headquarters for the Pacific fleet.

The economic impact of the Navy in Jacksonville is enormous. The Navy estimates that the total annual dollar impact of its bases in Jacksonville amounts to more than $1.7 billion. The annual payroll alone is $1.2 billion. That breaks down to $947 million for the military and $260 million for civilians. In addition, an estimated 20,000 military retirees live in the Jacksonville area, receiving $168 million annually in pensions.

In addition to the payroll, the Navy spends $323.7 million for such necessities as telephone and electric service, as well as contributing school impact funds. Local purchases and construction amount to $100 million annually. Shipyard contracts were $130 million in 1986, the last year for which figures are available. This represents a substantial increase from 1983, when shipyard work totaled only $65 million a year.

Ten years ago, military construction at the three bases was $24 million a year. In the first half of the 1980s, construction averaged $50 million annually. In 1986 that figure was up to $62.5 million, and 1987 figures were expected to equal that.

The Navy is more than just a set of bases that produce fascinating economic statistics. It is also men and women on active duty defending the interests, programs, and frontiers of the United States. Mayport ships and Cecil Field pilots are on duty wherever the interests of our country require them. That is why the *Stark* was in the Persian Gulf. That is also why pilots based at Cecil Field and flying from the aircraft carrier USS *Saratoga* intercepted the *Achille Lauro* hijackers as they attempted to flee in a jet in 1986.

Four-engined P-3 Orion submarine-hunting planes of the Navy are arrayed in squadron formation about their hexagonal maintenance hangar at Naval Air Station Jacksonville. Photo by Richard Kevern

A Marine drill team conducts an exhibition aboard the aircraft carrier USS Saratoga, *based at Mayport Naval Station. Photo by Richard Kevern*

During off-duty hours, these same men and women take active roles in all phases of Jacksonville community life, and the Navy regularly conducts public information programs to foster good relations with the people of Jacksonville.

At Mayport, for example, the Navy has established a tradition of opening at least one ship for civilian tours each Saturday, whenever possible. The tours are extremely popular. The USS *Saratoga* was opened for a day of civilian tours after returning from its 1986 exercise defying Libya's "Line of Death" in the Gulf of Sidra. Throngs of people overwhelmed the base, and only a fraction of the crowd was able to actually board the carrier.

From time to time, the Navy sends a smaller ship up the St. Johns River to tie up for several days at the bulkhead downtown along Coastline Drive. Tours at this location are always well attended.

This concentration of naval power in Jacksonville is the result of a strategic location and the friendship and cooperation that has marked Jacksonville's relations with the nation's military forces since the early twentieth century. At that time, the site that would become NAS Jacksonville was not within the city limits. Instead, the land at Black Point was generally unimproved, open, and agricultural.

In 1907 a state commission recommended that the tract be purchased for a permanent state camp. The commission suggested that

1,300 acres might be suitable and noted that it had an option on the property at $20 per acre. It went on to report that the citizens of Jacksonville had raised $6,000 toward the purchase and that there were $8,000 in federal funds available for the part of the camp that would be used as a target range.

The commission's recommendation was approved, and Jacksonville bought 300 acres and gave them to the state. Additional purchases were made until 1,000 acres were acquired. The first encampment of state troops occurred in 1909.

The reservation was federalized in September 1917, after the United States entered World War I. Additional land was leased from private owners, and Camp Joseph E. Johnston became a quartermaster training camp. As the war ended, construction was underway to expand the camp in order to train 50,000 men at a time. The capacity at the time was 27,000.

After World War I, the camp was demobilized and buildings were taken down. The state received 682 acres and 154 buildings for the use of the Florida National Guard and similar units. As a National Guard site, the camp was renamed Camp Foster.

In the late 1930s, the Navy decided to establish a major flight training base in the Southeast. Rear Admiral A.J. Hepburn headed a commission charged with seeking out a suitable site in Florida or

A Mayport-based warship returns from sea trials. Photo by Richard Kevern

The destroyer John Hancock *is at its berth at Mayport Naval Station. Photo by Joanne Kash*

adjoining states. After visiting Jacksonville twice in 1938, the Hepburn Board returned to the city early in 1939 with members of the House Naval Affairs Committee. The Navy needed a strategic location for its new base, with a landing field, a good harbor, and suitable year-round flying weather. Jacksonville met these requirements, but so did several other Florida locations.

Tipping the scales in Jacksonville's favor were efforts by members of the Jacksonville Chamber of Commerce, who persuaded Congress to pass legislation authorizing the aviation facility for Jacksonville. A companion appropriation measure authorized $15 million for construction, and the Navy narrowed its search from the entire Southeast to Jacksonville and vicinity.

The Chamber of Commerce had gained experience in lobbying Washington for the base through its failed attempt to persuade the Army to locate an air base here in 1935. The facility, MacDill Air Force Base, was eventually located at Tampa.

The existing Camp Foster was recommended for the airfield, and Ribault Bay at Mayport for the naval station. In July 1939, Duval County voters passed a $1.1-million bond issue for the two purchases. The money bought 3,260 acres at Black Point, now NAS Jacksonville, and 300 acres at Ribault Bay for "carrier berthing," now NAVSTA Mayport. The land at both places was deeded to the Navy.

Florida Air National Guard F16s on the line at their National Guard base at Jacksonville International Airport. Photo by Richard Kevern

Below: This is the control tower at Mayport Naval Air Facility, alongside the Mayport Naval Station at the mouth of the St. Johns River. Photo by Joanne Kash

Work commenced at both bases, and at NAS Jacksonville the first class of pilots was graduated in April 1941. Mayport originally served as a home port to patrol craft and target and rescue boats during World War II. The carrier berth was put on the shelf. The base served successively as a naval section base, sea frontier base, and then as a naval auxiliary air station.

At NAS Jacksonville, members of that first class of pilots had hardly reported to their duty stations when the Navy decided that a second landing field was needed in Duval County. It found 2,600 acres of forest and farmland 10 miles west of NAS Jacksonville in southwestern Duval County and bought the tract in 1941 for $16,851. It became the nucleus of what is now Cecil Field, one of four U.S. Navy master jet bases.

Six months after this purchase Cecil Field became operational as a naval auxiliary air station. By the end of World War II, four 5,000-foot runways were in use and pilots were being trained in combat flight operations.

Near Green Cove Springs, 17 miles south of Jacksonville along the St. Johns River, the Navy established a second auxiliary air station named Lee Field. After the war ended Lee Field was closed, but anchorages in the St. Johns River were developed for a mothballed fleet that eventually included 300 ships.

During the Korean conflict, 175 ships were reactivated from the Green Cove Springs fleet. After the truce in 1953, most were returned for mothballing. The ships were eventually removed or scrapped and in 1962 the facility, by then called Naval Station Green Cove Springs, was closed and sold to Reynolds Aluminum Corporation. Today, the old Lee Field site is the home of a developing industrial park complex.

During World War II there were three runways at NAS Jacksonville (each more than 6,000 feet long), seaplane ramps, and overhaul and repair facilities. These included the Naval Air Rework Facility,

Mayport frigates stand ready.
Photo by Richard Kevern

Below: Throngs of people over-
whelmed the Mayport base when
the USS Saratoga *returned in*
1986 from the Gulf of Sidra. Photo
by Richard Kevern

now operating as the Naval Aviation Depot. With 2,900 employees, it is the largest single industrial employer in Jacksonville and northeast Florida.

The first anti-submarine patrol began operation in April 1942. PBY seaplanes were a common sight taking off and landing on the St. Johns River. Today, they have been replaced by P-3 Orion four-motored airplanes and SH-3 Sea King and SH-60 Seahawk helicopters. Anti-submarine patrols have continued uninterrupted and remain the primary mission of NAS Jacksonville.

Toward the end of World War II a prisoner-of-war compound was established at NAS Jacksonville and 1,500 German POWs were housed there.

The end of the war brought about major changes at all of the Navy's First Coast bases. NAS Jacksonville's first role was to be a Navy separation center. It was the largest in the Southeast. Lee Field was closed down; Cecil Field was shifted to partial maintenance status. The peacetime Navy had about all the facilities it needed in NAS Jacksonville and NAVSTA Mayport.

In 1946, NAS Jacksonville became headquarters for the Seventh Naval District. The command remained there for two years. The Blue Angels, the Navy's flight demonstration team established to promote postwar aviation, flew its first public demonstration at the 1946 dedication of Craig Field. Located at Atlantic Boulevard and St. Johns Bluff Road, the airfield was named for Lieutenant Commander James Edwin Craig of Jacksonville, who was killed during the Japanese attack of Pearl Harbor. At that time a private airfield, today Craig Field is owned by the Jacksonville Port Authority.

By 1948, NAS Jacksonville had shifted its main mission from training to support of fleet units. The post of Commander Fleet Air Jacksonville was established, the forerunner of the present Commander Sea Based ASW Wings Atlantic, the senior command at the station.

At the end of 1948, Cecil Field was returned to operating base status for fleet aircraft units. The first jets assigned to Jacksonville arrived in early 1949 via Carrier Air Group 17. It was joined a month later by a second air group and Fleet Aircraft Service Squadron Nine. With major airstrips at NAS Jacksonville and NAS Cecil Field, half of the Navy's aircraft on the East Coast were stationed at Jacksonville.

At that time in Washington, D.C., the Navy was considering how to organize its air arm. Captain R.W.D. Woods submitted a report calling for the establishment of a small number of naval air stations designed specifically for the operation of jet aircraft. The stations had to be near enough to seaport bases to draw on them for logistical support, but far enough from major population areas to allow for future expansion.

Cecil Field was one of four bases designated by the Navy as a master jet base. The others are Oceana at Norfolk, Miramar at San Diego, and Coronado at San Francisco.

In 1951 Cecil Field was enlarged to 4,600 acres and construction began on four 8,000-foot runways. On June 30, 1952, the auxiliary field became Naval Air Station Cecil Field. Expansion since then has expanded the base to more than 19,000 acres, and the runways have been extended.

Below: All three Navy bases in Jacksonville have their own Officers' Club. This one is at Mayport Naval Station. Photo by Joanne Kash

A total of 51,050 military and civilian employees work for the U.S. Navy at three locations: Jacksonville Naval Air Station, Cecil Field Naval Air Station, and at Mayport. Photo by Richard Kevern

At Mayport, postwar development began with a report in late 1948 by the House Naval Affairs Committee to the Secretary of the Navy. The report proposed consolidating many of the Navy's Southeastern operations at Mayport. The proposal was to consolidate Green Cove Springs auxiliary air station, NAS Jacksonville, and other Jacksonville facilities at Mayport. Action was delayed, and the outbreak of fighting in Korea changed military thinking. The Navy began dredging Ribault Bay in 1950 and a carrier pier was built. Construction of the second aircraft carrier pier began in 1954. The first aircraft carrier homeported at Mayport was the USS *Lake Champlain.* It tied up at the carrier berth in 1952.

Four other aircraft carriers have been homeported at Mayport. They are the USS *Franklin D. Roosevelt,* the USS *Shangri La,* and the two carriers now berthed at Mayport, the USS *Saratoga* and the USS *Forrestal.*

The Korean War brought with it new and more sophisticated air surveillance techniques. Though seaplanes were still used for anti-submarine patrols, land-based P5M and P2 Neptunes were added.

In early 1960, the Naval Magazine Yellow Water was commissioned north and west of Cecil Field. The weapons reservation encompasses more than 10,000 acres, and its function is to procure, store, maintain, and issue all types of weapons used by the Navy's attack carriers. A guided missile service unit is attached to the weapons department.

The Cuban missile crisis in 1962 presented Mayport with a crucial challenge, which was ably met. Mayport was an advance staging area for the Second Marine Division and provided support to many vessels, including five aircraft carriers.

During the Vietnam War, many Mayport ships and Cecil Field planes saw action. The return in early 1973 of the first group of U.S. prisoners of war released by the North Vietnamese was an emotional experience at NAS Jacksonville.

In 1968, NAS Jacksonville added a huge hexagonal hangar, next to the intermediate repair facilities, that can house five squadrons under one roof. The hangar is within easy taxi distance of the runways and is considered a major improvement in aircraft intermediate maintenance.

Cecil Field became the base for all East Coast carrier-based anti-submarine warfare forces in 1975 after the northeastern base at Quonset Point, Rhode Island, was closed in an economy move.

The commitment of the City of Jacksonville to the Navy was exemplified in 1978 with the adoption by the City Council of an ordinance controlling development around the local Navy bases. The prime purpose of the ordinance is to prevent development so close to

With about 40,000 men and women in uniform, the U.S. Navy is an integral part of the community as well as Jacksonville's largest employer. Photo by Richard Kevern

Mayport ships and Cecil Field pilots remain on active duty to defend the interests of the United States. Photo by Richard Kevern

Far right: Anti-Submarine Warfare helicopters await their call to duty. Photo by Richard Kevern

the airfields that the Navy would find itself hemmed in. The ordinance was six years in the writing. It was overturned on a technicality in 1984 but was adopted again in the following year when the technical error was corrected.

The newest Navy base in the Jacksonville area is just across the state line at Kings Bay, Georgia, not much farther from the city than St. Augustine. The Navy is constructing a $1.8-billion Trident submarine base, which is virtually ready to go into active service. Another 15,000 officers and crew members will be stationed there.

Kings Bay is expected to cost $1.8 billion before it is completed. In 1986 construction costs totaled $184 million. In 1987 it was esti-

mated at $270 million. A large portion of that is being spent in North Florida and Jacksonville.

When it is fully operational, Kings Bay is expected to have an economic impact on Jacksonville comparable to that of Cecil Field. That would mean that with the 15,000 uniformed personnel, an additional 1,500 civilians would be employed on the base. The military payroll would be $370 million, and the civilian payroll would be $35 million.

When the Kings Bay base is opened, forecasts are that northside Jacksonville will begin to boom, responding to the need for housing and support services for servicemen and women and their families.

"An Exalting Experience"

. . .

The Arts

In this phase of our community's
development, there is no single
element of more importance than the
existence of arts-oriented institutions
with citizen-involving programs of
substantial merit, and capable of
producing personal satisfaction. Let's
make the City of Jacksonville itself ...
an exalting experience.

IRA MCK. KOGER
CHAIRMAN OF THE BOARD
CHIEF EXECUTIVE OFFICER
KOGER PROPERTIES, INC.

Roger Nierenberg conducts the Jacksonville Symphony Orchestra. After two seasons at the Florida Theatre, the Symphony is returning to the Civic Auditorium. Photo by Richard Kevern

In the early years of this century, English composer Frederick Delius lived in the Solano Grove area along the St. Johns River 35 miles south of Jacksonville. Several of his compositions expressing Florida themes are based on his observations and experiences in and around Jacksonville. The composer's connections to the area are celebrated each May with a Delius music festival; his home has been moved to the Jacksonville University campus, which also has an extensive collection of Delius notes and papers.

Jacksonville's arts connection has been gaining in strength in recent years. For more than four decades, Ira McK. Koger has championed the arts in the city, while building a $90-million business in the development and management of suburban office parks. A man of varied interests, he was elected a member of the South Carolina legislature while still in college, and worked 15 years in the broadcast and print media before moving into construction and real estate and establishing his home in Jacksonville. He has been a driving force behind such diverse cultural institutions as the Jacksonville Symphony Orchestra, the Jacksonville Art Museum, the public broadcasting station WJCT, and the St. Johns River City Band. A wing of the art museum bears his name and is home to his impressive collection of Chinese porcelains, and symphony orchestras throughout the country (wherever there is a Koger office park) have benefited from Koger foundation support.

Ira Koger's commitment to the arts has set the standard for a thriving business-arts partnership in Jacksonville. Since the 1972 establishment of the Arts Assembly of Jacksonville as the city's official arts agency, recognition of the value of arts-oriented institutions to the health of the community has increased dramatically. Its purpose is to promote the development of "a diverse and stimulating cultural environment in Jacksonville."

The Arts Assembly serves as an arts information clearinghouse and advocate of the arts on a local, state, and national level. The organization is funded by the National Endowment for the Arts, the Florida Arts Council, the State of Florida, and the City of Jacksonville, as well as by gifts from corporations, foundations, individuals, and membership dues. One of the initial accomplishments of the Arts Assembly was the purchase and restoration of the Florida Theatre, a movie and vaudeville palace originally opened in 1927. The Jacksonville Chamber of Commerce raised $5.7 million to purchase and renovate the theater, restoring the lobby's original decor of a Moorish courtyard at night, complete with a starry sky. It opened in 1983 as the Florida Theatre Performing Arts Center. The 1,978-seat facility is home to some of the concerts of the Jacksonville Symphony Orchestra, the Florida Ballet, and a variety of other events and performances requiring full theater facilities in a medium-sized house.

A 2005 Arts Vision Task Force, formed by the Chamber of Commerce in 1985, issued a set of 43 goals that its chairman, J. Shepard Bryan, Jr., described as "not a master plan but more than a wish list." It stressed "the interrelatedness of economic growth and the arts," pointing out that "strength in the arts is an aspect of our quality of life which is an important attraction to companies seeking new locations—a major factor of economic growth, and economic growth is the determining factor in improving the quality of life and building the arts."

The Alhambra Dinner Theater stages a new production every five or six weeks. This is a scene from "Little Shop of Horrors." Photo by Kelly LaDuke

This symbiosis has resulted in a renaissance for the arts in Jacksonville. The monthly arts calender, published by the Arts Assembly, is packed with opportunities for Jacksonville residents—plays, concerts, films, exhibits, lectures, poetry readings, opera, dance, and sometimes even world premieres of major motion pictures (thanks to the aggressive marketing efforts of the Mayor's Motion Picture and Television Liaison Office, which is working to again establish the city as a prime location for filmmakers). Three of Jacksonville's art institutions—the Jacksonville Symphony Orchestra, the Jacksonville Art Museum, and the Cummer Gallery of Art—have been designated as being among Florida's 14 Major Cultural Institutions by the Division of Cultural Affairs and receive substantial state funding. The symphony orchestra has been named as the State Touring Orchestra. The only orchestra chosen to be a part of the state's touring program, it performs both classical and pops concerts from Panama City to Key Largo.

Jacksonville was selected by the National Endowment for the Arts as one of five cities in the nation to produce a brochure about the impact of the arts on the community. The 32-page, four-color booklet was written and produced by the Arts Assembly and is used by businesses and government to illustrate Jacksonville's successful public/private partnership support of the arts.

The Jacksonville Symphony Orchestra is being expanded through a newly organized endowment program. The goal of the Permanent Fund endowment campaign is to raise $4.5 million; in addition to the permanent fund, the JSO also conducts an annual fund drive of more than $500,000 to meet regular operating costs.

The orchestra has 49 full-time members; other musicians augment the core orchestra on a per-service basis. Anticipating additions to the permanent fund and increases in the annual budget, the JSO has set a goal of utilizing 59 full-time musicians by 1990.

Under conductor and music director Roger Nierenberg, the number of annual concerts has increased substantially, and the symphony

The Cummer Gallery of Art in the Riverside section of Jacksonville faces a garden which extends to the St. Johns River. Photo by Richard Kevern.

*The best in the music world per-
form at the Jazz Festival. Photo by
Richard Kevern*

offers its patrons their choice of five subscription concert series. The popular Classical and Pops series have been joined by a Beethoven Series, four concerts in which all nine of Beethoven's symphonies are played; a Connoisseur's Series, featuring works less often performed; and a Coffee Concert Series at 11 a.m. on Fridays at the Civic Auditorium's Little Theater. A premiere event each year features such distinguished guest artists as Isaac Stern, Victor Borge, Kiri Te Kanawa, and Fredrica von Stade. For many, the appearance of Luciano Pavarotti with the Jacksonville Symphony Orchestra was *the* musical event of the 1980s.

The JSO has also developed an extensive Youth Program, reaching about 50,000 students annually in grades one through twelve. The orchestra performs a series of 10 concerts at the Civic Auditorium for grades four through six, and holds five other concerts in junior high schools throughout the city. Small ensembles visit elementary schools to introduce children to the orchestra by demonstrating the sounds that the various instruments make.

A popular new addition to the city's music scene, the St. Johns River City Band was founded in 1985 to re-create the atmosphere of the turn-of-the-century band concerts in the town square. The brainchild of Ira Koger and the only professional municipal brass band in the country, the band packs in the crowds every Sunday afternoon at Metropolitan Park, who come to picnic, socialize, and enjoy rousing renditions of American favorites from Copeland to Sousa to Duke Ellington. The versatile band also does its own memorable version of the *1812 Overture,* and even plays jazz—headlining the 1987 Jacksonville Jazz Festival with Al Hirt.

In September 1987 the band played Carnegie Hall, for the purpose of promoting brass band music throughout the country. New York critics received the concert warmly, and members of a committee formed by Koger to promote the concert—the New York Committee

for the Organization, Support, and Development of Large Brass Bands Elsewhere—showed an interest in furthering the spread of brass bands in their own cities. Meanwhile, the band is working to promote that idea closer to home by touring the state and giving free public concerts.

Jacksonvillians love their brass band marches, but come October, jazz is king. The Florida National Bank Jacksonville Jazz Festival, staged in Metropolitan Park, is a three-day celebration of the musical art form, and one of the biggest free outdoor jazz festivals in the United States. Each year, top-name artists like Dave Brubeck, Herbie Hancock, Miles Davis, Dizzy Gillespie, Della Reese, and George Benson draw tens of thousands to the riverfront park. The event is televised by WJCT and aired on PBS stations throughout the country.

A wide variety of concerts with smaller audiences in more intimate settings are offered throughout the year by the city's college and university music departments. Jacksonville University presents a world-class chamber music series featuring such eminent ensembles as the Beaux Arts Trio and the Juilliard String Quartet. Begun in 1984, the JU Chamber Music Series is presented in the university's Swisher Auditorium.

There is ample fare in Jacksonville for all kinds of music lovers— from rock concerts to country music shows in the Coliseum to folk singers and synthesizer musicians in the city's cafes and lofts. Operatic programs are performed locally by the Starlight Symphonette and the Lyric Theatre.

Mikhail Baryshnikov has performed in Jacksonville, as have the Martha Graham and Merce Cunningham troupes, Pilobolus, Alvin Ailey, and the Ballet de Monte Carlo. Dance is alive and well in the city, with performances by visiting companies and by the local professional dance company, the Florida Ballet at Jacksonville. Having celebrated its tenth birthday in 1988, the Florida Ballet offers a diverse

Above: Dizzy Gillespie and Al Hirt blow up a storm at the Jacksonville Jazz Festival. Photo by Richard Kevern

Mikhail Baryshnikov and Company take a final bow. Photo by Kelly LaDuke

repertoire from classic to contemporary. Its home stage is the Florida
Theatre Performing Arts Center.

Broadway comes to Jacksonville through Florida Community College's FCCJ Artist Series, which brings top touring productions to the
Civic Auditorium, and presents a variety of other performances at the
Florida Theatre. Shows like *Cats*, *La Cage aux Folles*, *Evita*, and *42nd
Street* consistently fill the auditorium's 3,000-seat main hall.

The Beaches Fine Arts Series has chosen the magnificent (and
acoustically superior) building of the St. Paul's-by-the-Sea Episcopal
Church as its home. Offerings range from plays and musical performances to exhibits of photography, sculpture, and weaving.

Professional and community theater flourishes in Jacksonville.
The River City Playhouse annually presents 24 different productions—
including original scripts—bringing audiences a total of 232 performances. The professional repertory company also offers special performances and workshops in its 578-seat house, the restored Five Points
Theatre. There are two other local professional repertory groups: the
Case Theatre, Incorporated, and the Jacksonville Actor's Theatre.

*Built in 1927 as a movie house,
the Florida Theater is now a performing arts center. Photo by
Steven Brooke*

The only resident Equity theater in Jacksonville is the Alhambra Dinner Theatre, operated by Tod Booth Productions, Incorporated. Booth has many years of acting and directing experience, mostly in Chicago, and presents shows that are consistently imaginative and well above the standard dinner theater fare.

Theatre Jacksonville, which has been offering community theater productions for over half a century, is the oldest continually performing nonprofessional group in the United States. Its playhouse on historic San Marco Square was built in 1938. Other community theater groups in the First Coast region include Players-by-the-Sea in Jacksonville Beach, Orange Park Community Theatre in Clay County, N.A.S. Jax Acts Community Theatre, the Amelia Community Theatre in Fernandina Beach, and St. Augustine's Ancient City Theatre. The First Coast Signing Theatre interprets performances for the hearing impaired and uses deaf actors in its presentations. Tots 'n' Teens presents children's theater with young performers, and Theatreworks, Incorporated, sponsors a season of quality musical theater for family audiences.

For film enthusiasts, the Film Institute of Jacksonville offers a full season of movies that are not likely to come to local movie theaters or be shown on cable television. Founded in 1979 by a group of local movie buffs, the Institute provides some 40 different offerings each year, including foreign films, experimental films, and Hollywood classics.

The literary arts are also alive and well in Jacksonville. Florida Community College annually sponsors a State Street Poets and Writing Festival, and its internationally distributed literary magazine *Kalliope, A Journal of Women's Art* celebrated 10 years of publication in 1988. The Women's Resource Network sponsors an annual playwriting contest that attracts entries from throughout the country.

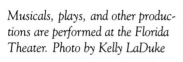

Musicals, plays, and other productions are performed at the Florida Theater. Photo by Kelly LaDuke

Right: The Florida Ballet, which calls Jacksonville its home, performs during the winter season at the Florida Theatre. Photo by Richard Kevern

The city is home to two major art museums and numerous galleries and art exhibition spaces. The Jacksonville Art Museum (JAM), founded in 1924 by a group of local artists, has maintained a strong commitment to contemporary creative artists by offering continuous classes, workshops, and lectures, by exhibiting the best in contemporary art, and by building a permanent collection of twentieth-century masterpieces. The JAM is also the home of the Koger Collection, one of the world's preeminent collections of Oriental porcelains, spanning the Neolithic period to the end of the Ch'ing dynasties, and a small but important collection of pre-Columbian art. It was also the JAM that brought the block-buster exhibit "Ramses II: The Pharaoh and His Time" to Jacksonville in 1986 to open the Prime F. Osborn III Convention Center.

In addition, the Jacksonville Art Museum offers noontime concerts, programs by special musical ensembles, films, workshops in various art media, and lectures relating to current exhibits.

Well-known to connoisseurs of fine porcelains for its 700-piece Meissen collection, the Cummer Gallery of Art houses some 2,000 pieces of art valued at more than $30 million. The collection ranges from a portrait relief of Ramses II dating from 1280 B.C. to Andre L'Hote's 1917 *Cubist Nude*. Twelve galleries of European and American art include works by Rubens, El Greco, Goya, Reynolds, Eakins, and Remington, as well as by lesser-known artists. A major acquisition program has added Egyptian and Roman sculpture and late Gothic works from central Europe as well as American colonial and early twentieth-century paintings. Works in the Cummer collection have been loaned to the National Gallery of Art in Washington, D.C., and the Metropolitan Museum of Art in New York.

The museum was founded in 1961 as the result of a bequest from the estate of Jacksonville collector Mrs. Ninah H. Cummer. The gift included the Cummer mansion and a core collection of 60 paintings,

Seen here is the "Pomodor" exhibit at the Jacksonville Art Museum. Courtesy, Jacksonville Art Museum

"Body and Soul" is one of the exhibits at the Jacksonville Art Museum. Courtesy, Jacksonville Art Museum

pieces of furniture, tapestry, and decorative art. Located in Riverside, the museum has two formal gardens—an English azalea garden designed in 1903 and an Italian garden designed after the famed garden of Villa Gameraia near Florence—as well as a lovely panoramic view of the St. Johns River.

A new art exhibition space has been opened at the Grande Boulevard shopping mall by the Jacksonville Coalition for the Visual Arts, and offers several major exhibits each year. The Coalition, formed in 1986, provides its membership (some 200 artists and art enthusiasts) with exhibition space, information about grants, commissions, and competitions, and a forum for airing the concerns and interests of the city's very active visual arts community.

Public art is becoming more in evidence as the city develops. A copy of the Navy Memorial in Washington has been erected along the Riverwalk, an equestrian statue of General Jackson welcomes shoppers to The Landing, intriguing outdoor sculpture graces several of the newer downtown buildings, and corporate art collections are becoming commonplace. The Jacksonville Chamber of Commerce has its own collection of works by area artists.

Another museum of note in the First Coast region is St. Augustine's Lightner Museum, housed in the former Alcazar Hotel built by Henry Flagler in 1888. The Lightner has gained national recognition for its collection of Victorian art, glass, ceramics, textiles, furniture, and mechanical musical instruments.

The pride of the Southbank Riverwalk is the Museum of Science and History. Having evolved from the Jacksonville Children's Museum, the institution offers children and adults the opportunity to explore an overwhelming range of cultural and natural phenomena, explained in ways that are especially understandable and enjoyable. The museum houses real Egyptian mummies, a reconstructed Florida trading post, an exhibit depicting a century of Florida Seminole Indian life, and the state-of-the-art Brest Planetarium, which offers "cosmic concerts," laser shows, and shows of the night sky. A marsh room features natural science specimens and live animals native to Florida, and another exhibit shows the way a city works. Changing exhibits have featured dinosaurs and sharks, robots and shipwrecks. In the fall of 1988 the museum opened its new $7.5-million science and space building, and its treasure trove will continue to be augmented to inform and delight visitors of every age.

One of the first recommendations of the Arts Task Force to be implemented was the creation of a school for the arts in the public school system. The Douglas Anderson School of the Arts opened in 1985, and offers especially talented youngsters professional training in the visual and performing arts along with their traditional high school education.

An Artist-in-the-Schools Program has been in existence in Jacksonville since 1972. Administered by the Arts Assembly with a grant from the Florida Arts Council and matching funds from the Duval County school system, the program allows for a professional artist to spend time in art classes throughout the system, doing his or her work while the students look on and ask questions. The artists also work with art teachers to assist in curriculum development.

Jacksonville is a community that demonstrates its commitment to the arts in many ways. Enlarging the scope of influence of the arts is a major focus of the Community Cultural Plan, which asserts that "the arts must be considered part of the infrastructure of our community," and recognizes that "a strong cultural community is one in which all segments meet to share the unique experience of being moved, delighted, challenged, educated and entertained, and on a daily basis, touched by the arts."

The budding art colony in Northeast Florida is nurtured by classes, both at the area's colleges and the several artists' cooperatives. Photo by Bob Milnes

Students walk across the campus at Bolles School, one of the oldest private schools in Jacksonville, having been founded in 1933. The school building began as the San Jose Hotel, a riverfront resort. Photo by Richard Kevern

CHAPTER 9

"THE ART OF THE POSSIBLE"

. . .

Education

In his roles as novelist, poet, song writer, essayist, critic, editor, historian, anthologist, and folklorist, as well as in his roles as diplomat and long-time leader of the NAACP, James Weldon Johnson was above all else an educator. He stands as a role model illustrating the art of the possible.

PROFESSOR RICHARD BIZOT
UNIVERSITY OF NORTH FLORIDA

151

Jacksonville's most remarkable native son was a man who overcame incredible odds to succeed in a staggering number and variety of endeavors. Born in Jacksonville on June 17, 1871, he was the son of James Johnson, headwaiter at the St. James Hotel, and Helen Louis Barton Johnson, a teacher at Stanton School. He graduated from Stanton, earned a degree from Atlanta University, and came back to Stanton as principal in 1894, gradually adding grades to the school until it became the first high school for blacks in Florida. During this time he also studied law and became the first black admitted to the Florida Bar by examination—a grueling two-hour oral testing by a panel of white judges, which attracted a standing-room-only crowd at the courthouse and which one attorney in the audience called the toughest examination he had "ever heard or heard of."

A contemporary inspiration to Jacksonville's educational community was revealed on July 1, 1987, when Mayor Tommy Hazouri took the oath of office, becoming the first mayor in the city's history to have received his education without having to leave the city to go to college. The mayor is a 1962 graduate of Andrew Jackson High School and a 1966 graduate of Jacksonville University. The mayor surrounded himself in City Hall with Jacksonville University alumni.

It was a long time coming, 166 years from the city's founding in 1821. It was more than 50 years after Jacksonville University's founding as William J. Porter University in 1934, later to become Jacksonville Junior College, and 30 years after the school became a four-year, degree-granting institution in 1956.

Hazouri's election and his unique Jacksonville educational roots indicate as well as anything the widening of the city's horizons as it advances into the ranks of the nation's major cities.

The future of any city, state, or nation is in its children. Jacksonville has recognized that it has major responsibilities for tomorrow's leaders, and the city is not taking that responsibility lightly. In 1987, the city's voters approved a $200-million school bond construction is-

The University of North Florida campus is located on a former tree and cattle farm. All its buildings are new and incorporate novel approaches to creating a Florida campus. Photo by Richard Kevern

The Downtown campus of Florida Community College at Jacksonville. Photo by Judy K. Jacobsen

Below: The Duval County School Board building faces the St. Johns River along the Southbank downtown. Photo by Richard Kevern

sue, allowing for construction of additional schools as well as improvements and expansions to existing schools throughout the system. But money, while an important part of the education equation, is only a small part of the story.

Jacksonville's public schools are consistently recognized on the state and national levels as having innovative and successful educational programs. One of the most interesting is a link with the local public television station by which education programs are broadcast daily, allowing students to have the benefit of instruction that would otherwise be available to only a few.

Eleven Duval County public schools have been named National Model Schools by the U.S. Department of Education: Kirby Smith Junior High School, Southside Junior High School, Stanton College Preparatory School, Ribault Senior High School, Jefferson Davis Junior High School, Terry Parker Senior High School, John Gorrie Junior High School, Sandalwood High School, Joseph Finegan Elementary School, John N.C. Stockton Elementary School, and Hendricks Avenue Elementary School. Since 1982, 33 Florida public schools have been named national model schools, and 11 of those have been in Duval County—the greatest concentration of honored schools in the country.

A number of private and church-affiliated schools are also found in Jacksonville. Among the largest are The Bolles School (coeducational, grades K-12), Bartram School (girls, grades 6-12), Episcopal High School of Jacksonville (coeducational, grades 7-12), and Bishop Kenny High School (Roman Catholic, coeducational, grades 9-12).

Postsecondary education is provided in Jacksonville by two public institutions—Florida Community College at Jacksonville and the University of North Florida—and three private institutions—Jacksonville University, Edward Waters College, and Jones College.

The oldest of these, and the oldest independent college in Florida, is Edward Waters College, established in Live Oak by the African

Pictured here is Jacksonville University Administration office building. Photo by Kelly LaDuke

The Davis College of Business moved into its new home in 1986. Photo by Kelly LaDuke

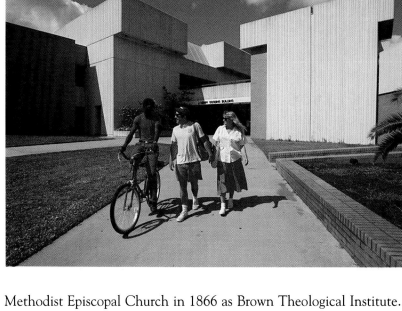

Methodist Episcopal Church in 1866 as Brown Theological Institute. Moving to Jacksonville in 1883, the school reopened as East Florida Conference High School, then expanded its curriculum to become Edward Waters College in 1892. When its buildings were destroyed by the 1901 fire that consumed much of central Jacksonville, the college acquired its present site on Kings Road. Administrative offices, classrooms, a library, and dormitories were constructed between 1912 and 1928. Other buildings were added between 1968 and 1982.

Edward Waters College was accredited as a junior college in 1955. In 1958, additional courses allowed expansion of the college into a four-year institution. In 1979 Edward Waters became an accredited four-year college, and in 1985 the college became the forty-third member of the United Negro College Fund.

The college offers bachelor of arts degrees in English, accounting, religion, philosophy, sociology, business administration, criminal justice, computer information systems, and psychology. Bachelor of science degrees may be earned in biology, chemistry, computer science, and mathematics.

Founded as a junior college in 1934, Jacksonville University now comprises three colleges—Arts and Sciences, Business, and Fine Arts—offering degrees in 60 undergraduate and 14 graduate programs. Master's degrees are awarded in education, business administration, counseling, and mathematics sciences. A unique Executive Masters of Business Administration program is open only to professionals. Entrance requirements, in addition to a bachelor's degree, include five to seven years in management and a recommendation from the employer. The 16-month course is offered on weekends to allow students to fit classes into their normal work schedules. JU also offers special courses of study in engineering and computer sciences in conjunction with Columbia University, the University of Florida, the University of Miami, and Georgia Tech.

The Davis College of Business moved into its new home, the Davis building, in 1986. The building was a gift of the Davis family, the founders of Winn-Dixie supermarkets and longtime supporters of the university.

Known for its College of Fine Arts, JU attracts outstanding faculty members in the arts, and its music faculty is recognized as being among the best in the country. The university owns an extensive collection of the notes and papers of the English composer Frederick Delius, who lived and worked in the Solano Grove area along the St. Johns River.

The college's Alexander Brest Museum houses a number of valuable permanent collections, including the Mussallem family's European and Oriental ivory collection, a collection of pre-Columbian artifacts, and the John R. Pace African art collection. In addition, there are collections of Boehm porcelain, Royal Danish porcelain, and Steuben glass.

Through the efforts of JU President Frances B. Kinne, leaders in the fields of entertainment, theater, and national politics have appeared at the university. Paul Volcker was awarded an honorary degree and spoke at the 1987 commencement ceremonies shortly before he retired as chairman of the Federal Reserve Board. Jack Benny and Bob Hope made one of their few joint appearances on a Jacksonville University stage. The Juilliard String Quartet appears at the university annually.

The university's 27 buildings are situated on a 214-acre shaded campus in Arlington on the banks of the St. Johns River. Its 2,300 students come from 40 states and 40 foreign countries.

The University of North Florida is the newest of the nine state universities in Florida, having been authorized in 1965 and opened to students in 1972. It opened as an upper-division institution, offering college work on the junior and senior levels as well as some graduate programs. UNF admitted its first group of freshman students in the fall of 1984.

Through its three colleges (Arts & Sciences, Business Administration, and Education and Human Services) and three divisions (Computer & Information Sciences, Nursing, and Technologies), UNF offers both pre-professional and vocational programs of study. In addition to eight baccalaureate programs, the university offers degrees at the master's level and a cooperative program with the University of Florida leading to the Doctor of Education and Specialist in Education degrees.

The UNF computer science program is one of only 48 such accredited programs in the country, and the John E. Mathews Jr. Computer Science Building has recently been opened.

Jacksonville office park developer Ira McK. Koger has funded an Eminent Scholar's Chair in American Music at UNF, which has been filled by jazz musician Rich Matteson, establishing the university as a center for the serious study of jazz.

This is the main entrance to the University of North Florida. Photo by Joanne Kash

Here is the entrance to Jacksonville University on University Boulevard North in Arlington. Photo by David Dobbs

The campus is situated on 1,000 acres of designated wildlife preserve between the city and its beaches. Plans are underway to develop a research park next to the UNF campus, and 275 acres have been donated to the city by the family of the late A.C. Skinner for that purpose. The property is under the control of the Duval County Research and Development Authority.

Almost 70 percent of the university's 6,500 students attend classes part-time, taking advantage of UNF's flexible schedule, which accommodates classes throughout the day and into the evening hours. Most UNF students are commuters. The addition of the freshman and sophomore programs and student apartments on campus have fostered enhanced student activities programs and intramural and intercollegiate athletics.

Many of UNF's upper division students earned associate degrees at Florida Community College at Jacksonville (FCCJ) before transferring into the university's baccalaureate program.

The second largest of Florida's 28 community colleges, FCCJ is a vital force in the Jacksonville community. It serves more than 70,000 students a year in a variety of college-credit, vocational education, adult general education, community outreach, and personal enrichment programs and classes throughout Duval and Nassau counties.

With four main campuses, the Geis maritime training center, and more than 250 off-campus centers, the college is easily accessible geographically to all First Coast residents. Its open-door policy and college preparatory instructional programs ensure educational opportunities for all.

The college offers 35 associate degree programs covering a wide range of academic and technological specialties. The average age of college-credit students is 28. Through an articulation agreement with the State University System, students earning associate of arts degrees at community colleges are eligible to enroll in any state university.

Recent studies have shown that FCCJ graduates rank high among transfer students.

FCCJ also offers certificate programs in a number of vocational fields, and continuing education classes vary from gourmet cooking to motorcycle repair.

Opened in 1977, the Downtown Campus is on 21 acres in the heart of urban Jacksonville. The campus includes classrooms as well as laboratories for instruction in such programs as building trades, engineering technology, automotive technology, and metal trades. The college offers outreach programs for widowed persons, senior adults, displaced homemakers, and other special segments of the community. A fully equipped television studio offers students experience in television production, and a variety of programs are taped for broadcast on the college's cable channel.

The Geis Marine Center is five miles north of the Downtown Campus on the banks of the St. Johns River. Named for Rear Admiral Lawrence R. Geis, former commander of Fleet Air Jacksonville, the facility offers occupational training in a variety of marine trades, and operates under the administration of the Downtown Campus.

FCCJ's suburban North Campus, on 160 acres in the northern portion of the county, serves that area of Jacksonville as well as Nassau County residents, offering a comprehensive mix of specialized programs as well as basic general studies. Built in 1970, the campus is the site of FCCJ's health related programs, as well as a modern data processing lab recognized as among the best such training facilities in the Southeast. The Disabled Student Center provides college-wide services to disabled students.

South Campus, opened in 1971, offers all basic studies courses and is the home of FCCJ's musical, theatrical, and visual arts programs. Because of the strong arts programs, the city located its Douglas Anderson High School of the Performing Arts nearby. South Campus also houses training programs in criminal justice and fire science.

The newest of FCCJ's campuses, Kent Campus, opened in 1979 on 38 acres at Roosevelt Boulevard and Park Street. In addition to a strong academic program in arts and sciences, the campus offers special programs in real estate, banking, marketing, insurance, and transportation, and a comprehensive home economics program. The Kent Gallery exhibits work by local, regional, and national artists and craftsmen and is open to the public.

FCCJ provides an extensive program of evening classes in a number of convenient community locations such as public schools, churches, business firms, hospitals, and retirement homes, and has just opened a new center in the Grande Boulevard Mall.

Jones College, a school of business administration, is in Arlington on the banks of the St. Johns River. It has branch campuses in four other locations in Jacksonville and Orange Park, and other branch campus operations in Tampa and Orlando. The college offers two- and four-year programs in business-related fields such as accounting, broad-

Courtyard green of the Kent Campus of Florida Community College at Jacksonville. Photo by KBJ Architects, Inc.

The statue of Henry M. Flagler stands guard at the entrance to Flagler College in St. Augustine. The building began in 1888 as Flagler's first resort hotel, the Ponce de Leon. Photo by Joanne Kash

cast management, computer accounting, data processing, management, marketing, and secretarial sciences. These programs also train medical receptionists and medical and nursing assistants. Among the most popular programs is data processing, with more than 300 of the school's 1,500 students enrolled in the two-year program.

In St. Johns County, Flagler College, a four-year liberal arts college founded in 1968, occupies the building that Henry Flagler built as the Ponce de Leon resort hotel. The college began as an all-girls school, but became coeducational in 1971. The 1,100 students are from 30 states and 13 foreign countries, and attend classes amid a myriad of reminders of the building's resort origins. A $2-million campaign is nearing completion to fund the restoration of the dining hall and parlors to their original elegance.

The dining hall is typical of late-nineteenth-century palatial public dining rooms, with Tiffany stained glass windows, 18- and 24-karat gold stencils, vaulted ceilings, murals depicting early life in St. Augustine, and other similar embellishments. The ceiling and murals have been restored, the stencils regilded, the stained glass and oak floor restored, and a climate-control system has been installed.

Originally an all-girls school, Flagler College is a four-year liberal arts college founded in 1968. Photo by Kelly LaDuke

The restoration was completed in late 1987, and on January 12, 1988, a celebration was held in the dining room and parlors to mark the 100th anniversary of the opening of the hotel. This celebration included an open-house for the college and the community.

Flagler is a four-year liberal arts institution that awards a bachelor of arts degree in a variety of disciplines. In addition to the standard liberal arts program, Flagler has a special Philosophy/Religion major that can be coordinated with pre-professional training in youth ministry offered by the Young Life Christian Youth Organization.

Also located in St. Augustine is the Florida School for the Deaf and Blind, and Flagler College works closely with this school. Among the strongest programs at the college is special education for the hearing impaired, for students with specific learning disabilities, and for the mentally retarded. Flagler's women's tennis team also claims the National Championships of 1987-1988.

The famed 17th hole at the Tournament Players Club at Sawgrass in Ponte Vedra during The Players Championship. Spectators sit and stand on mounds built to provide a clear view of the golf course. Photo by Richard Kevern

CHAPTER 10

THE GOLF AND TENNIS CAPITAL OF THE WORLD

...

Putting Green and Clay Court

In the professional sports headquarters game the current score is New York: 4, Jacksonville: 2.

ARTHUR "CHICK" SHERRER, JR.
EXECUTIVE DIRECTOR, JACKSONVILLE
CHAMBER OF COMMERCE

The 17th hole of the Players
Course at Sawgrass is on an island.
An alligator inhabits the lagoon sur-
rounding the island. Photo by Kelly
LaDuke

Each year millions of Americans watch on television as some of the best golfers on the pro tour take a bath at the 17th hole of the Tournament Players Club. It happens during THE PLAYERS Championship, held in late March at the Tournament Players Club course in Ponte Vedra. Golfing fans are never disappointed.

Of the six major professional sports with headquarters in the United States, four—football, baseball, basketball, and hockey—call New York home. Florida's First Coast lays claim to the other two, golf and tennis. Jacksonville's new status as the "Golf and Tennis Capital of the World" is the result of an aggressive marketing campaign by the city's business community and the residents of nearby Ponte Vedra, just south of the city in St. Johns County, where the PGA TOUR and the Association of Tennis Professionals (ATP) have recently located their international headquarters.

The First Coast area hosts two nationally televised golf tournaments—THE PLAYERS Championship (TPC) and the Mazda Senior Tournament Players Championship—and two major tennis tournaments—the Bausch and Lomb Championship and the Dupont All-American Tennis Championship. The ATP plans to sponsor a major international tournament, and the First Coast has been formally designated "An Official World Golf Destination of the PGA TOUR."

THE PLAYERS Championship, which boosts the First Coast economy by an estimated $67 million each year, has been played at the TPC course since 1982. Before that (beginning in 1977), it was played

on the original Sawgrass course, on the ocean side of Highway A1A. The first winner at Sawgrass was Mark Hayes with a one-over-par 289. In 1978, Jack Nicklaus was the winner, also with a one-over 289—the highest winning score ever recorded for the Players.

But in succeeding years, March winds off the Atlantic Ocean plagued the tournament at Sawgrass, and it was with a sigh of relief that the pros moved across the highway to the new Tournament Players Club course in 1982.

The new TPC course exacted its own respect from the pros, especially the 17th hole (one of the most photographed golf holes in the world) with its wide expanse of water protecting the island green and its unusual additional hazard—the TPC resident alligator.

Don January has called the TPC "the only course where you tee off on the first hole, thinking of the 17th." Ben Crenshaw agreed: "There's no other hole like it in the world. I just pray to get it on the green." And according to Lee Trevino, "The hardest part about playing this hole is to convince your arms that it's OK to start moving."

The worst year for bathing at the 17th was 1984, when 98 balls went into the water, 64 of them during the very windy first round. Wind velocity was clocked at 25 mph with gusts to 40 on that disastrous day.

The 132-yard 17th hole is, of course, a prime candidate for a hole in one, though most pros follow the safer strategy of just attempting to land on the green. There has been only one ace there in PLAYERS competition, shot by Brad Fabel in the first round in 1986. It was the second year that he qualified for the tournament, but he failed to make the cut after two rounds, as was his fate the previous year.

In the first five years of tournament play, the 17th saw 1,378 pars, 358 birdies, 182 bogeys, and 172 double bogeys. Only the 18th hole, a slight dog leg to the left around a lake, has a tougher record for bogeys—512 with 187 double bogeys.

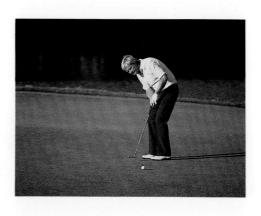

In 1988, Jacksonville's own Mark McCumber scored a record-breaking 15-under-par 273 to win the tournament before thousands of wildly cheering hometown fans. The best 18-hole score was carded by 1984 winner Fred Couples, an 8-under 64 in the second round.

Though the TPC course was built as a stern test for the pros, it was also built with spectators in mind. Stadium golf, a new concept in golf course constructon developed by PGA TOUR Commissioner Deane R. Beman and golf architect Pete Dye, was introduced at the TPC. Earth mounds are placed strategically and terraced so spectators can follow play on at least one hole and frequently on two or more holes from the same mound, seeing over the heads of the fans in front of them. The idea has since been adopted by many courses that are the scene of tournament play during the year. The PGA TOUR is including this feature in all of its new courses as well as in the renovation of existing courses.

THE PLAYERS Championship, in addition to being a major sports event and spectator draw, has become one of the prime marketing tools of the Jacksonville Chamber of Commerce, which hosts a TPC/Florida Showcase during the week of the tournament. Key executives from industries and market segments throughout the nation, as well as from some foreign countries, are invited to visit Jacksonville to enjoy golf, tennis, fishing, yachting, tours of the area, and general socializing with community leaders.

In 1987 the First Coast was designated an Official World Golf Destination of the PGA TOUR. Fifty area golf courses range from those easily mastered to the challenging championship courses of the TPC and Sawgrass.

The U.S. Golf Association and the Florida State Golf Association both rate the 27-hole Sawgrass course as the toughest in the area, no matter how it's played: East-West and South-East combinations carry a slope (or difficulty) rating of 133. The South-West combination is ranked at 132.

Tied for second are two of the three nine-hole courses at Amelia Island Plantation—Oysterbay and Oakmarsh—as well as the course at the Ravines in Clay County, all ranked at 131. Then comes Baymeadows at 130 and finally the TPC at 129.

The TPC and Sawgrass oceanside courses have been ranked by *Golf Digest* as among the 20 best in Florida. Among the factors considered in the ratings are shot values, resistance to scoring, design balance, memorableness, aesthetics, conditioning, and tradition. The TPC is ranked third and Sawgrass eleventh. *Golf Magazine* rates the TPC course among the top 50 in the world.

Beginning in 1987 the TPC Seniors Tournament, played in June, moved to the Valley Course at Sawgrass from Cleveland, Ohio, where it had been played for several years. That move puts two major tournaments a year in the Jacksonville area.

THE PLAYERS Championship has raised more than $2.5 million for area charities, and is building the Nancy Reagan/TPC Village for drug and alcoholic rehabilitation of adolescents.

Jacksonville's growth as a golf mecca dates from 1977 when the PGA Tour relocated its headquarters to Ponte Vedra from Washington, D.C. In the years since then, many golf courses have been added in the First Coast area.

Sawgrass offers 27 holes at Sawgrass Country Club, 36 at Tournament Players Club, and 18 at Marsh Landing. All of the courses were designed by golf architect Ed Seay except the new Valley Course, which was built by Pete Dye and Jerry Pate. The first Sawgrass course opened in 1972.

Other courses in Ponte Vedra include the 18 holes at Oak Bridge north of the TPC, 18 at The Plantation south of the TPC, and 36 at the Ponte Vedra Inn and Country Club. The Plantation, an Arnold Palmer Course, is the newest; it opened at the end of 1987.

Three other courses in the Beaches area are Selva Marina in Atlantic Beach, Mayport at the Mayport Naval Station, and Jacksonville Beach Golf Club, a public course at Jacksonville Beach.

In addition to the Mayport course, the Navy also has golf courses at Naval Air Station Jacksonville and Naval Air Station Cecil Field. All three courses are restricted to military personnel, their dependents, and military retirees.

At Amelia Island Plantation northeast of Jacksonville along the ocean in Nassau County there are three nine-hole golf courses—

Facing page, top: Golf pro Payne Stewart tees off during the 1988 Players Championship. Photo by Kelly LaDuke

Facing page, bottom: These golfers have made it safely onto the island green of the famed 17th hole at the Tournament Players Club at Sawgrass in Ponte Vedra. Photo by Judy K. Jacobsen

Above: Lee Trevino at The Players Championship. Photo by Judy K. Jacobsen

Oysterbay, Oakmarsh, and Oceanside—and a new 18-hole course at Long Point, designed by Tom Fazio. The three nine-hole courses can be played in a 18-hole configuration if desired.

Golf courses are becoming integral parts of upscale housing developments. Among those under construction are Deer Creek just south of Deerwood (which itself has a golf course winding through its homesites), Orange Park Country Club, and Julington Creek.

Those already open, aside from Deerwood, include Marsh Landing, Summer Beach at Fernandina, Hidden Hills in Arlington, Baymeadows in the Baymeadows area, and Deer Marsh Creek in St. Augustine. Marsh Landing and the new holes at Hidden Hills were developed by Arnold Palmer.

In addition to being a major sports event, the Players Championships and other PGA Tours events draw tourists to Jacksonville. Photo by Kelly LaDuke

Plans are also underway for a family golfing center and 18-hole municipal golf course as part of a residential development on the Westside. Included would be a junior golf program that would use a driving range, practice putting greens, and sand bunkers, as well as miniature golf. The project would comprise 180 acres, with 140 coming from the developers and 40 from the city, which owns abutting land.

Deane Beman, commissioner of the PGA TOUR, has pointed out that the city's link with pro golf goes back to the early postwar years. At that time, the Jacksonville Open was played on the Hyde Park and Brentwood courses, municipal courses that were sold to private operators in the 1960s.

The Tournament Players Club's course has won respect from the pros, especially at the 17th hole, with its wide expanse of water protecting the island green. Photo by Kelly LaDuke

Martina Navratilova keeps her eye on the ball at WTA at Amelia Island. Photo by Kelly LaDuke

"Hyde Park's sixth hole is ever known as 'Hogan's Alley,' reminiscent of an 11 Ben Hogan took on the hole during the 1947 tournament," Beman said. Today, the Hyde Park Golf Club has a slope rating of 119 from the back tees. Opened in 1925, it is one of the oldest golf clubs in the First Coast area.

The oldest First Coast golf course is at the Ponce de Leon Resort, just north of St. Augustine on U.S. 1, which opened in 1917. Next came the San Jose Country Club, opened in 1921, the Timuquana Country Club, opened in 1923, and the Hyde Park Golf Club, 1925. The Fort George Golf Club, now the public Fairfield Fort George Island course, dates from 1928. All courses except Fort George were designed by Donald Ross.

Another pre-World War II course, the Ponte Vedra Inn and Club Ocean Course, was designed by British golf course architect Herbert Bertram Strong and opened in 1933. Golf pro Bobby Jones played Ponte Vedra regularly in the early postwar years, and criticized it. He felt it was "too severe for a resort course—it was a course to challenge professionals." Jones recommended that Robert Trent Jones redesign the course, and the work was completed late in 1947. In 1961, Robert Trent Jones returned to Ponte Vedra to add the West Nine, which increased the course's versatility.

While the championship courses draw most of the attention, lesser-known courses are being upgraded. Hidden Hills east of Arlington has undergone major renovation in conjunction with the development of single-family homes overlooking the golf course. Pine Lakes, a public course off U.S. 17 north of the Imeson Industrial Park, is another under renovation. Previously with only seven traps and little grass, Pine Lakes' upgrading has resulted in a course with four lakes, 37 traps, several hundred new trees, and grassy fairways.

Both Hidden Hills and Pine Lakes are responding to growth patterns that are being influenced by the new Broward Bridge, which opened in the last half of 1988, linking Arlington near Regency to the Northside. The Northside is expected to boom because of the bridge and because of the Kings Bay Trident submarine base, just across the state line in Georgia, 35 miles away.

Other public courses in the First Coast area are Magnolia Point near Green Cove Springs, Fernandina Beach Golf Club at Fernandina Beach, Deerfield Lakes Golf and Country Club at Callahan, Reynolds Golf Course at Green Cove Springs, and West Meadows Golf Club and Willow Lakes Golf and Country Club, both on the Westside.

At the end of 1987, the Association of Tennis Professionals (ATP) decided to move its headquarters to Ponte Vedra Beach. Influencing its decision was the fact that the PGA Tour—the association of professional golfers—is based at Sawgrass in Ponte Vedra Beach.

The flowering of professional tennis on Florida's First Coast was heralded by the Women's International Tennis Association Championships, begun at Amelia Island Plantation a decade ago, and Amelia was once the home court of tennis superstar Chris Evert. But 1987 was a watershed year for tennis in the Jacksonville area: not only did the $300,000 Bausch and Lomb Championships (successor to the WITA tournaments) attract record crowds who came to watch tennis greats like Martina Navratilova and Steffi Graf, but the DuPont All-American Tennis Championships were inaugurated in September at the Plantation's Racquet Park, and in early December the Association of Tennis Professionals announced plans to move its headquarters to a site next to the PGA TOUR headquarters at Sawgrass.

The ATP decision came at the urging of its executive director, Hamilton Jordan, former chief of staff to President Jimmy Carter, whose friendship with PGA TOUR Deputy Commissioner Tim Smith, also a former Carter aide, was a factor. According to Jordan, the ATP headquarters call for a 15,000-seat stadium facility that will begin to host major international tournaments in the early 1990s. The first phase of development will include eight courts and a clubhouse. Two of the courts will be grass, two will be European clay, two American clay, and two hard courts, offering a variety of surfaces for the practicing pros. The site for the ATP complex had been owned by the PGA Tour, and a swap was arranged to secure the land.

But like golf, tennis is more than a spectator sport in Jacksonville. Public and private courts abound within the city, and nearby resorts like Amelia Island Plantation and the Marriott at Sawgrass offer first-class tennis facilities. There are 19 courts at Amelia's Racquet Park, three of them lighted for night play, and Marriott guests have access to 33 clay courts, 10 of them lighted.

Golf and tennis have been the sports of choice for business executives, and it's safe to surmise that many crucial decisions are made on the courts and links of Florida's First Coast.

The crowd cheers on golf favorite Arnold Palmer. Photo by Richard Kevern

Each September, Amelia Island Plantation is the site of the du Pont All American Tennis Championships. Here, Jimmy Connors prepares to serve. Photo by Judy K. Jacobsen

Some of the thousands of competitors in Jacksonville's annual River Run distance race. Photo by Richard Kevern

CHAPTER 11

FROM GRIDIRON TO GREENSWARD
...
Sports, Resorts, and Recreation

We Want the NFL.

MAYOR TOMMY HAZOURI

Seen here is the Gator Bowl in early November during the Florida-Georgia football game. In center background is the Matthews Bridge to Arlington. Photo by Judy K. Jacobsen

Jacksonville is a football town. Despite the fact that it has no college or university team, and no NFL franchise (as yet), the city is strongly committed to the game and at least twice a year packs its 80,000-seat Gator Bowl with avid football fans. The Gator Bowl Classic has been played here for 40 years, and the annual Florida-Georgia clash in early November, played in the Gator Bowl since 1933, is always a sellout. The town enthusiastically supported its ill-fated USFL team, the Jacksonville Bulls, drawing near-capacity crowds for home games—the only city in the league to do so. Fans turned out 50,000 strong in the Gator Bowl to greet the owner of the then-Baltimore Colts, trying to persuade him to move his team to Jacksonville.

Jacksonville residents also enjoy a gentler sport. The St. Johns Croquet Club has planted and groomed a croquet lawn, or greensward, in Ortega's riverside Seminole Park, where they play throughout the year.

The diversity of sports and recreational opportunities in Florida's First Coast is one of the region's main attractions. The area is famous for year-round golf and tennis, and some contend that if you're a scuba diver, there's no better place to live in the country.

Where else can you find wreck-diving and spearfishing in your own backyard, spring and cavern diving within an hour's driving time, and magnificent coral reefs just 250 miles south where the Gulf Stream

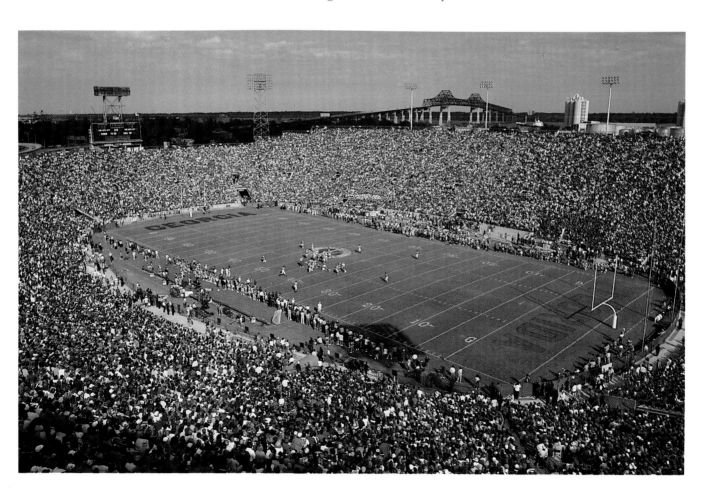

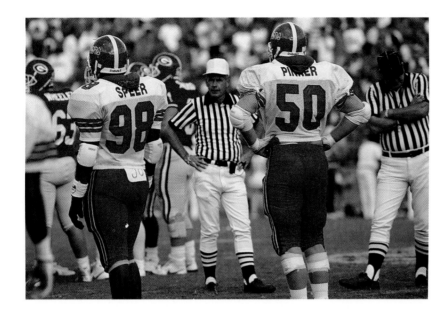

*The 80,000-seat Gator Bowl is the
site of the annual Florida-Georgia
college football game. It is always a
sellout. Photo by Judy K. Jacobsen*

*Below: There's always plenty of
time to wet a line at one of the tide-
water fishing piers along Florida's
First Coast. Photo by Bob Milnes*

swings near Florida's east coast? Offshore Jacksonville is a favorite
hunting ground for spear fishermen, the many artificial reefs created
over the years by the Jacksonville Offshore Sports Fishing Club. One of
these reefs was created by sinking the old Gator Bowl press box in 90
feet of water.

The present football stadium, having just undergone a $10.5-mil-
lion renovation, is considered the best non-NFL facility in the nation,
and the city is aggressively courting the National Football League with
the Mayor's NFL Task Force and a committee of the Chamber of Commerce specifically devoted to bringing a professional franchise to the
community.

The city has prepared a detailed proposal for an NFL franchise,
developed in the summer and fall of 1987. The 10-year package, worth
about $125 million, includes additional skyboxes at the Gator Bowl as
well as a practice facility that would be built at the University of North
Florida campus between the Gator Bowl and the Beaches, several miles
to the east.

In the same sports complex with the Gator Bowl is the 10,000-
seat Jacksonville Veterans Memorial Coliseum, and Wolfson Park, a
baseball field where the Southern League Jacksonville Expos play. A
farm club of the National League Montreal Expos, the team is one of
the Southern League's most successful, both on the field and in the box
office.

The Coliseum is home to the annual Gator Bowl basketball tournament; school basketball tournaments; touring rock concerts; rodeos;
The Ringling Brothers, Barnum and Bailey Circus; and, in the heat of
summer, is a popular ice-skating rink. During one of his visits to
Jacksonville in 1987, President Ronald Reagan spoke in the Coliseum
to thousands of Duval County high school students.

Basketball fever seized Jacksonville in 1970 when the Jacksonville
University Dolphins, sparked by an amazing young player named Artis

*Below: The River Run replaces
cars and trucks on Jacksonville's
Isaiah D. Hart bridge. Photo by
Richard Kevern*

*Bottom: In the annual Mug Race
along the St. Johns River, sailboats
race from Palatka to Jacksonville.
Photo by Richard Kevern*

Gilmore, progressed to the championship game of the NCAA tournament. The Dolphins are still a highly respected team in college basketball, with an enthusiastic local following. Professional basketball is back in Jacksonville with the 1988 opening season of the Jacksonville Hooters, a team of the United States Basketball League.

Three other important sporting events draw attention to Florida's First Coast each year: The River Run, The Mug Race, and the Greater Jacksonville Kingfish Tournament.

The River Run, a 15K run that begins and ends downtown, includes two St. Johns River bridges in its course. Each spring it draws thousands of runners from all over the nation and from other countries. The Mug Race, a 35-year-old competition on the St. Johns River, is billed as the world's longest river sailboat race. Beginning in Palatka, it stretches northward for 38.5 nautical miles to Orange Park. Open to all, it has drawn as many as 400 boats.

The Greater Jacksonville Kingfish Tournament held in mid-July was established in 1980 and draws an increasing number of entrants each year. Boats taking part in past years have come from 21 states and the British West Indies. More than $275,000 is offered in cash and prizes.

Tournament officials estimated that 80,000 spectators were on hand for the weighing-in at the 1987 tournament. First prize for the

largest fish was $35,000. A $100,000 bonus prize was offered for catching a kingfish larger than the 90-pound record catch in Florida waters, but was not claimed.

Demonstrating the First Coast's quantum leap to international sports stardom is the rebirth, reorganization, and recognition of the Jacksonville Sports Hall of Fame, which operates in cooperation with the Boys & Girls Clubs of Northwest Florida, Incorporated, and the City of Jacksonville. More than 70 outstanding athletes of the community have been named to this important list, plus another 50 to the Sports Honor Roll. Plaques listing Hall of Fame members hang in a display at the Coliseum.

The most obvious recreational asset in the First Coast area is the beach and the Atlantic Ocean. There are miles of beaches along Duval, Nassau, and St. Johns counties—and while much of the beachfront property is privately owned, all of the beaches are open to the public to the high-water mark excluding one mile within Mayport Naval Station.

The beaches stretch from Fort Clinch State Park at the northernmost tip of Amelia Island in Nassau County to Anastasia Recreation Area on Anastasia Island south of St. Augustine in St. Johns County. Other public parks along the shore include Little Talbot State Park on

A summer festivity, mug racing on the St. Johns. Photo by Wendell Metzen/Southern Stock Photo

Talbot Island, Huguenot Park, Hanna Park, Jacksonville Beach, Mickler's Landing, and Vilano Beach. Many of the public beaches have public parking lots, and there is public access where roads and streets end against the beach.

The most heavily used section of the beach is downtown Jacksonville Beach, where Beach Boulevard meets the ocean, followed by Anastasia Beach. The voluntarily manned Red Cross lifesaving station is at Jacksonville Beach, providing protection for more than a mile of beach. A short walk south of that corner is the fishing pier, a popular local surf spot.

Hot air balloons make a colorful sight as they drift lazily above Jacksonville. Photo by Richard Kevern

The Atlantic Ocean is not as good for surfing big waves as the Pacific, but surfing enthusiasts are out riding their boards practically every day of the year. The First Coast boasts some very good east coast surfing, including "Blow Hole," "Middles," the Vilano Inlet in St. Johns County, and "The Poles" in Hanna Park. Summertime surf is always fairly crowded, especially in post-hurricane winds. In the winter the surfers plunge in wearing wet suits to protect themselves from the ice-cold water.

Deep-sea fishing is another popular sport, and charter boats are available at Fernandina Beach, Mayport, and St. Augustine, as well as at some marinas along the Intracoastal Waterway and along the St. Johns River in Jacksonville.

The Atlantic Intracoastal Waterway is an integral part of the three oceanfront counties. It links Chesapeake Bay with the Florida Keys through a series of canals, channels, and bays sheltered by the barrier island chain that marks the southeastern U.S. coastline.

The channel's authorized depth of 12 feet is designed to accommodate boats and yachts of almost any size. The height of sailing craft that can use the waterway is limited by fixed bridges to about 65 feet.

By its very existence, the waterway encourages boating activities. There are innumerable miles of protected waterway and tributaries, some of which can be navigated only by very shallow-draft vessels, and many marinas scattered along the banks. Some areas are more easily reached by boat than by car or pickup truck.

With so many miles of waterways, including the St. Johns River and its tributaries, other creeks, lakes, and ponds, fishing is one of the

Above: One of the required Jacksonville pastimes is sunning at the beach. Photo by David Dobbs

Jacksonville Beach, in season. Photo by Richard Kevern

most popular outdoor pastimes on the First Coast. Bass, bream, and catfish are especially popular catches.

While recreationists on the First Coast tend to gravitate toward the beach, the waterways, and golf courses, there are additional recreation facilities in many parts of Jacksonville. There are 87 public tennis courts throughout the city and another 135 private ones located in various health clubs, country clubs, and similar establishments.

There are 11 city-owned swimming pools throughout Jacksonville. Funds are now being sought to add 11 more at high schools throughout the city to increase public availability and encourage student athletic participation. In addition, there are pools at YMCAs, country clubs, athletic clubs, apartment complexes, and subdivision developments.

A lone fisherman greets the morning sun at the Jacksonville Beach fishing pier. Photo by Richard Kevern

The tourists who filled Jacksonville's rebuilt hotels in the first two decades after the Civil War eventually began to leave for destinations farther south. The disastrous 1901 fire spelled the end of Jacksonville's reputation as a winter capital.

The loss of the northern visitors was a devastating blow to Jacksonville's tourist trade. It was not until the last 20 years that tourists have begun to return to Jacksonville in any real numbers. The city had become a stopover place on the way to destinations farther south. In the meantime, Jacksonville became a resort mainly for parts of Georgia and Northeast Florida, and people continued to enjoy the river and beaches. They also hunted in the thousands of acres of woodlands.

St. Augustine, however, fared much better. It was the oldest city in the nation, having been settled in 1565; it had real year-round tourist attractions in the Castillo de San Marcos, an Alligator Farm, and attractions relating to its antiquity. It also had the world's biggest indoor swimming pool in the Alcazar casino where Gertrude Ederle trained for the 1924 Summer Olympics. Beyond that, the winter weather was generally a bit warmer than in Jacksonville.

In the 1960s, a restoration program was undertaken along St. George Street, the Old City's main thoroughfare. Buildings were restored or rebuilt to re-create the appearance of part of St. Augustine's

Top: Greeting the sunrise at the Atlantic Ocean, a fleet of Hobie Cats stands ready to race again. Photo by Richard Kevern

Above: The 50-meter swimming pool at the University of North Florida campus has roll-up sides to take advantage of Florida's weather. Photo by Joanne Kash

Fishing off the deck behind your house is a well-honored pastime in Florida's First Coast. Photo by Richard Kevern

business section in the late eighteenth century. Since 1933, the Spanish fort has been maintained by the National Park Service as a national monument. About 500,000 people tour it each year.

Today, St. Augustine hosts 1.3 million visitors annually. They spend more than $100 million, the majority along the St. George Street plaza, which stretches south for several blocks from the 1808 city gate. The coquina-paved street is lined with restaurants and shops that offer souvenirs, curios, crafts, art, and sweets. Other narrow streets and small shops downtown also offer a variety of shoppers' wares.

With the glory days of Flagler's hotels long gone, many of St. Augustine's visitors today are day-trippers. There are fewer than 2,500 hotel and motel rooms around the nation's oldest city, although the supply of rooms did increase 6 percent in 1987 and 1988 with the addition of three motels.

Resort living in the St. Augustine area has developed along the lines of condominiums and time-sharing plans. Anastasia Island's beachfront is lined with condominiums, many of which are available for weekly rentals. Other condominiums are tied in with time-share vacation plans. There is no count of the number of condominium units included, but estimates are more than 1,000 and probably approaching 2,000.

There are two other historic forts in the First Coast area, both of which are open to visitors. First is Fort Caroline, a reproduction of the wood fort built in 1593 by the French Huguenots under Jean Ribault. The original fort was destroyed and the colony wiped out in 1565 when the Spanish marched up from St. Augustine to assert their claim on the area by force of arms. The site is operated as a national monument by the National Park Service. The Park Service runs a reception center in which the history of the fort is detailed and some artifacts are displayed. A replica of the original column that Ribault erected to mark his landing and territorial claim for France has also been restored. The original site of Fort Caroline and Ribault's landing disappeared in the nineteenth century when storms and channel work eroded the St. Johns River bluff where the fort had been constructed.

The other battlement is Fort Clinch, in Fort Clinch State Park at the north end of Amelia Island, close to Fernandina Beach. Fort

Above: At the ocean in Jacksonville Beach is the serpentine Seascape Condominiums, one of many condominiums which line the First Coast ocean front. Photo by Richard Kevern

Resort-style living is the big attraction at Sawgrass in northern St. Johns County, where condominiums, apartments, and upscale homes are the rule. Photo by Richard Kevern

A lagoon with a fountain and tall pines provides the setting for Coopers Hawk Apartments. Photo by Richard Kevern

Clinch was constructed early in the nineteenth century as part of a system of forts designed to protect the coast. It was never finished.

During the Civil War the fort was occupied by Confederate forces until 1862, when the Union Army, transported to Amelia Island by the Navy, seized the fort and held it as part of the blockade strategy used to wear down and eventually defeat the Confederacy.

The oldest destination resort in the First Coast is the Ponce de Leon Resort and Convention Center, just north of St. Augustine on U.S. 1. It dates back to 1917 when the golf course was opened and Flagler's downtown hotels were still drawing crowds. The resort has recently been renovated and is being expanded. The conference center includes eight meetings rooms, the largest of which will seat 400 for dinner. The original building has been given a facelift and is now the main lodge. There are 194 rooms, mini suites, and bedroom-parlor suites, a swimming pool, six tennis courts, and an 18-hole golf course, which is the oldest in the region. The golf course is ranked by the U.S. Golf Association as the fifth most difficult on the First Coast.

Modern resort life in Jacksonville dates from 1927, when the National Lead Company built a 12-room log cabin at what is now Ponte Vedra for its executives and other guests. British golf course architect Herbert Bertram Strong was brought in to build a course, and it was completed in 1932, during the depths of the Depression. Construction of the course was very much a hand- and animal-labor operation. Thirty men and 100 mules undertook the necessary earth moving projects. From that beginning has grown an upscale resort and residential community, which is also home to the PGA TOUR and the Association of Tennis Professionals.

The Ponte Vedra Inn & Club opened in 1937. The resort rose out of mined-out sands when the National Lead Company turned to Telfair Stockton Company, a major land developer in Jacksonville, to provide a master plan for the property. (Telfair Stockton Company later became Stockton, Whatley, Davin & Company, and at the beginning of 1988, SWD Division of BancBoston Mortgage Corporation.) The Ponte Vedra Inn & Club is now owned by Gate Petroleum Co. of Jacksonville.

When the inn opened, Jim Stockton, a 1916 Princeton graduate, used the best mailing list he had—his class yearbook—as a mailing list to promote the resort. Princeton grads from throughout the country responded by coming down for a look, and many bought or built vacation homes in the developing resort area.

In 1942 National Lead became completely involved in war work and sold its Ponte Vedra holdings to the Ponte Vedra Corporation.

Today, the Ponte Vedra Inn & Club has 164 rooms (all but 22 of them on the beach), two 18-hole golf courses, 15 tennis courts, five swimming pools, half a mile of beach, two main dining areas, and two main lounges.

Ponte Vedra has always had its share of visiting celebrities, and some have made it home. One of the better known guests in the early years was CBS newsman Edward R. Murrow, who vacationed incognito in January 1942 before returning to England to report on the war.

Other celebrities have included Bob Hope, Art Linkletter, President Gerald Ford (to see the TPC), Federal Judge Harold Medina,

Park Suite Hotel is one of the many hotels which have opened in the Baymeadows office and light industrial area since mid-decade. Photo by Richard Kevern

Left: The Ponte Vedra Inn and Club is located on the beach at Ponte Vedra. Homes and one of the Ponte Vedra golf courses share the lagoon in the background. Photo by Richard Kevern

One of the newest hotels to open in Florida's First Coast is the Marriott Resort Hotel in Ponte Vedra, overlooking the Tournament Players Course. Photo by Richard Kevern

Right: The Omni Hotel lobby welcomes visitors and conventioneers. Courtesy, Fey & Associates

and, at a series of forums, retired General Lauris Norstad, former Ambassador U. Alexis Johnson, Allen W. Dulles, Wernher von Braun, Frank Pace, and newsman James Reston.

Thirty miles to the north and across the Mayport Ferry is Amelia Island Plantation, located on 1,250 acres between the Atlantic Ocean and the Intracoastal Waterway. There are 256 hotel rooms and 368 rental condominiums.

While Ponte Vedra Inn developed first as a vacation spot, Amelia Island Plantation, constructed in the last 15 years, was built from the outset as a vacation and convention location as well as a residential area. Prominent among its facilities is a 22,500-square-foot meeting center that can accommodate 500 people, as well as additional meeting facilities in the Amelia Inn, overlooking the ocean.

The First Coast's newest resort destination is the Marriott at Sawgrass Resort, which opened in 1987. The resort consists of 650 guest rooms, suites, and villas with 17,000 square feet of meeting-conference space in two ballrooms; two executive board rooms; and seven conference rooms plus an additional 17,000 square feet of exhibit space. The hotel lobby features a seven-story atrium with interior waterfalls, extensive foliage, and a view of the TPC 13th hole.

Resort guests have access to five championship golf courses of 99 holes, including the Tournament Players Club and Sawgrass courses; 33 clay tennis courts, including 10 lighted courts; six swimming pools; two croquet courts; stables; and the beach.

Hotels, motels, and inns are distributed evenly throughout Jacksonville. There are 1,280 rooms downtown in four hotels, including the Omni, which opened in 1987; 1,660 in 10 locations at the airport area; 3,003 in 14 resorts, hotels, motels, and inns at the Beaches, including Amelia Island Plantation and Ponte Vedra-Sawgrass; and 4,707 in 34 hotels and motels in suburban locations. That totals 10,650 rooms, and construction now under way will push the total past 11,000 by the end of 1988.

In the five-county First Coast area, it is estimated that there are more than 16,000 rooms in resorts, hotels, motels, and inns. Tourism is again big business for Florida's First Coast.

Below: Comfortable and spacious accommodations are offered at the Omni Hotel. Courtesy, Fey & Associates

Bottom: A mass of contrasts and zebra stripes is created by the Omni Hotel in the background and the reflection of the Southern Bell Building in the mirrored wall of the Omni's atrium. Photo by Richard Kevern

Downtown's Southbank is dominated by Gulf Life Tower at left and Prudential Plaza Two at right. Photo by Richard Kevern

PEOPLE AND PLACES

. . .

Neighborhoods and the Quality of Life

Once you've seen the full moon
reflected in the St. Johns, you never
want to leave.

A LONGTIME JACKSONVILLE RESIDENT

Below: The three-lane Acosta Bridge, a lift span, is scheduled to be replaced in the next few years by a high-level fixed span of at least six lanes. At left is the railroad bridge. Photo by Kelly LaDuke

Bottom: The venerable Florida Yacht Club, basin and tennis courts are at the end of Yacht Club Road in Ortega. Photo by Richard Kevern

Flowing through the heart of Jacksonville and Florida's First Coast, the St. Johns River touches the city and the region in ways that are both obvious and subtle, influencing how people live and their quality of life. The river's size and its crossing points also affect where people live and where they work.

Eight bridges and one ferry cross the St. Johns River along its 50 miles that wind through the First Coast. Seven of those bridges and the ferry are in Duval County. The eighth bridge links Green Cove Springs, the Clay County seat, with Orangedale in St. Johns County.

The ferry is less than a mile from the mouth of the river at Mayport. Moving upstream, the bridges are the spectacular new Broward Bridge linking the Northside and Arlington, then the Mathews, Hart, Main Street, Acosta, and Fuller Warren bridges and the twin spans forming the Buckman Bridge.

The Music Man's River City was in Iowa, but Jacksonville is very much a River City itself with both commercial traffic and pleasure boats on the river. Its River City Band, a local brass and woodwinds ensemble, was formed in the early 1980s to recall the heritage of a century ago when weekly municipal band concerts were big attractions. In fact, the River City Band played a concert at Carnegie Hall in New York City in 1987.

The St. Johns River, as well as the Atlantic Intracoastal Waterway, the Atlantic Ocean, and the innumerable rivers and lakes

Expecting their supper, seagulls follow a homeward-bound shrimp boat as it sails up the St. Johns River to its dock at Mayport. Photo by Richard Kevern

of Florida, all shape the quality of life and point Jacksonville and Florida's First Coast toward a water-oriented life. Developers reach out for waterfront of all kinds to enhance their properties. They landscape storm water retention basins, making them into small lakes, frequently with fountains. They dredge waterfront acreage for canals and channels so that residents can buy waterfront lots and moor their boats at their own docks, only a few steps from their back doors.

The water-oriented life is even more pervasive. There are at least 40 marinas in Florida's First Coast counties, as well as innumerable marine contractors, supplies stores, and boat and yacht dealerships and repair shops. It is commonplace to see boats on trailers parked alongside garages throughout the city and taking up parking spaces at apartment complexes. Any day of the week boats are being launched or pulled out of the water at one of the many boat ramps throughout Florida's First Coast.

There is a small but growing group of residents who have chucked the good life ashore for what they consider the better life afloat. They live on their yachts, houseboats, pleasure craft, or sailboats at marinas or their own moorings.

Jacksonville is filled with natural waterways of varying lengths and importance. In addition to the St. Johns River, among those navigable for at least some distance by small craft are Trout River, Ribault River, Broward River, Fort George River, Moncrief Creek, Dunn Creek, Clapboard Creek, Hannah Mills Creek, Cedar Point Creek, Sisters Creek, Pablo Creek, Greenfield Creek, Arlington River, Pottsburg Creek, Ortega River, Cedar River, Christopher Creek, Goodbys Lake, Julington Creek, Doctors Lake, and Swimming Pen Creek.

In the same way, Nassau and St. Johns counties are laced with streams and small rivers as well as the Intracoastal Waterway. The St. Johns River separates St. Johns and Clay counties. The St. Marys River forms the northeastern boundary of Baker County and the northern boundary of Nassau County. The northwestern portion of Baker County is part of the Okefenokee Swamp, most of which is in Georgia.

Many of the First Coast's restaurants, including several of its better ones, are located on the various waterways and provide docks so they can be patronized by boaters. Some restaurants are actually located in marinas to attract the yachting crowd, and some are easier to find by boat than by car.

Boating is high on the preferred list of participation sports, along with tennis, golf, fishing, and bowling. The younger set adds surfing to the fun. The Atlantic is not as generous as the Pacific in providing the right curl to its waves, but the surfing along the First Coast is as good as any within 3,000 miles.

Fishing is what you make it, whether it be dropping a line into the river from the bank of a city park, or bringing in a kingfish during a day of deep-sea fishing. Almost every bridge is wide enough for a sidewalk, or at least a catwalk, where anglers can wet their lines.

Fish camps dot the banks of First Coast rivers, streams, and the Intracoastal. At first, they were places where fishermen could get bait, gasoline, or a new lure. They added food and drink until many fish camps are now renowned for catfish and hush puppies. Deep-fried fish and seafood and beer top the menus. They are part and parcel of North Florida life.

The population of the First Coast region is growing rapidly. The increase is directly responsible for the low unemployment rate because more workers are needed to serve the increasing number of residents. The area's jobless rate is below that of the state of Florida and the entire country.

Almost half of the population gain in Duval County between 1970 and 1980 was from in-migration. In the remainder of the First

Rainclouds hover over this community church. Photo by Kelly LaDuke

Coast area, in-migration accounted for nearly 90 percent of the growth.

The 1980 census listed the five counties of Florida's First Coast as having 737,541 persons, an increase of more than 100,000 from the 1970 census total of 621,827.

In 1986 the metropolitan area population was estimated by the U.S. Census Bureau to be 852,700, up from 825,400 in 1985.

These may be impressive figures, but they are only part of the story. Duval County grew from 528,800 in 1970 to 571,000 in 1980, and was estimated in April 1986 to be 652,000. The county population is expected to be 690,000 in 1990; 769,000 in 2000; and 827,000 in 2010.

Jacksonville is ranked as the seventeenth-largest city in the country. Projections say it will be thirteenth largest after the 1990 census.

Growth in Jacksonville and Duval County is concentrated in the southeast quadrant of the city, including the census tracts of Mandarin-Loretto, Pottsburg, and Southside Estates.

Orange Park, in the northeast corner of Clay County, was responsible for two-thirds of the growth in Clay County between 1970 and 1980, when the county population totaled 67,000 residents. In St. Johns County, growth is concentrated in the north around Ponte Vedra on the ocean and Fruit Cove on the St. Johns River opposite Orange Park, and in the south at Matanzas, south of St. Augustine.

Nassau County grew 59 percent to 32,800 residents in 1980. The Callahan-Hilliard area grew 87 percent, Yulee more than doubled with 102 percent growth, and Fernandina Beach grew 19 percent.

Baker County, with 15,000 residents in 1980, increased 65 percent from 1970 to 1980. Growth was fairly uniform in the county. Macclenny led with a 70 percent increase, Sanderson had a 59 percent increase, and the remainder was in the unincorporated areas of the county.

By percentages, the greatest growth was in St. Johns County. Matanzas grew 802 percent to 3,000 residents in 1980, Fruit Cove 210 percent to 4,100, Ponte Vedra 209 percent to 5,500, and St. Augustine, 40 percent to 33,870.

Florida's First Coast is home to a diversity of religions with approximately 1,000 congregations representing more than 60 Christian denominations as well as synagogues and mosques representing Judaism and Islam. The largest congregation is First Baptist Church in downtown Jacksonville with 15,000 members. The church complex covers several city blocks at the northern edge of the business district.

The Jacksonville Interfaith Council is an organization composed of representatives from most denominations and faiths. The Council discusses ways to improve brotherhood and understanding among different congregations and addresses matters of moral concern in the community.

Race relations have improved greatly since the confrontation days of the 1960s, and black citizens are numbered among the community's

These kids take a field trip through the city. Photo by Kelly LaDuke

Memorial Park, a tribute to soldiers who died during World War I, is on the banks of the St. Johns River in Riverside. Photo by Richard Kevern

leaders, serving as City Council members, School Board members, and state legislators, as well as in high positions within city agencies.

The Jacksonville Chamber of Commerce has recognized the importance of economic development initiatives in traditionally black neighborhoods and has a special program that seeks new businesses and industries for those areas.

Among those representing the black business community in the Chamber of Commerce are Ms. Willye F. Dennis, a longtime leader of the local NAACP, who is a member of the Board of Governors, and Ronnie A. Ferguson, a member of the Chamber's executive committee and head of the Small Business/Area Councils Board. The chamber named Ferguson, who is also president of the Jacksonville Urban League, as its Outstanding Young Leader in 1987.

Area festivals, mostly with a nautical bent, punctuate the First Coast calendar. During the first weekend in May there is a Shrimp Festival at Fernandina Beach. It has become a major arts and crafts show, with as many as 100,000 visitors during the festival.

During festival time, the shrimp fleet is moored at the municipal dock at the foot of historic Centre Street, which is closed to vehicular traffic during the celebration. From the dock, there is a spectacular view of the marshes and flats between the Intracoastal Waterway, which passes by the dock, and the mainland.

In St. Augustine on Palm Sunday more than 250 powerboats and shrimping boats pass in review for the annual Blessing of the Fleet— the highpoint event of the spring arts and crafts festival. August brings the Days in Spain Festival, marking the city's founding in 1565.

The Jacksonville Arts Festival is held in April of each year, and Jacksonville Beach stages an arts festival in late April. Mandarin has an arts festival as part of that community's drive to maintain its heritage as one of the oldest settlements on the First Coast, predating Jacksonville by many years.

A Jacksonville festival that is gaining popularity since its inauguration in 1985 is the annual boat Parade of Lights, which is part of the Gator Bowl festivities at the end of the year. Yachts, pleasure craft, and small boats are decorated and pass in review. In 1987, there were more than 50 entries. Thousands of spectators line the Riverwalk along the south and north banks of the river to see the spectacle.

Deciding where to live in Jacksonville or anywhere in the First Coast region is a problem; there are so many desirable places to settle down. Anyone who wants to live along a navigable waterway can do so—providing he or she can afford it. Waterfront property premiums cost from $10,000 for a lot in a marginal location to $200,000 or more for one along the St. Johns River and $300,000 or more for oceanfront lots.

A prime residential area in Jacksonville as the decade of the 1980s winds down is Epping Forest. It is a development of individual homes and condominium units on the former Alfred I. du Pont estate. The original estate home and formal gardens overlooking the St. Johns

The Florida-modern Hillwood Condominiums face a private lagoon. Photo by Richard Kevern

Below: The Epping Forest Yacht Club has rebuilt and modernized the small yacht basin on the St. Johns River that existed at the former Alfred I. du Pont estate. The estate is being converted into single-family homes and condominiums. Photo by Richard Kevern

River have been restored as the Epping Forest Yacht Club. The loblolly pines and live oaks have been thinned out to allow for construction of individual homes. The houses and condominiums are priced from about $275,000 to more than $500,000.

The location, which requires only a short, easy drive from downtown, is the last major riverfront property close to central Jacksonville. That, plus the du Pont mystique (presidents and royalty have visited there), have turned the development into one of the most desirable residential locations in the city.

Home for "Old Jacksonville" is Ortega, on the west side of the St. Johns River. There, on an island that once was called Maxton's Island, homes are not so much sold as they are willed.

Ortega has been fully developed for many years and has developed its own distinction on the First Coast. Its location, not too far from downtown, adds to its desirability, and the view of the central city from Sadler Point is one that is hard to beat.

The result is that families tend to stay in Ortega. Children—or nieces, nephews, and close friends—often take over the homes occupied by their parents, aunts, or uncles. Fewer homes are sold on the open market than in newer areas.

In other close-in Westside neighborhoods, including Avondale and Riverside, houses are more readily available. Those areas, being in the original city, were built out years ago, and to buy there means buying an older home because of the lack of vacant lots.

That is not the situation on the Southside or throughout Arlington and the Beaches. In most of the rest of Jacksonville residential lots are available, and the newcomer to Jacksonville has a choice to buy or to build almost anywhere he or she might wish.

It is possible in the First Coast area to buy much more house for the money than in many other parts of the country. One of the reasons is the fact that there is so much land available. In most neighborhoods, it is possible to find a vacant lot on which to build. It is also possible to find a summer house or rental house to buy and rehabilitate, or even tear down and start all over.

Top: Located within the Epping Forest community is the Fitness Center. It includes a Nautilus-equipped gym, four swimming pools, and much more. Courtesy, Fey & Associates

Above: Is there any lovelier sight than a child discovering the wonders of the beach? Photo by Richard Kevern

Many of Riverside's homes have been converted to office buildings. This trend has resulted in many of the big, older homes being remodeled and restored instead of being torn down. The mix of offices and homes in this district is about 50-50.

One of the reasons that the Riverside-Avondale Preservation Society came about was to control the expansions of St. Vincent's Medical Center and Riverside Hospital. Now, there are many delightful restorations, and the mix of offices and homes is considered one of the charms of the neighborhood. There are antique stores and offices of various kinds. Along Riverside and St. Johns avenues medical and health-related offices are more concentrated.

River locations in Arlington and east of Arlington are also becoming highly desirable. Before the Mathews Bridge—the so-called "bridge to nowhere"—was built, there was little in Arlington but great fox hunting. That area has developed into Jacksonville's best example of the typical postwar suburban residential area. The Broward Bridge is expected to add to Arlington's desirability.

As the decade winds down, it appears that Arlington will surpass Mandarin in popularity to potential homeowners. In 1986, the latest year for which figures are available, Mandarin was still No. 1 in new housing and real estate transfers, with Arlington No. 2, but that could well change in 1988 and during the years ahead.

From the intersection of Fort Caroline Road and the Broward Bridge road, there are 35 residential and commercial developments taking place within a two-mile radius. There could be 6,000 lots or more in those plats.

Arlington homes along the St. Johns River, in places like Charter Point opposite the mouth of the Trout River, range in price from $40,000 to millions. Charter Point homes range from $200,000 to $800,000. The average price for an Arlington home is $80,000.

Home associations in Arlington and elsewhere in the city and on the First Coast are helping to maintain a desirable quality of life. Strong homeowners' associations have resulted in attractive neighborhoods with steady or increasing property values.

Developers are putting together larger pieces of property and ensuring that property values will be maintained by providing such amenities as side entrances for garages, which present a nicer appearance from the street. Banning clotheslines, and similar considerations, also create sustainable value within the neighborhoods.

Though many areas compete for the title of most desirable neighborhood, the Beaches retain what they have always offered: great life on the oceanfront, which is available nowhere else on the First Coast.

The desire for beachfront and beach living is continuing to grow, and the growth is greatest among the higher priced properties and areas from one end of the First Coast to the other. Prices for oceanfront lots—when they are available—range from $200,000 to $400,000. The current rule of thumb is $4,000 per foot of oceanfront for bare land in a good location.

From north to south, some of the most desirable beach residential areas include Amelia Island Plantation and the Summer Beach section on Amelia Island in Nassau County; Oceanwalk at Atlantic Beach in Duval County; Sawgrass-Ponte Vedra in northern St. Johns County; and the condominium strip along the shore at Matanzas south of St. Augustine.

Except for Oceanwalk, all the top oceanfront areas share the fact that they have been developed for resort-style living, with golf and tennis making up a large measure of their appeal. As a result, the homes and condominiums are frequently bought by retirees and couples with teenagers or grown children.

Oceanwalk, on the other hand, caters more to family-style living and attracts younger affluent families with children. In Oceanwalk, homes run from $105,000 up to $500,000 or more, depending on location and size.

Some oceanfront homes in Ponte Vedra Beach sell for $1 million and more. Boosting real estate values in that area are the Mayo Clinic, just across the Intracoastal at San Pablo Road; the headquarters of the PGA TOUR at the TPC Club; and the Association of Tennis Professionals headquarters next to PGA TOUR.

With the widening of coastal Highway A1A, real estate people say there is an entirely new set of rules taking effect in Ponte Vedra

Older homes in Jacksonville's Springfield, Riverside, Avondale and San Marco neighborhoods are being restored, some as homes and others as offices for professional people. Photo by Judy K. Jacobsen

Beach. Its link to Jacksonville via Butler Boulevard has expanded its accessibility to the city, and additional strong growth can be expected.

Some areas in downtown Jacksonville Beach have been under-developed, awaiting plans for redevelopment. As a result, there is a significant strip of beachfront that will be transformed in future reconstruction. Overall, Jacksonville Beach development has produced commercial uses within one or two blocks of the ocean, leaving a strip one or two blocks wide for residential/retail/entertainment uses.

Years ago, the entire beachfront was dotted with summer cottages that were closed in the winter when people moved back into town. Many of these have been converted to year-round residences while others have been torn down and replaced. As that replacement continues, Jacksonville Beach is expected to undergo a sharp rise in land values.

Ponte Vedra Beach began as a mining property, even including railroad tracks on the beach, until the beginning of the Depression. Then redevelopment as a resort began, and the area has since blossomed into an upscale residential community.

In the three Beaches communities of Jacksonville Beach, Atlantic Beach, and Neptune Beach, it is generally recognized that properties west of Third Street (Highway A1A and the main street of the Beaches) are much less expensive than properties east of Third Street, which are that much closer to the ocean.

The west side of the Beaches communities tails off into marshes and swamps that run down to the Intracoastal. The adverse building conditions inhibit, but do not stop, Beaches growth to the Intracoastal.

The highest-priced area off the beach in Ponte Vedra is the new Plantation, a golf course community with a course designed by Arnold Palmer. The Plantation lots range up to $190,000 and single-family home prices are $350,000 and up. The Plantation attracts golfing enthusiasts from all over, including those from the Northern and Western United States.

Growth in Jacksonville on the west side and toward the southwest is limited by Naval Air Station Jacksonville and Cecil Field. Zoning restrictions to minimize interference with Navy flight patterns limit growth west of NAS Jacksonville. Those restrictions overlap into the Cecil Field restricted areas. This has created a gap in development from south and west of Ortega to the area around I-295 and Argyle Forest and into Orange Park.

Development is just beginning in southwest Duval County toward I-295 and east of Cecil Field. Projects there offer new single-family homes for $60,000 to $90,000. They are all eligible for FHA and VA financing.

The FHA and VA programs are very important in financing Jacksonville housing, and are involved in almost half of all housing deals in the city. Builders and developers in Jacksonville pay close attention to the requirements of the VA and FHA.

In northeastern Clay County, Orange Park is not growing as fast as it was in mid-decade. Heavy traffic along Blanding Boulevard is proving to be an obstacle. Growth is now pushing along Highway 17 and onto Fleming Island in the Doctors Lake area.

Another area of growth in the last half of the 1980s is Middleburg, southwest of Orange Park. For those urbanites who want large pieces of property, Middleburg offers the closest location with multi-acre building sites.

Before the days of bridges across the St. Johns River, Jacksonville was mostly a Northside and Westside city. The only way to get across the river was by ferry. When the Acosta Bridge opened in 1921, it marked the start of real development of the Southside. The St. Nicholas and San Marco neighborhoods were the first to be developed; St. Nicholas around Atlantic Boulevard at the start of Beach Boulevard, and San Marco, a mile west, at San Marco Square and along the river.

In the refurbished San Marco Square shopping area, boutiques offer specialty merchandise of all kinds. Photo by Kelly LaDuke

Quaint homes characterize the Springfield area. Photo by Kelly LaDuke

St. Nicholas history reaches back to colonial days when it was fortified by the Spanish in 1788 and 1789. The small fort was abandoned and its site obliterated.

Both neighborhoods have twins across the river, San Marco with Avondale, and St. Nicholas with Riverside Manor. This is not unusual, since both were developed by the same companies—Stockton, Whatley, Davin and Company for San Marco and Avondale, and Crabtree for St. Nicholas and Riverside Manor.

The San Marco area, along the river and near downtown, is a desirable neighborhood, and the rehabilitation of the shopping district is helping to enhance home values.

An interesting neighborhood somewhat off the beaten path is Secret Cove, off Belfort Road just north of Southpoint. Houses there range up to $200,000. The development includes a swimming pool, tennis courts, and a lake.

The area that has undergone the greatest growth in the 1980s is Mandarin, stretching from the San Jose section south along the river to the county line at Julington Creek. Mandarin is one of the oldest areas in Jacksonville, having been settled before Jacksonville was founded.

Harriet Beecher Stowe, author of *Uncle Tom's Cabin,* and her family wintered at a riverfront home in Mandarin for many years following the Civil War.

The community is marked by huge live oaks and sizable estates along the St. Johns River. It had been a rural community until the 1960s when developers began building homes. Now, it is all but full.

The Mandarin Community Club has worked very hard to maintain the integrity of the community, and has both succeeded and failed at the job. Florida Highway 13, once a two-lane country road winding through pine forests, is now a five- and six-lane highway lined with shopping strips, fast-food outlets, and marked every few hundred feet with traffic lights.

With all that water, sailboat races are inevitable. Photo by Richard Kevern

Off the main street, there are many subdivisions, some of them among the highest quality in the First Coast. The entire community is perceived as maintaining or increasing its value.

When downtown Jacksonville was wiped out by the 1901 fire and more than 8,000 residents were left homeless, Hogan's Creek saved Springfield. The old neighborhood is north of downtown Hogan's Creek, and like so many close-in neighborhoods in many cities across the country, it fell on hard times during the Depression, but is now attempting a comeback.

Springfield has some very nice areas, and rehabilitation is taking place there. But one of Springfield's strengths is also one of her drawbacks. There are many very large houses in the community. In earlier eras they were occupied by extended families or were two-family homes. Today, many of them have become halfway houses in response to contemporary approaches to human rehabilitation programs. Springfield therefore suffers from the perception of undesirability that is attached to the group homes and halfway houses. There is a concentration of those in Springfield because many of the larger houses can be adapted to those uses and because the neighborhood is convenient to downtown governmental services, both in location and in terms of available mass transportation. Some claim that half of all First Coast congregate-living homes are in Springfield.

Above: A dragon comes to life at a sandsculpting contest. Photo by Richard Kevern

Top: Fireworks fill the sky above The Jacksonville Landing, marking its first birthday. At right is Independent Square, Jacksonville's tallest building. Photo by David Dobbs

*Condominiums and hotels are sil-
houetted by the afternoon sun at
Jacksonville Beach. Photo by
Richard Kevern*

Still, individual rehabilitation of homes continues and there are some truly magnificent late-Victorian period homes in the neighborhood. In addition, condominium units have been built on the south edge of the area, next to downtown.

If proposals to redevelop the fringes of downtown for housing come to fruition, then Springfield will stand an even better chance of revival, once again becoming a gracious neighborhood, only a short walk away from the heart of the city.

One of the outstanding qualities of life in Florida's First Coast is its pace, which is more relaxed than in many other parts of the country. Perhaps it is because of the ever-present opportunities for recreation anywhere in the area. Perhaps it is that Jacksonville—Florida's business city—and Florida's First Coast know how to mix business with pleasure and get the most out of both.

EPILOGUE

Named for a general who never set foot in the town and claiming little more in common with glitzy South Florida than palm trees and sunshine, Jacksonville is a city of surprises. Since its founding by a little group of settlers more than 150 years ago, the town has never ceased to challenge the assumptions of those who think they know it. People who thought of it simply as a winter retreat for rich northerners—a role it played magnificently during the latter part of the nineteenth century—were surprised to see Jacksonville develop into the financial and commercial capital of the state. Those who saw it in the twentieth century as a big, overgrown South Georgia cowtown were caught off guard when it shed its ultraconservative image to undertake a bold new experiment in city government which has been astonishingly successful. Some who have seen Jacksonville as simply a place to hurry by on the way to playgrounds farther south will now find ample reasons for pause—perhaps at Sawgrass, Amelia Island, or Ponte Vedra.

Jacksonville is a sparkling new city with a healthy respect for its past. The Oriental Gardens are gone, but Epping Forest, the lovely du Pont estate, has become a posh residential development. KBJ Architects, the firm which designed most of our ultramodern landmark buildings, makes its home in a restored Victorian mansion downtown. Many of the bridges and streets are named for politicians and developers, but other place names resound with the region's Spanish, British, and French heritage.

Anyone who has lived in Jacksonville more than two decades knows that "Dora" was a hurricane and "Cora" a sporting house madame who became the wife of the famous nineteenth-century writer Stephen Crane. (Hurricanes often threaten the northeast coast of

Florida, but seldom come ashore. Dora, in 1965, was a devastating exception.)

Jacksonville is a city of three seasons—the best three—and no snow, except for the surprise of huge fluffy flakes that sometimes drift down in a February dawn and send pajama-clad Florida children rushing outside shrieking with glee, to find them as ephemeral as soap bubbles, and as much fun!

We are a city of a surprisingly rich ethnicity. The mayor is of Lebanese extraction. There's a Greek Festival and an African Festival each year, a German-American Club and a close-knit community of Vietnamese immigrants. Spanish is spoken here, as is French and Yiddish and West Indian and American Southern.

Sometimes the surprises come in the form of a phalanx of bright spinnakers unfurled against the backdrop of the city skyline, or the magical appearance of hot air balloons hovering low and enormous over the river, emitting sounds like the breathing of dragons.

Jacksonville is more than a thriving, populous city—it is deep woods and sun-spangled waters, windswept dunes and tide-washed marshlands. It's a working city, but our citizens know how to play—and office workers routinely put on their walking shoes for a lunch-hour stroll down the Southbank Riverwalk.

It is a place for the adventurous in spirit where men and women of vigorous individuality have left their indelible marks—Rene de Laudonniere and Daniel McGirtt, James Weldon Johnson and Henry John Klutho, Henry Flagler, Ed Ball and Ira Koger, Dr. Malvina Reichard and Harriet Beecher Stowe. Their spirit is Jacksonville's heritage, the source of its unique legacy. If Juan Ponce de Leon were to discover Jacksonville today, he would find a tradition of innovation and a youthful exuberance that would surely cause him to give up his search for the Fountain of Youth and settle down right here on Florida's First Coast.

—Peggy Friedmann

The fishing pier at Jacksonville Beach. Photo by Richard Kevern

Most of downtown Jacksonville lies on the north bank of the St. Johns River between the Acosta Bridge (left) and Main Street Bridge (right). In the foreground are the towers of the developing Southbank downtown area. Photo by Judy K. Jacobsen

Part Two

FIRST COAST ENTERPRISES

CHAPTER 13

NETWORKS

Jacksonville's energy, communication, and transportation providers keep products, information, and power circulating inside and outside the area.

207

CONTINENTAL CABLEVISION OF JACKSONVILLE

Under the leadership of Jeff DeLorme, vice-president and general manager (right), Continental Cablevision's 500 employees have worked diligently to improve the quality and speed of service to its subscribers.

HBO, TBS, CBN, USA—a decade ago the abbreviated titles of these popular cable services would have been nothing more than an unfamiliar string of letters to Jacksonville residents. Today Home Box Office, Superstation TBS of Atlanta, the CBN and USA Cable Networks, plus more than 30 other programming services, are a part of the daily life-style of thousands of Jacksonville families.

More than 150,000 households in Jacksonville subscribe to cable television service provided by Continental Cablevision of Jacksonville, the largest system in the country of its parent company, Continental Cablevision Inc.

Rated the best cable company in the nation by the respected industry trade publication *Channels,* Continental Cablevision Inc. is the third-largest cable operator in the United States, serving more than 2 million subscribers in 300-plus communities.

Continental came to Jacksonville in February 1984, when it purchased Area Communications, Inc., the existing cable system, from its local ownership. Jacksonville's first cable company, Area Communications began delivering cable service to the community in June 1979.

Since purchasing the system Continental has expanded programming and improved customer service in the Jacksonville market, resulting in a 55-percent increase in subscribers. The Jacksonville system today consists of

New studios opened in October 1987 provide video training and programming access to numerous community organizations.

more than 3,000 miles of cable plant, and is one of the 20 largest cable service areas in the United States.

Continental Cablevision offers 52 channels of programming, including children's, sports, news, business, health, music, premium services, and the national networks, plus extensive community programming.

Continental has a staff of nine professionals who produce as much as 60 hours of local programming each week. Local programming includes shows such as "People and Politics," "The Jacksonville Money Report," "Senior Citizens' Issues & Updates," "Women on the Move," "To Your Health," and many others.

In addition, Continental Cablevision has pioneered the development of the Sunshine Network, which is a statewide network of cable programming. Local programs produced by member systems in Orlando, Tallahassee, Fort Lauderdale, Tampa, Broward County, and Jacksonville appear on the network on cable systems statewide.

Continental Cablevision also has joined eight other Florida cable operators to form a new sports network that will provide 400 live or tape-delayed

telecasts each year, 100 of which will be produced by Florida systems. Home Sports Entertainment of Houston was chosen to manage the new sports service. It will feature collegiate sporting events from around the country as well as boxing, tennis, wrestling, horse racing, and high school football.

Continental Cablevision of Jacksonville is located at 5934 Richard Road in Jacksonville's Southside and has branch offices in Westside and Northside. Leading the company is vice-president and general manager Jeff DeLorme, who has been with the parent company since 1980 and with the Jacksonville system since 1984.

Continental has a work force in Jacksonville of 500 employees, which includes programming production personnel, installation and repair technicians, and customer service and sales representatives.

Continental's primary goal is to deliver cable service of the highest quality and value to its Jacksonville sub-

Continental Cablevision expanded its service in 1988 with the addition of 10 new satellite-delivered channels.

scribers. To meet customer needs, Continental has extended the operation of its installation and repair services from 7 a.m. to 7 p.m. seven days a week.

To improve customer service, a $250,000 telephone system was installed that has allowed Continental Cablevision to respond to customer inquiries up to 90 percent faster than the previous system. Featuring the latest in telephone answering technology, response time has been reduced to 30 seconds or less on every incoming call.

The innovative telephone system, coupled with enhanced employee training in customer service techniques, has ranked Continental Cablevision of Jacksonville number one in the country in overall customer satisfaction according to a survey of cable subscribers conducted by Response Research Inc. of

Chicago, Illinois.

The Jacksonville system also ranked high in other categories in the survey, which measured customer attitudes regarding 79 cable systems nationwide. Continental Cablevision of Jacksonville was found second in value for the money, third in overall customer service, and fourth in variety of programming.

Continental Cablevision of Jacksonville also receives high marks from the Jacksonville community for the support it has given to civic and charitable organizations and events. The company has participated directly in a number of fund-raising, and education projects, and has also provided public service programming time for a large number of groups. These include the Jacksonville Zoo, Florida Special Olympics, the Dorcas Drake Annual Christmas Party, the Jacksonville Blood Bank, the Mental Health Association of Jacksonville, and the Spina Bifida Association of Jacksonville.

PEOPLES GAS SYSTEM

Below the streets of Jacksonville lie hundreds of miles of gas mains that supply much of the energy needs of Jacksonville's major manufacturers and thousands of city residents.

The Peoples Gas System is the city's natural gas supplier, serving 15,000 customers—12,000 of whom are residences. The firm is also a major supplier of propane gas in areas not served by natural gas mains. By far the bulk of Peoples' gas supply in Jacksonville (more than 95 percent) is distributed to businesses, particularly to large industrial manufacturers.

The company has seen unprecedented growth in recent years in its commercial business because of the economy of gas compared to other fuels. Today Peoples serves nearly every major manufacturer, business concern, and hospital in northeast Florida, and continues to expand to meet the needs of new commercial customers.

One of Peoples' largest customers in Jacksonville is the Jacksonville Electric Authority, which uses natural gas to fuel its massive generators. The electric authority uses approximately 15

This modern office building, showroom, and service center opened on Phillips Highway near Emerson Street in late 1985.

percent of Peoples' total annual gas distribution in Jacksonville.

In one of its most significant expansions ever, Peoples recently completed construction of 11.5 miles of high-pressure main to serve the JEA and other major Northside customers, such as U.S. Gypsum, Anheuser-Busch, and Jefferson Smurfit. The pipeline is the largest-diameter main installed in Florida since 1959. The 18-inch-diameter pipeline is more than six times the capacity of the average gas main. The project also involved an 1,800-foot underwater crossing of the Trout River.

Peoples Gas in Jacksonville is part of the statewide Peoples Gas System, Inc., headquartered in Tampa. The firm is the largest natural gas distributor in Florida, totaling more than $200 million in sales revenue annually. Its affiliate, Peoples Gas Company, is also the state's largest independent propane

distributor.

Peoples Gas System, Inc., is a Lykes Energy company owned by the Lykes family of Tampa, which is also known for its longtime Florida business interests in citrus and meat packing. Peoples has a statewide employment of nearly 1,000.

Previously serving primarily South Florida and the Gulf Coast of Florida, Peoples expanded into northeast Florida in 1979 with the purchase of Florida Gas Company. Florida Gas had a long history of supplying Jacksonville with its natural gas needs.

The gas industry in Jacksonville dates back to 1854, the year the Citizens Gaslight Company began manufacturing gas from coal and pumping it through hollowed-out cypress logs to light the streets of the city. The enterprise later became known as the Jacksonville Gas Company, which expanded and prospered through the years and eventually became Jacksonville Gas Corporation. In 1958 a natural gas pipeline was constructed to Jacksonville, and the firm was purchased and renamed Florida Gas Company.

One of 10 divisions of the state-wide Peoples Gas System, the Jacksonville offices were on Adams Street in downtown Jacksonville for many years. In late 1985 a new $2.5-million office building, showroom, and service center opened on Phillips Highway near Emerson Street. The two-story structure includes 30,000 square feet of general office, retail, and warehouse space.

The Jacksonville division receives gas to serve the city through a gate station in the Normandy section of the city's westside. At the "city gate," gas is measured and regulated into the Jacksonville system from the statewide transmission pipeline of Florida Gas Transmission Company, from whom Peoples purchases its gas. Florida Gas

Distribution lines are continually upgraded and expanded to meet the needs of industrial and residential customers.

Transmission Company pipes the natural gas in from the rich gas fields of Texas, Louisiana, and the Gulf of Mexico.

In Jacksonville, Peoples employs nearly 100 people in its four major departments:

The distribution department is responsible for laying the underground pipes to extend gas service around the city to a growing number of commercial customers.

The service department serves primarily residential customers. Through the department, service lines and house piping are installed off the main lines; gas appliances are installed and repaired; and residential gas systems are adjusted and serviced.

The sales department offers for sale a full line of gas appliances—including ranges, water heaters, clothes dryers, furnaces, central heat and air conditioning, and others.

Large industrial accounts are served primarily by the administrative

Sixteen thousand meters are read by Peoples' meter readers each month.

department, as are other essential financial and personnel concerns of the operation.

In the future, Peoples Gas System, both locally and statewide, will continue to expand its facilities and strengthen its service and distribution capabilities to meet the increasing demand for gas as an energy source.

WJKS-TV

WJKS-Channel 17 is an Emmy Award-winning television station that is dedicated to its news effort and public affairs programming.

The WJKS news staff produces four 30-minute news programs each day at 6:30 a.m., 12 noon, 6 p.m. and 11 p.m., as well as provides live coverage of special events and short updates during the day to keep the public informed of the latest news.

Bearing the slogan "First on the News Scene," WJKS is Jacksonville's only television station with its own helicopter. The station's full-time helicopter pilot is on call 24 hours a day to fly *Sky 17* to the scene of breaking news events.

Channel 17 reporters are able to telecast directly from the familiar bright-orange helicopter using sophisti-

Award-winning WJKS-TV, Channel 17, keeps on top of breaking news events with Sky 17 and sophisticated live remote equipment.

cated live remote equipment. For coverage of important events outside the station's broadcast area—such as a launch at Cape Canaveral—the station makes use of a state-of-the-art satellite linkup facility that can broadcast or pick up signals from anywhere on the planet. Persons or events photographed at WJKS studios or remote locations can be viewed instantaneously anywhere in the world via the satellite connection. In addition to the helicopter and satellite capabilities, the station's news staff has five mobile microwave units designated specifically for live remote telecasts.

In efforts not going unrecognized, the WJKS news staff has won numerous awards for its local news coverage, including two Emmy awards for spot news reporting. The station has also made great strides in the local television ratings.

A major network affiliate in Jacksonville since it opened in 1966, WJKS has grown dramatically during the past

two decades, keeping pace with the growth of the city. Today WJKS is aired to a quarter-million homes in the North Florida/South Georgia area. More than three-dozen cable systems carry its telecast, the largest of which is Jacksonville's Continental Cable.

Since 1982 the station has been owned by Media General Broadcast Group, which also owns WXFL in Tampa and WCBD in Charleston, South Carolina.

WJKS presently has a total employment of 100 professionals, technicians, and administrative staff. Approximately 35 are on the news staff.

Another major component of the station is its television-commercial production capabilities. The WJKS production staff of nearly 25 has produced hundreds of commercials for local, state, and regional markets.

The Channel 17 staff handles the entire creative and technical process, including creative design, writing, supplying the talent, building the sets, and

This satellite linkup facility broadcasts or picks up signals from anywhere in the world.

creating the graphics. The station's state-of-the-art production facilities have sophisticated graphic and video capabilities. Commercials produced in the WJKS studios have won numerous awards, including the Addy Award.

WJKS has a strong commitment to public affairs programming, and has shown that commitment in many areas of broadcasting. Each year the station does a telethon, devoting hours of continuous air time to the Children's Miracle Network in support of local children's hospitals.

WJKS has also been a major supporter of the For Kids Sake nationwide, syndicated campaign. In the campaign, stations air programs dealing with issues of importance to young people today, such as scholastic achievement, health, and family.

In addition to the For Kids Sake special series of 30-minute and one-hour specials, WJKS has broadcast educational and safety programs aimed at young people and sponsored Jacksonville's fingerprinting for children program. Within the community, the station is also an active supporter of numerous community and charitable activities, including Volunteer Jacksonville, the Blood Drive, and United Way.

In the future, WJKS plans to expand its local programming and continue its strong commitment to local news and public affairs through expansion of its staff and technological capabilities.

Familiar to the Jacksonville area are WJKS' five mobile microwave units for live remote telecasts.

WJXT-TV

The award-winning WJXT-TV first brought television to Jacksonville in 1949. Today, with the latest in modern technology and a staff committed to excellence, the station continues to provide Jacksonville viewers and advertisers the finest in news and entertainment programming.

Don't defend the status quo. Report hard and aggressively, and let the people draw their own conclusions about the information presented to them.

That philosophy has been the benchmark of journalistic quality at WJXT TV-4 for nearly 40 years. The winner of an unprecedented two Alfred I. du Pont-Columbia awards —the broadcast equivalent of the Pulitzer Prize—WJXT has set a standard of journalistic excellence recognized nationwide.

The public acceptance of the Post-Newsweek station's newscasts through the years has been unparalleled. WJXT has consistently attracted more viewers to its 6 p.m. news than Jacksonville's five other television stations combined.

The respect the station has earned through its news operations has permeated throughout WJXT's entire programming schedule, from sign-on to sign-off. One of the highest-performing CBS affiliates in the country, the station's position in the community is so strong that it consistently retains ratings leadership in Jacksonville regardless of the performance of the CBS network nationwide.

One of the oldest CBS affiliates in Florida, WJXT was the first television station between Atlanta and Miami, and one of the original 62 stations in the country. It was founded by Glenn Marshall in 1949, a time when few households even owned television sets.

"Not only did we pioneer television in Jacksonville, we've been here 40 years. Four generations have grown up with us," says Gus Bailey, Jr., WJXT's general manager. "We've made a real difference in the community. You don't make a difference by talking about it. You make a difference through your actions."

In 1953 the station was purchased by the Washington Post Company. Following journalistic standards established by the esteemed newspaper and its publisher, Philip L. Graham, WJXT soon developed a solid news team with an investigative unit, hard-hitting documentaries, and on-air editorials.

During the 1960s the station's investigative team unearthed widespread corruption in Jacksonville's city government. Its aggressive reporting helped bring about the indictment of a number of city officials, and its widely acclaimed documentary, "Government by Gaslight," served as a catalyst for consolidation of city and county governments. "Government by Gaslight," was only one of many important documentaries produced by WJXT to direct attention to community issues, and bring about reform.

The Alfred I. du Pont-Columbia Award-winning documentary "The Smell of Money"—about local odor pollution problems—eventually led to the passage of a tough pollution-control ordinance that has improved the quality of life throughout Jacksonville. "Jacksonville's Roads: The Deadly Drive Home," WJXT's second du Pont-Columbia Award winner, chronicled numerous driving hazards on the city's streets and highways, and has resulted in policy review and changes by the city agencies responsible. Other thought-provoking programs that have made a difference in the community are "Wards of the Street," highlighting the plight of teenage runaways; "Premature Mothers," a startling look at factors contributing to the area's teen pregnancy dilemma; and "Execution in the Sun," an examination of the controversial subject of capital punishment.

In addition, the station's news coverage of the inefficiencies of the city's toll collections were key in bringing about a voter referendum that resulted in the abolishment of tolls on area roadways. For overall excellence in electronic journalism, the Eyewitness News team has twice received the prestigious Edward R. Murrow Award from their colleagues in the Radio and Television News Directors Association who cited the station for the most outstanding news coverage and presentation in the Southeast.

WJXT's long history of stability in ownership is mirrored by the stability in its professional staff.

The late Bill Grove, the station's news anchor and director during the 1950s, 1960s, and 1970s, was Jackson-

ville's most respected newsman for three decades. When he was honored at his 25th anniversary with WJXT, his counterpart on the national level, Walter Cronkite, made a special trip to Jacksonville to join the festivities.

The station's popular weatherman, chief meteorologist George Winterling, recently celebrated his 25th year with WJXT. He joins longtime anchors Tom Wills and Deborah Gianoulis, and sports director Sam Kouvaris in daily broadcasts throughout the northeast Florida-southeast Georgia region.

WJXT is also the leader in area community service, with a substantial commitment to provide production and air time free of charge to local nonprofit organizations working to bring a better quality of life to area residents. Through the years the station has broadcast a wide variety of local informational, agricultural, public affairs, religious, and children's programming. The Sunday morning Bible-study program "Sunday School Forum" is the longest-running local religious program in the country.

The WJXT sales and marketing staff works with area businesses to develop television advertising plans that enable them to grow and prosper. Believing that results are the primary goal,

To keep up with technology, WJXT-TV will occupy this multimillion-dollar, state-of-the-art facility in 1989.

WJXT marketing specialists provide expertise in budget development, media planning, and vendor funding. The station's state-of-the-art commercial production unit is also a key component in WJXT's client service.

WJXT's research department, established in 1962, is one of the oldest and most respected operations of its kind in Florida. Using an extensive resource network that includes computerized data, syndicated studies, local market surveys, and annual consumer research, the department provides in-depth demographic profiles, purchasing habits, retail trends, and sales forecasting.

Technologically, WJXT is also a leader nationwide, spearheading innovative technological breakthroughs in a wide variety of areas. It was the first station in the country to mount a full-service camera on its tower. The "tower cam," located 450 feet high, gives a panoramic view of downtown Jacksonville and the suburbs, and has proven itself an important tool in covering such breaking news stories as fires, oil

spills, and return-to-port of major ships, as well as providing a bird's-eye view for important weather stories.

The station's closed captioning system for the hearing impaired was also the first of its kind in the nation. Used during newscasts and editorials, it provides real-time captions directly from the scripts used by news reporters and anchors. WJXT also pioneered mobile satellite uplink capabilities with the Florida News Network, enabling the station to provide viewers news coverage from around the state.

WJXT's current facility, built in 1960, will be replaced in 1989 with a new state-of-the-art building that will be one of the finest broadcast facilities in the Southeast. The multimillion-dollar facility signals a continuing commitment to Jacksonville by WJXT.

"Our goal remains the same as when we first arrived," Washington Post-Company chairman Katharine Graham recently told WJXT's staff, "to keep everyone informed about what is happening throughout this community so that growth can be managed intelligently, so that all citizens can share in Jacksonville's prosperity, and so that all of the community's resources can be brought to bear on the challenges we confront."

WAIV-WOKV

Jacksonville's dramatic growth during recent years—particularly in its Baby Boom-age population—has created the need for an outstanding news and information service, as well as adult-oriented entertainment.

Two sister radio stations—97 WAIV-FM and 60 WOKV-AM—fit the bill for both.

WAIV is the dominant adult-contemporary station in Jacksonville, playing classic hits of the 1960s, 1970s, and 1980s. WOKV is northeast Florida's only all news, sports, and talk station, featuring established news personalities and Jacksonville radio's largest news-gathering team.

Both stations are owned by E-Z Communications, Inc., of Fairfax, Virginia, and are operated under the same management at the stations' Westside offices of 6869 Lenox Avenue.

"We have retooled and reoriented our radio stations to reflect the tremendous population growth that has taken place in Jacksonville during the past five years," says Jeff Dorf, vice-president and general manager for more than four years. "We've seen the impact of both stations grow dramatically during the past couple of years, in part because Jacksonville's white-collar, professional, and biomedical-related industries have expanded."

The stature of WAIV-WOKV in the community has grown as they have

With a changing population, the impact of WAIV/WOKV has grown dramatically. Personnel keep abreast of the challenge to provide ever-changing programming.

taken leading roles in involvement in major community and civic events.

WAIV or WOKV has served as the official broadcast station for such events as the spectacular opening of the Jacksonville Landing, the annual Tournament Players Golf Championship, political debates, the annual Jacksonville Christmas tree lighting, the Dorcas Drake Christmas toy drive, and many other community activities. The

The station's production room where the commercials are readied for airing.

stations have hosted such charitable functions as the March of Dimes Walk America Campaign and the Muscular Dystrophy Telethon.

WAIV boasts Jacksonville's strongest signal, broadcasting south to Orlando, north to Waycross, Georgia, and west to the Gulf of Mexico.

A family-oriented radio station, WAIV's programming is aimed primarily at adults between the ages of 25 and 54. Some of northeast Florida's most established on-air personalities entertain listeners with a mix of top contemporary hits of the past three decades, with the exception of hard rock. Known as "Your 10 in a Row Station," WAIV plays 10 songs in a row each hour without commercial interruption.

Regular features include a lunchtime oldies show each weekday, and a special program of love songs each weeknight from 9 p.m. to midnight. Weekend programming features a live, all-request oldies show Saturday night, and two popular Dick Clark programs—"Countdown America" and "Rock, Roll, and Remember"—on Sunday.

The station brings its audience the latest news updates, complete weather service, and regular traffic advisories. Thousands of Jacksonville residents rely on the WAIV traffic reports of Jacksonville Sheriff's Office Sergeant Sonny Connell as they drive to work each morning.

In addition to the station's drive-time popularity, WAIV maintains a massive at-work listening audience. "Our station is very popular with local businesses. We do a lot of special programming during the day for at-work listeners," Dorf says. "WAIV does the most business-to-business advertising of any station in Jacksonville."

WOKV, also popular in the business setting because of its continuous news, sports, and informational programming, has a diverse audience that cuts across demographic guidelines with its broad range of programming. Appealing primarily to listeners age 25 and older, informational programming ranges from a Saturday-morning garage sale roundup to personal financial advice to a psychology talk show. Local and national experts in a wide variety of subjects conduct the programs, primarily in the weekday morning time slot.

The station's news operation provides the most up-to-date news coverage available on a local, state, and national basis. WOKV utilizes a number of network news services, including CBS Radio News, ABC Talk Radio, and NBC Talk Network, as well as the Associated Press wire service and the Florida Network.

On the local level WOKV has the largest local news-gathering team of any radio station in Jacksonville, covering all major local and regional happenings of interest. The station also provides special continuing coverage of such important Jacksonville news events as the return of naval carriers to the Mayport Naval Station and local elections.

Utilizing a number of network news services, WOKV provides the most up-to-date news coverage available on a local, state, and national basis.

WOKV devotes many hours of its broadcast time to the coverage of sports, including the airing of athletic events, interviews with leading sports personalities, and overall sports news of the day.

Veteran sports announcer Jay Solomon conducts a two-hour sports program each weekday evening, interviewing athletes, coaches, and other experts about topical events of interest in the sports world. WOKV is the flagship station of the University of Florida Radio Network and originates all sports broadcasts for this nationally recognized university. The station also broadcasts all Miami Dolphin football games, the Monday Night Football game, a professional baseball game of the week, all professional football and baseball play-off games, and various other games.

Each year the station provides continuous, in-depth coverage of Jackson-

Behind the scenes is a professional staff taking care of the business end of production.

ville's major sporting events. WOKV broadcasts hole-by-hole coverage of the Tournament Players Club Golf Championship and the Seniors Tournament Players Club championship. The Women's Tennis Association championship and the Du Pont Tennis Classic, both held at Amelia Island Plantation, are among other world-class events for which the station provides live coverage.

WAIV and WOKV were purchased by E-Z Communications in December 1986 from Affiliated Broadcasting, a subsidiary of the *Boston Globe,* which had owned both stations since 1981. E-Z Communications owns 13 radio stations across the country from Seattle to Miami.

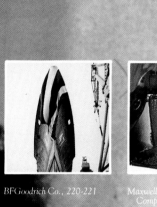

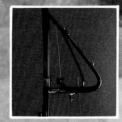

CHAPTER 14

MANUFACTURING

Producing goods for individuals and industry, manufacturing firms provide employment for many Jacksonville area residents.

219

Courtesy, Sally Industries

BFGOODRICH CO.

A sonar dome rubber window mounted on a hydrotest fixture, which simulates actual ship insulation.

There's a type of window that can be heard through, not seen through, and it's made of rubber, not glass.

The large sonar windows produced by the BFGoodrich Co. in Jacksonville provide protective coverage for the ultrasensitive, very sophisticated sonar equipment installed in antisubmarine warfare frigates, destroyers, and cruisers.

The BFGoodrich Marine Products and Services Unit in Jacksonville is the free world's only producer of rubber sonar bow and keel domes for naval surface ships. The company produces up to 20 each year at its 16-acre manufacturing facility on Blount Island. The rubber windows and keel domes are provided for the U.S. Navy as well as for the navies of foreign allies, such as Australia, Spain, Japan, and West Germany.

"This business unit makes a vital contribution to the defense of the United States," says Laurence "Tyke" Furey, senior executive and general manager of the Marine Products and Services Unit and a retired Navy captain whose background includes serving as commanding officer of two Navy destroyers. "We are the sole producer of rubber sonar domes for U.S. Navy surface ship antisubmarine warfare (ASW) combatants, whose principal mission is to ensure access to the world's sea lanes."

The protective windows are designed by computer to withstand the dynamic loads that might be encountered during shipboard service in a hostile marine environment. Resembling a medium-size whale, the 40-foot-long bow domes eliminate acoustical interference caused by the ship's movement through the water.

These nine-ton windows are precision hand-crafted to strict specifications in two separate halves within large molds. The halves are then cured separately in a huge, pressure-cooking device called an autoclave. They are then joined by a splicing operation on a special fixture that serves to structurally hydrotest the windows.

Once completed, the domes and windows are transported via C5A aircraft, ocean barge, or truck to their final destination—shipyards or storage sites. Some go directly to the nearby Mayport Naval Station for vessels stationed there.

In addition to the production facilities, the Blount Island plant includes a laboratory where rubber formulations are physically tested for quality and compliance to strict performance specifications.

Always at the forefront of development and research technology, BFGoodrich is developing fiberglass-reinforced plastic composite material for use in future shipboard applications. In the future the firm will begin production of relevant programs for submarine application.

Total employment by the company in Jacksonville is 175, with 120 working at the Blount Island facility and the others at the administrative offices located in the Regency North Executive Square in Arlington. Yearly sales of the Jacksonville operation surpass $18 million.

The Blount Island manufacturing facility office building.

The 30- by 45-foot steam autoclave—the largest in the world.

The Marine Products and Services Unit in Jacksonville is a part of the BFGoodrich Aerospace and Defense Division. BFGoodrich Co., a highly diversified *Fortune* 500 corporation founded in 1870, is one of the world's largest chemical and aerospace firms—with plants, laboratories, research and development facilities, and sales offices throughout the world.

The corporation began research, development, and production of marine acoustical materials 50 years ago. The sonar-enhancement technology began in 1938 with the development of Rho-C rubber compounds possessing the same acoustical properties as sea water. BFGoodrich's original prototype rubber bow window, a forerunner of the contemporary model, was first tested in 1966.

Jacksonville was chosen as the new site for the Marine Products and Services Unit for a number of reasons, not the least of which were a skilled labor force, the river's deep-water channel for shipping, and local naval air, sea, and submarine presence.

The leadership of the unit has made a concerted and successful effort to take an active role in North Florida. The firm has played a progressive role in community, military, and charitable activities, including a significant donation to the establishment of the U.S. Navy Memorial on the Riverwalk, paying tribute to those men and women who have served in the Navy.

The management of the Marine Products and Services Unit emphasizes the value of each of its employees to the organization, and follows a well-received participatory style of management.

"We sincerely encourage participation from everyone in our organization. My door is always open, and each of my staff functions in the same manner," Furey says. "As much as possible, we want everyone here to be an effective, contributing asset to the organization. We keep our people motivated, dedicated, and very well-informed."

Because construction and quality of the product are the focal point of the company, every employee—from clerical workers to upper management—is invited to spend a day a month working hands-on in the production phase to gain a better understanding of the production/delivery cycle.

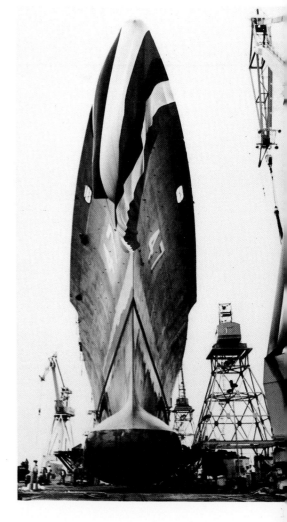

A bow-mounted SDRW on the USF Ticonderoga, *an AEGIF cruiser.*

MAXWELL HOUSE COFFEE COMPANY

The Maxwell House trademark is as familiar to Jacksonville as freshly roasted "Good to the last drop" Maxwell House coffee.

Jacksonville's Maxwell House Coffee Company plant has been a downtown landmark since the turn of the century. Since first opening its doors in 1910, the Jacksonville plant has grown from a facility employing 30 people who produced 40,000 pounds of coffee per day, to the largest Maxwell House plant, employing more than 500 people, who produce hundreds of thousands of pounds of coffee each day.

Today the Jacksonville plant produces more than half of all Maxwell House coffee sold in the United States. Green coffee beans are roasted and ground into both regular and instant coffee that is packaged into cans, jars, and vacuum bags of all sizes.

The company that today is the nation's largest manufacturer, commanding more than one-third of the domestic market, was created in 1892 in Nashville, Tennessee, by a young coffee salesman named Joel Cheek.

An ardent connoisseur of the beverage, Cheek was not satisfied with the taste of the coffee he was selling. He left his job and spent five years experimenting with the roasting and blending of coffee beans until he created what he considered "the perfect blend."

To gain a market for his new product, Cheek featured the coffee at the prestigious Maxwell House Hotel in Nashville, and the aromatic blend soon acquired a large following—as well as a new name. According to legend, President Theodore Roosevelt sampled a cup of the coffee while visiting in Nashville in the early 1900s and gave the firm the slogan still used today when he pronounced the coffee "Good to the last drop."

As the popularity of Maxwell House coffee grew, Cheek took on a partner, John Neal, and together they established the Cheek-Neal Coffee Co. and opened a small roasting plant in Nashville.

Demand soon surpassed production capacity at the small plant, and Cheek-Neal began looking for strategic cities in which to open new facilities. In 1904 a plant opened in Houston, Texas, and in 1910 Jacksonville was selected as the site of the company's next major plant, owing to the city's centralized location and excellent rail and port facilities. Leon Cheek, one of Joel Cheek's sons, was the first Jacksonville plant manager.

In 1915 Maxwell House became a registered trademark in the United States.

The original Jacksonville plant was located on the St. Johns River across Bay Street and to the east of the present location. Coffee was roasted over "coke" fires in electrically powered ovens. Power failure meant mustering a bucket brigade to extinguish fires in the roasting cylinder to keep the coffee beans from burning.

Sales increased and a new and

Hundreds of thousands of cans are produced daily in the only Maxwell House can plant in the world.

larger plant was erected in 1924 that is today still the plant's main production building. Located on 12 acres downtown at 735 East Bay Street, modern-day Maxwell House operations include nine buildings housing administration, storage, and production facilities. In addition to its coffee production, the Jacksonville operation also includes the only Maxwell House can-producing plant, which makes hundreds of thousands of Maxwell House coffee cans each day.

General Foods purchased Maxwell House in 1928. Today the coffee company is part of General Foods Worldwide Coffee & International, one of three General Foods operating companies. In 1985 Philip Morris Companies Inc. purchased General Foods.

Shortly after General Foods bought Maxwell House, Bill Dowling became manager of the plant, a position he held for 28 years. The plant underwent major expansion and improvement during his tenure, including the addition of new roasting ovens and the expansion of packing, receiving, shipping, and general office facilities. In 1951 a new business was born—Instant Maxwell House—and two new buildings were constructed to produce

Roasted beans are checked for color as they are discharged from the roasters.

Coffee levels and appearance are closely monitored by filler operators for Instant Maxwell House.

and pack the new coffee.

From the beginning of the firm through present day, Maxwell House has enforced stringent quality control measures to ensure that the flavor and taste of the coffee is maintained in every jar, can, or vacuum bag of coffee produced.

A highly technical and complex process, the production of the brew that starts the morning routine for so many Americans begins simply enough—with the green coffee bean. Maxwell House coffee beans are grown in South America, Central America, and Africa, and are purchased through the Maxwell House Green Coffee Division on Wall Street, the heart of the world's coffee market. The green beans used to derive the distinctive Maxwell

House blend arrive in Jacksonville through the Port of Jacksonville or the Port of Miami.

The beans, which are received in burlap or grass woven bags, are dumped into hoppers where they are cleaned and stored by type to await roasting and blending. At this point the coffee beans can go one of two ways—to regular processing for ground coffee or to soluble processing to make instant coffee. In the regular process, the beans are placed according to their flavor type in one of many large rotating cylinders where they are roasted at temperatures of more than 300 degrees.

The roasting process usually takes 10 minutes or more with the temperature in the cylinders increasing dramatically during the last few minutes.

Attendants visually inspect vacuum bags for defects to ensure that the quality of the packaging is as good as the quality of the product.

A Quality Systems technician pulls cans off the line to test vacuum against the prescribed standard.

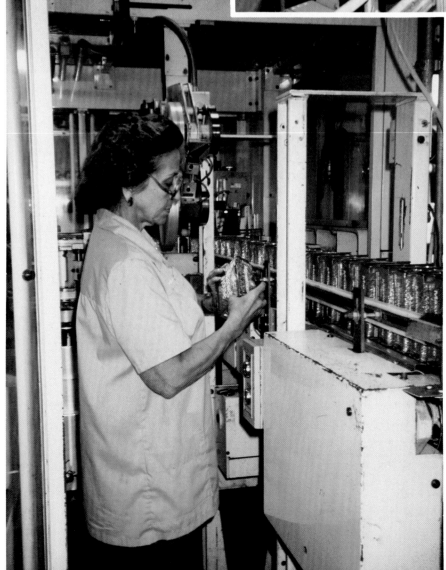

Under the intense heat the beans swell, unfold slightly, and begin to make a noticeable cracking sound, similar to popcorn popping.

After the roasting process is complete, the beans are blended with other beans to meet very exacting specifications in order to create the unique Maxwell House flavor. The blended beans feed down into grinders where the whole beans are crushed into small particles that consumers will later brew with hot water to create the rich, dark beverage. Quality-control experts test the coffee at each step to ensure that the specific taste and flavor unique to Maxwell House has been achieved.

After the beans have been ground, they are weighed and packaged into the familiar blue Maxwell House cans, jars, or vacuum bags by means of a long, weaving conveyor belt. Once the cans have been filled, an end is applied and a vacuum is produced to remove the air. The can is then sealed and placed in a case for shipping. From there the coffee is distributed to supermarkets, restaurants, hotels, and other commercial establishments throughout the country.

The process for making instant coffee is similar, but after the beans are roasted and ground, they are placed in giant percolators. In the percolators, the particles of the ground coffee that dissolve in water are removed, and the remaining roasted grounds are dried and burned in the boiler house to provide energy.

A fine instant powder is produced by drying. Prior to 1970 this powder was packaged and sold as instant coffee. However, since 1970 an agglomerator has been in use that performs the task of combining several of the particles together into chunks, which have become known as agglomerated instant coffee. Once the agglomeration process is complete, the instant coffee is packed into jars.

With production at millions of pounds of coffee each year, the Jacksonville Maxwell House plant is one of the city's largest manufacturers—and the most notable manufacturing facility located in the downtown area.

The company has always played an

The Maxwell House Coffee Company (foreground), located at 735 E. Bay Street, is proud to have been a part of the Jacksonville community since 1910.

active role in Jacksonville's economic growth as one of the city's major, and most stable, employers. Maxwell House has a payroll in excess of $30 million per year in Jacksonville, which includes a work force of more than 500 employees.

Statewide the firm supports the Florida economy by spending more than $40 million for service industries, using nearly 1,500 vendors across the state.

Maxwell House Coffee is also a

Pallets of "Good to the last drop" Maxwell House coffee are loaded into tractor trailers for distribution to grocery stores, restaurants, hotels, and other consumers all over the country.

community leader as a supporter of educational, cultural, and charitable activities. The corporation gives ongoing monetary and volunteer support to such organizations as the United Way; WJCT, Jacksonville's public broadcasting station; Jacksonville University; the YMCA; YWCA; and Junior Achievement.

In addition to Maxwell House, General Foods maintains a district sales service office in Jacksonville and a coffee and grocery products distribution warehouse.

Maxwell House is proud to be a part of the Jacksonville community and proud of its tradition—producing coffee that's "Good to the last drop."

SCM GLIDCO ORGANICS

Fragrance chemicals are the firm's major products. Some of these are sold to the perfume industry. In addition, Glidco produces nature-identical flavor chemicals—spearmint, peppermint, lemon, lime, and cinnamon.

Located on the Northside is one of Jacksonville's oldest companies that has quietly become the world's foremost producer of chemical fragrances and flavors.

Tide, Prell, Spic and Span, Head and Shoulders, and numerous other products used every day in homes around the world have the refreshing scents they do because they use the type of fragrances developed at SCM Glidco Organics in Jacksonville. "Chemicals that we produce here are probably in every home in Jacksonville," says SCM

The Glidco plant, valued at $300 million, covers 55 acres and employs 200 people.

Glidco president George W. Robbins.

A longtime producer of concentrated pine oil, SCM Glidco today produces more than 20 million pounds of the substance each year at its 55-acre, $300-million facility. But it is a series of terpene-based chemical fragrances, flavors, and intermediates from which vitamins are made that today have become the company's major products.

The top fragrance sold is a citral-lemon aroma that is used in numerous detergents and cleaning products. A total of 250 different fragrance chemicals are produced, including a large variety of floral and wood scents that are popularly used in many soaps and personal care products. SCM's next major product line is flavor chemicals, particularly peppermint, spearmint, and many other flavors used in toothpaste. Root beer, licorice, cinnamon, and many other flavors are used in such products as candy, liquor, and menthol cigarettes.

The company's product line has greatly diversified since it was founded in 1910 by the Cummer family, for whom the Cummer Gallery of Art is named. When first opened, the plant was strictly a turpentine-processing facility. Located at its present site off Elwood Avenue in Jacksonville's Northside, the firm was a half-day's buggy ride into town.

In its nearly 80-year history the manufacturing facility has had 12 different names. It was purchased in the 1930s by the Glidden Paint Co. and used the name Glidden for nearly 40 years. But, contrary to common belief

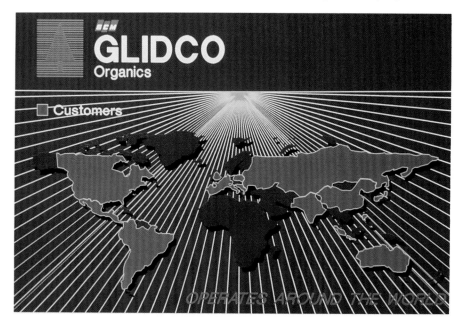

Glidco, recognized worldwide as the technological leader in the field of sophisticated terpene chemistry, exports 60 percent of its products.

Glidco produces the fragrances in many of the best-sellers on this aisle—detergents, soaps, household cleansers. The Jacksonville-based company is the world's largest producer of pine oils.

by many Jacksonville residents, paint was never manufactured at the plant. Pine oil and turpentine products continued to be the major part of the product line, with production of the current line of fragrances and flavors beginning in the 1960s. Glidden Paint Co. was the first firm to develop a route to fragrance chemicals from turpentine.

"We're the world leader in terpene chemistry," says Robbins. "We're a very high-technology company. We practice state-of-the-art techniques in our field." At one time turpentine was derived directly from tree sap for use in the firm's products, but today the source of turpentine is from pulp mills, where turpentine comes off as a gas in their production process, and is saved and sent to Glidco. Suppliers are primarily in the United States and Canada.

SCM Corporation purchased Glidden in the 1960s, and SCM was later purchased by Hanson PLC of England. In 1987 the name of the Jacksonville company was changed to SCM Glidco Organics.

Today the firm has roughly $80 million in annual sales. Approximately two-thirds of the sales are in the fragrance chemical line, with the rest divided between pine oil, vitamin intermediates, and flavor chemicals.

The corporation has grown to employ in excess of 200 people, including chemists, chemical operators, a research and development staff, flavorists, perfumists, and marketing and sales personnel.

In addition to the Jacksonville facility, SCM Glidco operates a manufacturing plant in Brunswick, Georgia, that employs approximately 30 workers. SCM Glidco also has sales offices in New Jersey; Brussels, Belgium; and Tokyo, Japan.

"We are truly a global business. More than 60 percent of our products are sold outside the United States,"

Many of the personal care items used every day—toothpaste, mouthwash, shampoo, and shaving cream—contain flavors and fragrances from Glidco.

states Robbins, who came to the Jacksonville plant as the company president in 1982. "We're a big exporter of chemicals. We believe we are the worldwide leader in our product line."

On the home front SCM Glidco Organics plays an active role in community events and is a regular supporter of a number of local charities and civic organizations.

In the future Robbins sees a much increased demand for Glidco's chemical fragrances, as there is continuing demand for the products that use Glidco's chemicals.

ALLIED-SIGNAL AEROSPACE COMPANY

There's nothing quite so breathtaking as a huge jet roaring down the runway for takeoff and then lifting into the sky.

For the People at Allied-Signal Aerospace in Jacksonville, that sight is particularly satisfying.

The Bendix Engine Controls Division plant, located in Deerwood Center, manufactures the ignition systems that get those jets—and any other kind of turbine-powered plane that flies—airborne. The Jacksonville plant is the world's top producer of the "exciter" units that are the main energy source for the ignition systems used in turbine engines. The more than 12,000 ignition systems manufactured each year in Jacksonville are used by every major airline in the world.

With more than 60 years of experience in the research and development of aircraft engines, Allied-Signal Aerospace is known for its engineering technology and high-quality products. In the Jacksonville area, the firm is clearly one of the most sophisticated, technologically advanced manufacturers in the marketplace. Its engine parts are built and tested to meet stringent governmental and Federal Aviation Administration (FAA) regulations.

A typical advanced commercial aircraft utilizes ignition systems on each of the engines (insert). The ignition system converts electrical energy to spark energy to ignite the fuel/air mixture in the turbine engine. Design, manufacture, and service support of these systems is performed in the Jacksonville facility of the Allied-Signal Aerospace Company.

The corporation's choice of Jacksonville as the home of its engine ignition system product line in 1981 marked a major coup for the city's economic development efforts. Relocating from its former headquarters in Sidney, New York, Allied-Signal Aerospace selected Jacksonville over 30 other cities because of the area's large labor force, the pleasant Florida environment, and, most of all, because of the enthusiasm of the city toward the company.

Allied-Signal's confidence in Jacksonville has proven to be a turning point for the city's economic development, as numerous other large northern businesses have followed the firm's lead and chosen Jacksonville.

Locating in a parklike complex in Deerwood Center, Allied-Signal Aerospace brought along 100 of its employees from New York and hired several

hundred from the Jacksonville market. With a total work force today surpassing 500, Allied-Signal not only develops, designs, and manufactures aerospace products, it also services them. Approximately 40 percent of the Jacksonville plant's business is involved with customer and product service and worldwide support.

While the ignition systems represent the firm's primary product line in Jacksonville, Allied-Signal also produces such engine accessories as magnetic speed and torque sensors, engine cabling systems, permanent magnet generators, and helicopter control grips.

The Bendix Engine Controls Division is part of the Allied-Signal Aerospace Company of Allied-Signal Inc. with operating offices worldwide. Allied-Signal Inc. has more than 240,000 employees in 70 major divisions and subsidiary companies.

EXCEL INDUSTRIES OF FLORIDA, INC.

A newcomer to Jacksonville's manufacturing community, Excel Industries of Florida, Inc., is the nation's leading producer of ventilator windows for trucks, vans, and other ground transportation vehicles.

Located off Phillips Highway in south Jacksonville, within easy access of Interstate 95, the 266,000-square-foot facility includes a large metal fabrication plant, an assembly plant, and a chronologically controlled warehouse. The 25-acre Jacksonville manufacturing facility was purchased in 1986 from Irvin Industries, a producer of automotive accessories.

Since Excel began operations in the South Jacksonville Industrial Park in January 1986, the company has significantly increased its sales and multinational work force. Today more than 700 people are employed at Excel, producing more than 16,000 vent assemblies each day. The Jacksonville firm—which exceeds $50 million in sales each year—is a major supplier of windows for Ford and Chrysler vehicles. In addition, Excel began producing vent assemblies for General Motors during the second half of 1988.

Excel of Florida is one of eight subsidiaries of Excel Industries, Inc., of Elkhart, Indiana, the leading independent supplier of window systems for ground transportation in North America. Founded in 1928, Excel designs, manufactures, and markets products for passenger cars, trucks, buses, recreational vehicles, and military vehicles.

Since being acquired by Excel, the Jacksonville plant has undergone extensive renovations. Equipment improvements include state-of-the-art welding capabilities and a modernized paint department. The electrostatic powder-coating paint system includes a computerized system that allows for the painting of more than 50,000 parts each eight-hour shift.

Other significant additions include five numerically controlled rubber injection-molding machines used in the production of weather-stripping. The company has fully implemented a statistical process control system to ensure product quality and continuous improvement. The production process includes a series of steps from stamping, forming, welding, and assembly of vent window components. Employees at the plant are comprised of assembly workers, machine operators, and tool and die makers, as well as engineers, and quality-control and administrative personnel.

Excel Industries of Florida, Inc.,

The Excel Industries of Florida plant produces 16,000 ventilator windows each day, totaling more than 3.8 million per year. These vent windows are used on trucks, vans, and other ground transportation manufactured by most of the major U.S. automakers.

considers its employees its most valuable asset, and has established several employee recognition programs and developed a participatory style of management. Excel is fully committed to customer satisfaction, quality attainment, employee involvement, and continuous improvement of its products to be competitive in the world market.

An assembly inspector at the Excel plant in South Jacksonville Industrial Park checks a completed ventilator window for quality, and performs her duties of water testing.

ST. JOE PAPER COMPANY

Alfred I. duPont, whose will established The Nemours Foundation, moved to Florida in 1926 with his wife, Jessie Ball duPont, and built Epping Forest, their Jacksonville home.

Jessie Ball duPont was Alfred I. duPont's devoted wife and the sister of Edward Ball. Jessie duPont spent much of her life in Jacksonville promoting cultural and humanitarian endeavors.

When Alfred I. duPont moved to Florida in 1926, he came to build upon the opportunities awakening in an area destined for growth and development. He and his wife, Jessie Ball duPont, were attracted like many others to the unspoiled beauty and warm climate.

The couple settled in Jacksonville, and with the resources available to them as members of a world-famous family, they built their beautiful estate called Epping Forest.

The year was 1927, and Florida was in the middle of an economic collapse brought on by land speculation. Alfred duPont became determined to develop companies that would help stabilize the volatile Florida economy and devote his resources to benefit citizens throughout the state.

"We are now in Florida to live and work," he said. "We expect to spend the balance of our days here. Our business undertakings should be sound, but our primary object should not be the making of money. Through helpful works, let us build up good in this state and make it a better place in which to live."

Alfred duPont and his business associate, Edward Ball—Jessie duPont's brother—shared a no-nonsense philosophy based on hard work. This was balanced by the belief that wealth should be used wisely to promote education, the arts, and health care. Alfred duPont believed deeply that children must be able to become good citizens without the burden of a crippling disease or illness.

He would live only nine years in Jacksonville, but upon his death in 1935, Alfred duPont left his estate as a charitable trust. He also provided for the establishment of The Nemours Foundation, which would make available treatment for crippled children and the elderly.

The earnings from his estate went to Jessie duPont during the remainder of her life, but she unselfishly made no effort to maximize her personal income. Instead, along with Edward Ball and other trustees, she worked to make the trust assets appreciate. In addition—while Jessie duPont was receiving the income from the trust, from 1935 until 1970 when she died—she personally funded The Nemours Foundation, which operated the Alfred I. duPont Institute in Wilmington.

The businesses within the Alfred I. duPont Trust grew and prospered under the guidance of Edward Ball, from 1935 until his death in 1981. Throughout his long career Ball displayed business talents that commanded respect from his allies and created confusion among his adversaries.

In his will Ball left his estate to The Nemours Foundation for the care and treatment of physically handicapped children in Florida, stating:

"Mr. Alfred I. duPont was my friend and benefactor, and I can think of no better purpose than leaving what I have accumulated to The Nemours Foundation."

In all, duPont and Ball participated in some 30 companies. From ambitious beginnings in the 1920s through the Depression, World War II, the postwar boom, the Baby Boom, the turbulent 1960s and 1970s, and into the uncertainty of the 1980s, these farsighted individuals left a legacy that has both changed and become a part of Florida. On the business side of the legacy, two companies best exemplify the dynamic growth in Florida and the need to balance such growth with careful management of the state's natural resources.

Stretching out into the Florida Panhandle are hundreds of square miles of evergreen forests. In 1933 Ball added 240,000 acres to the duPont holdings across four counties in western Florida. From a rundown, sparsely populated area dependent on fishing has evolved a major enterprise.

The town, called Port St. Joe, is the site of a large paper mill operation, part of the St. Joe Paper Company—a venture built from the land. The mill produces more than 400,000 tons of kraft linerboard each year. Kraft, a German word for strength, is a sturdy paperboard used in making corrugated boxes. Eighteen box plants produce containers for manufacturers and service companies throughout the eastern United States.

The firm is dedicated to preserving the resources from which it prospers, so millions of pine seedlings are planted each year. Extensive wildlife sanctuaries are maintained for song and aquatic birds, alligators, deer, bears, and many other species.

The St. Joe Paper Company is based on sound, long-term planning, utilizing the natural resources of the area and providing a major source of employment for the Panhandle portion of the state. Not only did Ball build upon the natural resources, he also had the ability to recognize the potential of underutilized properties. Such was the case with the Florida East Coast

Edward Ball was Alfred I. duPont's loyal business associate. From 1935 until his death in 1981, Ball managed some 30 companies, including the St. Joe Paper Company and the Florida East Coast Railway. He also left the bulk of his estate to The Nemours Foundation.

Railway.

The financially plagued railroad had been in receivership and/or trusteeship for 30 years, yet it served the entire east coast of Florida where phenomenal growth was to occur. Under Ball's leadership St. Joe Paper Company acquired the majority of the bonds of the railroad, and subsequently became the majority stockholder on January 1, 1961.

Originally started as the Jacksonville, St. Augustine and Halifax River Railway, the fledgling line was purchased in 1885 by industrialist Henry M. Flagler, a partner with John D. Rockefeller. Under Flagler's leadership the F.E.C. was constructed to Miami and eventually went overseas to Key West, until the devastating Labor Day Hurricane of 1935 left miles of track and support facilities in ruin.

Violent storms and major construction programs just before the Great Depression created an untenable financial position for the F.E.C. management, and in 1930 bondholders forced the line into receivership.

After St. Joe acquired the F.E.C., Ball made sweeping changes in its management and accounting procedures to improve efficiency. The number of employees was reduced, and the operations and maintenance divisions became increasingly mechanized. Hit with a long and bitter strike, the newly reorganized firm still pulled through.

Today the F.E.C. and its associate industries are successful contributors to Florida's booming economy. They share a philosophy in keeping with Alfred I. duPont. "Our basic strategy,"

The St. Joe Paper Company's mill operation produces more than 400,000 tons of kraft linerboard each year for companies throughout the eastern United States.

a director writes, "remains the molding of a corporate structure not only to prosper during the best of times but also to weather the worst of times."

Combined with St. Joe Communications, Inc., the Apalachicola Northern Railroad Company, and the Talisman Sugar Corporation in Palm Beach County, the Jacksonville-based St. Joe Paper Company thrives by attentive management of its varied assets.

Gran Central Corporation, a subsidiary of Florida East Coast Industries, has constructed the new duPont Center on the south bank of the St. Johns River in Jacksonville. This project will serve as headquarters for the Alfred I. duPont Testamentary Trust, The Nemours Foundation, St. Joe Paper Company, and F.E.C. Industries.

The many ventures already discussed represent only the business side of Alfred I. duPont's legacy. There is a humanitarian side as well, represented by an unparalleled effort to provide quality health care to children and the elderly.

American medicine has undergone a revolution in just the past few years. In the realm of medical service, The Nemours Foundation has demonstrated a remarkable ability to research

As the early-morning sun casts its light on downtown Jacksonville, a Florida East Coast Railway train heads south across the St. Johns River.

and even anticipate the future of American medical practice, then translate patient wants and needs into health care programs that are among the world's best.

These programs are implemented through three outstanding organizations: the Alfred I. duPont Institute in Wilmington, Delaware; the Nemours Health Clinic in Wilmington; and the Nemours Children's Clinic in Jacksonville.

The institute evolved from a small Delaware children's orthopedic hospital into a state-of-the-art, multispecialty hospital for children. The most talented pediatric specialists from around the world are being recruited to its medical staff. New programs in rheumatology, surgery, sports medicine, rehabilitation, orthopedics, and other fields attest to the dynamic changes occurring in pediatric care.

At the Nemours Health Clinic in Wilmington, outpatient eye, ear, and dental care and pharmaceutical prescriptions provide better, more accessible health service to thousands of Delaware's senior citizens.

Nowhere is Nemours' ability to anticipate future medical practice better articulated than at the Nemours Children's Clinic in Jacksonville. Recent medical practice has tended to reduce hospitalization in favor of outpatient care. This is especially helpful for children. Many childhood diseases or surgical disorders may be diagnosed and treated on an outpatient basis. Young patients feel less apprehensive and more responsive at home with their families. Skyrocketing medical costs are also reduced.

The Nemours Foundation's goal is to fashion a system of pediatric care similar to that of the Mayo Clinic for adults. The main components are outstanding physicians and support staff, a multispecialty approach to illnesses and surgical disorders, and the cutting edge in medical technology.

To meet this ambitious goal the Nemours Children's Clinic dissolved its hospital component and moved from the historic Nemours/Hope Haven location, which was a landmark to many Jacksonville residents, to interim headquarters on the Baptist Medical Center Campus. There a team of outstanding pediatric subspecialists have been recruited representing medical fields from allergy and immunology to urology. Nemours has also acquired state-of-the-art equipment such as a new magnetic resonance imaging center.

Working closely with referring physicians, and spending time with patients and parents alike, inspires the traditional patient-doctor relationship—based on trust and understanding. From 1985 through 1988 there were more than 73,000 clinic and outpatient visits to the Nemours Children's Clinic. While most patients are privately insured, Nemours is open to patients and their families regardless of their ability to pay.

Looking to the future, Nemours is building an 11-story multimillion-dollar pediatric clinic complex. The new clinic is scheduled to open in 1990.

Through a legacy carried for more than 60 years—as citizens, as career people, and as humanitarians—family and employees associated with The Nemours Foundation and the Alfred I. duPont Trust have carried on duPont's vision.

The Nemours Children's Clinic in Jacksonville has made an unparalleled effort to provide quality health care to children, recruiting the most talented pediatric specialists from around the world for its medical staff.

VISTAKON, INC.

multipatented manufacturing process that produces the highest-quality product possible. In 1986 Acuvue received the Food and Drug Administration (FDA) approval and was test-marketed in Florida and California before being introduced to the U.S. and international marketplace.

The main difference in the manufacture of the lenses is that they stay in the soft state throughout the production process, unlike other lenses. Typical soft lenses are made through a process in which lenses go through a soft stage, then a hard stage, and then are softened again. This method can

An international leader in research and development in the visual care industry, Vistakon, Inc., manufactures and distributes millions of contact lenses each year from its two Southside laboratories on San Marco Boulevard (left) and Richard Street (below).

One of Jacksonville's most rapidly growing companies, Vistakon, Inc., is a national leader in the production of contact lenses, and the world's first producer of disposable contact lenses.

A Johnson & Johnson company, Vistakon manufactures millions of contact lenses each year in its two Southside laboratories on San Marco Boulevard and Richard Street. The firm is an international leader in research and development in the visual care industry, and distributes its lenses worldwide.

In 1987 Vistakon began marketing a product that represented a major breakthrough in the industry—Acuvue—a disposable contact lens. The lenses look and feel like traditional soft lenses.

The Acuvue Disposalens System allows contact lens wearers the ultimate in comfort, convenience, and safety by providing them with a quantity of extended-wear lenses that are worn for one or two weeks each and then discarded.

The disposable lens system eliminates the problem of long-term deposit buildup on the lenses that can result in decreased vision sharpness, discomfort, and, occasionally, eye health problems.

The system also does away with the cleaning and disinfecting routine that contact lens wearers often find tedious. Eye patients testify to the comfort and clearness of vision that new lenses bring.

The concept for the disposable lenses was originally conceived by a Danish ophthalmologist. In 1983 Vistakon purchased the concept, and Johnson & Johnson researchers worked for four years to develop the refined,

create variations which reduce lens reproducibility. Acuvue is produced by a process called stabilized soft molding, which assures virtually 100-percent reproducibility.

Vistakon has developed disposable lenses to the point that any variation between lenses is so miniscule that it is not noticeable to the wearer. However, the increased comfort of a new lens is very noticeable.

The Acuvue lenses cost about the

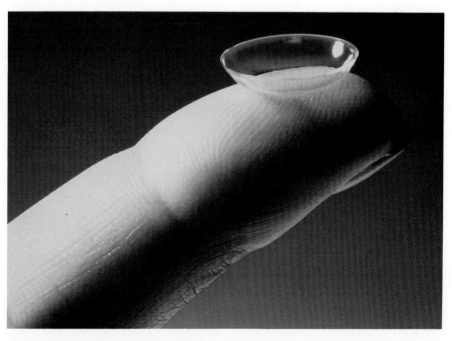

same as regular extended-wear lenses, and savings result in not having to purchase sterilization solutions and kits, or insurance.

Johnson & Johnson, the largest and most diversified organization in the medical field, moved into Jacksonville and the contact lens business in 1981 when it purchased Frontier Contact Lens of Florida. Opened by Semour Marco in the early 1970s, Frontier was a high-quality producer of both hard and soft contact lenses that were distributed in Florida and throughout the Southeast. Frontier had also developed a toric lens for patients with astigmatism.

When Johnson & Johnson decided to expand in the optical care field, it was attracted by Frontier's quality reputation and its development of the toric lens. A year after the firm was purchased, the name was changed to Vistakon.

Following Johnson & Johnson's philosophy of its companies making major contributions to the medical world and striving to become the best in their field, Vistakon immediately undertook state-of-the-art research and development activities that have resulted in the development of the disposable lens.

The operation has grown tremendously since Johnson & Johnson took over in 1981. The amount of production and the manufacturing facilities have both grown 15 times their original size, and could grow to more than 25 times by 1991. The number of employees has increased from approximately 80 in 1981 to more than 700. The only major contact lens producer in Florida, the firm commands more than 5 percent of the national market.

Headquartered on several floors of the TRECO building in San Marco, the primary production facility of the Acuvue lenses is in a 150,000-square-foot structure on Richard Street. Soft

Extended wear disposable lenses eliminate the problems associated with traditional lenses— deposit buildup, discomfort, decreased vision sharpness, and occasional health problems.

extended-wear contact lenses have traditionally been produced in the firm's second production facility on San Marco Boulevard near the TRECO building. In the future, that facility may manufacture the disposable lenses as well.

Leading Vistakon is president Bernard W. Walsh, a longtime Johnson & Johnson executive. Employees of the company come from a vast number of professions and trades, including chemists, biologists, engineers, line supervisors, and a broad range of manufacturing technologists.

The corporation uses a team approach in tackling its problems and setting its goals. Representatives from all levels of the firm, from upper man-

This advertisement heralded a major breakthrough in the industry—Acuvue—a disposable contact lens marketed by Vistakon.

agement to line workers, meet together regularly to address issues and involve employees in the decision-making process. Management finds the input invaluable, and employees see—and become part of—the direction of the company.

Together, the Vistakon, Inc., staff is working on correcting today's vision care problems with the technology of tomorrow. In so doing, the organization is becoming a leader in two of Jacksonville's foremost, and most rapidly growing, industries: high technology and medicine.

SALLY INDUSTRIES, INC.

The company's namesake, Sally, plays and sings everything from popular standards to country in restaurants and night spots throughout the world.

One Sally Industries, Inc., worker has spent the major part of a day inserting hairs one by one into the beard of an incredibly lifelike silicone figure of Abraham Lincoln.

Another is fine-tuning the electronic controls that allow latex turtle faces to blink their eyes.

A third is carefully synchronizing the audio track with the body movements of a lifesize robot of Mark Twain.

Such are the everyday jobs of the artists and technicians who work at what may be Jacksonville's most unusual—and most fascinating—business.

Sally Industries, Inc., designs and builds "animatronic" characters and robotic productions for major theme parks, amusement centers, fairs, and museums, as well as for use in business and industry.

Sally characters have performed in three world fairs, and today appear in entertainment centers worldwide. One of the largest entertainment robot makers in the country, the company has the distinction of having designed and built not only one of the tallest audio-animated robots in the world but also the world's largest animated theater show.

With the reputation Sally enjoys in its field, and the number of projects the firm has under way worldwide, it is difficult to believe that it was little more than a decade ago that Sally Industries was born in the garage of a local dentist.

Dr. John Rob Holland began building robots in 1977 as more of an avocation than an occupation. With an undergraduate degree in engineering, Dr. Holland believed that robotics could be more than just entertaining. He believed that by combining creativity and sound mechanical design, he could produce powerful marketing and communications tools.

As the popularity of the robots grew for both business and entertainment use, Dr. Holland moved his new company into its present production headquarters at 803 Price Street and named the enterprise after the first robot he ever built.

Today the firm has grown to the point that it is owned by 120 stockholders. Dr. Holland serves as chairman of Sally's board of directors, which through the years has included some of Jacksonville's most prominent citizens—including Prime F. Osborn III, J.J. Daniel, John Buchanan, Wilbur Margol, and John Thomas of Atlanta.

Howard W. Kelley, Jr., a longtime Jacksonville broadcast executive, became president and chief executive officer of Sally Industries in 1985. Under Kelley's leadership the company has expanded from being primarily domestic in scope to encompassing a truly international market. Today 60 percent of Sally's creations are exported outside the United States. Employment at the Jacksonville headquarters approaches 40.

During the past three years Sally has built characters, animated shows, exhibits, and rides for entertainment facilities from Australia to Mexico to England to Japan. The company operates sales offices in London, Madrid, Tokyo, Kuwait, and Seoul.

Also falling under the Sally Industries umbrella are three associated businesses: Sally Animatronics Pty. Ltd. in Sydney, Australia; Scenesetters Animations Ltd. in London, England; and Exhibit Resources Inc. in Jacksonville.

Sally characters don't just move, they perform. Likenesses are studied, costumes researched, and realistic movements examined. They are given individual voices, dialect, style, and facial expression, making each character unique.

The star of the world's largest animated theater show, Electro—he's the one in silver—can walk as well as talk and sing.

SEMINOLE KRAFT CORPORATION

The opening of the Seminole Kraft Corporation paper mill in 1987 brought new life into the manufacturing economy of Jacksonville.

Seminole Kraft invested more than $20 million in recommissioning the former St. Regis and Jacksonville Kraft paper mill—for years one of the city's leading industrial employers until it was shut down in 1985.

Many of the paper mill workers— a work force of 360—who formerly worked for the mill have been hired by Seminole. Today the mill's total payroll exceeds $15 million a year, and the company's annual purchasing power tops $40 million, most of which is spent in Jacksonville.

Seminole Kraft is owned by an investor group and a *Fortune* 500 company, Stone Container Corporation of Chicago, the world's largest producer of brown paper and paper bags. The Jacksonville plant's general manager is Frank Lee.

The company was named for the huge Seminole Chief paper machine that runs the length of a football field inside the mill. The Seminole Chief is a premier paper machine that has set standards in the industry.

The mill produces both the liner board that is used in corrugated shipping containers and the brown paper that is used in grocery bags. Each day the Seminole Chief and a second paper machine turn out 1,000 tons of liner board and 300 tons of brown bag paper. In all, the mill produces 450,000 tons of liner board and paper each year.

Seminole distributes its products across the United States, as well as overseas through the Jacksonville Port. The liner board and paper are made into boxes and bags in other factories around the country, including some of Stone Container's other plants.

The 650,000 cords of pine and hardwood timber used in the mill come from throughout North Florida and

Since the reopening of the paper mill by Seminole Kraft in 1987, a work force of 360 people has provided a boost to the Jacksonville economy.

South Georgia. The wood arrives in chips or is cut into chips in a special chipping facility at the mill.

The chips are then cooked into a wood pulp. The turpentine residue produced in the process is sold to such area companies as SCM Glidco, Union Camp, and Hercules Corporation. A soap product that is recovered in the cooking process is also sold.

In the future Seminole plans significant capital improvements to the

Seminole Kraft Corporation lights up the night in Jacksonville.

plant, and the company intends to become involved in community and charitable activities.

Management of the plant wants to make one point clear to its employees and to the city's corporate community: Seminole Kraft Corporation is in Jacksonville to stay.

CASTLETON BEVERAGE CORP. (BACARDI)

An aerial view of the Bacardi Corporation facility in Jacksonville.

In the midst of Jacksonville's industrial Northside lies the 100-acre hamlet of Daiquiri, Florida.

Named for the popular rum party drink, the "town" of Daiquiri actually is the home of Bacardi Corporation's only bottling plant in the United States. The plant, with its brightly colored holding tanks and well-manicured lawns, bottles 89 percent of all Bacardi rum sold in the United States. On the back label of almost any light or amber Bacardi rum bottle sold anywhere in the country are the words, "Bottled by Castleton Beverage Corp., Jacksonville, Florida."

Proofing of Bacardi Rum determines the tax liability. Castleton has paid in excess of $1.6 billion in taxes since 1972.

Castleton Beverage Corp., the official name of the wholly owned Bacardi Corporation subsidiary, imports high-proof rum produced in Bacardi's Puerto Rico distillery through the Port of Jacksonville. Jacksonville's sea, rail, and highway access for distribution purposes was the primary reason the city was selected as the site of the U.S. plant in 1972.

Bacardi is not only the best-selling rum in both the United States and the world, it is also the top-selling brand of any distilled liquor—and has been since 1979. Bacardi sold 20 million cases of rum worldwide in 1987—7.4 million cases in the U.S. as compared to 5.8 million sold by the second-leading brand, Smirnoff Vodka in the United States.

Founded in Cuba in 1862, Bacardi includes 13 corporations worldwide with nine distilleries and bottling plants in Brazil, the Bahamas, Mexico, Martinique, Canada, Panama, Spain,

Trinidad, and Puerto Rico. In addition to the Jacksonville plant, Bacardi includes seven other bottling plants in Australia, New Zealand, Austria, Costa Rica, the United Kingdom, and West Germany.

The Jacksonville facility bottles 6.5 million cases—or nearly 120 million bottles—of rum each year on its seven high-speed production lines. The seventh line was added in 1985, a German-made system that is the Mercedes Benz of automated bottling machines. The line works at higher speeds than any other machine in the world.

"When we went looking for a new line, we were looking for the best," says Manuel Diaz, vice-president and general manager of Castleton Beverage Corp. since 1980. "Our manufacturing facility has the best equipment and the best people. That's a great combination."

Every size container sold by Bacardi is bottled in Jacksonville, from the small plastic miniatures used by the air-

Bottles are filled with extreme accuracy at high speeds.

lines to the largest 1.75-liter jugs. The miniatures are bottled on the new high-speed machine at a rate of 850 bottles per minute. The 1.75-liter bottles also are bottled at the world's fastest pace, coming off the line at a rate of 200 bottles per minute. The production lines run 16 hours per day.

The bottling process begins when cases of empty bottles are placed on the production line. The bottles drop from the boxes upside down and move down the line where they are air-cleaned, filled with rum, capped, labeled, and then repacked into the boxes.

When the high-proof rum first arrives in Jacksonville from Puerto Rico, it is placed in huge holding tanks that have a total capacity in excess of nearly 6 million gallons. Approximately 65 percent is amber rum, and the remainder is dark rum. The plant has its own water-treatment facility and adds water to bring the rum down to 80 proof.

Quality control is an area of utmost concern at Castleton Beverage. The quality-control laboratory runs lab tests to ensure that the mixture conforms to the standards of the Bacardi Corporation in areas such as purity, color, and proof. A taste panel of experts performs the final analysis of aroma, smoothness, and flavor.

The Jacksonville facility also tests all new products introduced by Bacardi internationally in a specially equipped research and new products laboratory. Jacksonville is currently one of six test market cities nationwide for the new Bacardi Breezer rum refresher.

In addition to distributing the light and amber rum bottled in Jacksonville, Castleton Beverage Corp. also acts as the distributor for other Bacardi products from other plants, as well as non-Bacardi products. Castleton is the distributing organization for Bacardi Imports, Inc., sole U.S. distributor for a line of French wines, Martini & Rossi, and Irish Cream Liqueur.

The entire 100-acre plant includes a separate administration building, the bottling plant, a 160,000-square-foot warehouse facility, a separate employee lounge area, a water-treatment facility, and numerous huge, half-million-gallon storage tanks. The tanks and some of the buildings are colorfully painted, some in bright solid colors and others in a variety of designs, including the Bacardi corporate trademark of a black bat on a red background.

"We're very proud of our facilities. Making our buildings and tanks pleasing to the eye is part of our corporate culture," Diaz says. "We want our facility to represent the quality of our product to the community. And we want our employees to have a pleasant place to

Final product inspection is done prior to the placement of the bottles in the cases.

work."

The bottling plant employs 180 workers, more than 140 of whom work directly in the bottling process. The remainder are research and technical personnel, testers, and the administrative staff.

Castleton has a number of progressive employee benefits, including an employee-assistance program offering counseling services for a wide variety of personal and professional problems. The company also offers an innovative program in which sons and daughters of employees are offered summer jobs at the plant during their time off from school.

Diaz, who benefited by summer work at the Bacardi plant in Puerto Rico during his college days, initiated the program nearly 10 years ago. "In the summers I used to come home from college in New Jersey and work at the plant in Puerto Rico. It was so helpful to me that I wanted to offer the opportunity to others," the general manager explains.

Castleton Beverage Corp. is also a leading corporate citizen, lending its support to a variety of charitable and community concerns, in particular the city's educational institutions, the arts, and campaigns such as United Way. Diaz sits on the commission of Keep Jacksonville Beautiful, and is a member of the International Development Board of the Jacksonville Chamber of Commerce.

ANHEUSER-BUSCH, INC.

The front entrance of Anheuser-Busch's Jacksonville home.

Known worldwide for the quality of its beer products, Anheuser-Busch, Inc., produces more beer in its 12 U.S. breweries than any other company in the world. Anheuser-Busch commands more than 40 percent of the world beer market, almost double that of the second-leading competitor.

Anheuser-Busch's Jacksonville brewery, which opened in 1969 on the city's Northside and is the firm's sixth-largest plant in capacity, is part of a system that stresses quality and is number one in all areas of operation. Anheuser-Busch believes that strict adherence to quality is the fundamental ingredient in successful performance.

"Under no circumstances will quality be compromised," plant manager John Wilchek says. "We preach quality in every aspect of work, and we believe the final product reflects that."

Producing 6.8 billion barrels of beer each year, the Jacksonville plant brews all of the Budweiser, Michelob, Busch, Bud Light, Michelob Light, and Natural Light beer sold throughout the greater part of Florida and the southeastern United States. Jacksonville's sister brewery in Tampa produces beer for the Tampa-St. Petersburg area and southwest Florida.

In order to comprehend the massiveness of Jacksonville's Anheuser-Busch plant, consider these facts: Each day the plant produces roughly 300,000

cases of 24 cans or bottles to the case; the physical size of the plant encompasses more space than Jacksonville's tallest skyscraper or largest shopping mall—1.3 million square feet, all under one roof; and eight rail cars of grain are shipped to the plant each day.

Total employment at the Jacksonville facility surpasses 850, with 640 of those being hourly workers directly involved in the production process. The

The brewhall where the product officially starts.

plant runs 24 hours a day, 365 days a year.

Anheuser-Busch beer is made from a unique combination of the highest-quality barley malt, hops, rice, yeast, and water. Every Anheuser-Busch beer is completely natural without any artificial ingredients or preservatives.

In the brewing process the ingredients are blended together to the exact specifications of the brand of beer being produced. The beer then goes through two stages of fermentation. The second stage of fermentation includes the beech wood aging process, which is done exclusively by Anheuser-Busch. Beech wood aging adds an extra measure of natural clarification and maturation. The long, natural brewing process takes in excess of 30 days.

The entire brewing process is strictly maintained, using state-of-the-art computer controls in a highly detailed program of quality assurance. Quality assurance begins with the testing of ingredients before brewing ever begins, and extends through the smallest detail of packaging the beer for distribution.

The most exacting test of the beer's quality is the judgment of a brewmaster panel and a quality-assurance panel. The members of each panel scrutinize the aroma, appearance, and taste of packaged, filtered, and unfiltered beer.

"Constant attention to detail is the way we control the quality of our beer, until we get the exact character we're looking for," explains Tom Walter, brewmaster at the Jacksonville plant. "The beer is taste-tested daily to be sure it has been brewed exactly the same way and the taste is consistent."

Quality control continues in the canning and bottling process, with close attention paid to cleanliness, safety, and consistency. High-speed production lines operate at 95-percent efficiency, the highest in the industry. Most of the plant's cans are produced at the Metal Container Corporation in Jacksonville. Metal Container is

the can-manufacturing subsidiary of Anheuser-Busch.

Founded in St. Louis in 1852, Anheuser-Busch is a diversified corporation that includes ownership of numerous entertainment theme parks, food product companies, real estate, a railway company, and the St. Louis Cardinals baseball team, in addition to its breweries and other beer-related operations. Leading the organization since 1974 is August A. Busch III.

On both a national and local level, Anheuser-Busch is a leading corporate citizen in terms of community involvement and charitable contributions. The corporation is deeply concerned about the problems of alcohol abuse and driving while intoxicated. It supports a wide number of organizations in all areas of alcohol awareness and education.

Anheuser-Busch strongly supports community activities in the Jacksonville area. Locally its hallmark program is Operation Brightside. Conducted during the summer months, the program gives minority students employment opportunities in the beautification of the city. With its ongoing charitable program, Anheuser-Busch supports local colleges and organizations such as the United Way, the

Chip cellars where Anheuser-Busch products are aged to perfection.

symphony, the YMCA, and the zoo.

Anheuser-Busch also is involved in land applying its agricultural waste from the beer-production process. The high-nitrogen by-products, which are beneficial as nutrients for plants, are used to grow turf that is sold to golf courses and landscaping companies throughout the Southeast. The program has drawn widespread attention from environmentalists and was honored with the Lee and Mimi Adams Environmental Award.

Anheuser-Busch's conservation ef-

forts also include the use of cogeneration to maximize the efficient use of energy. In 1987 the Jacksonville plant joined the company's St. Louis plant in cogenerating energy through a process in which waste heat is used to produce steam required in the brewing process. Locally, 80 percent of the electrical energy used by the plant is made by cogeneration.

The Anheuser-Busch, Inc., plant is open to the public for self-guided tours, with a free tasting at the end. More than 65,000 people take the tour each year.

Cans of Bud Light transiting from the filler to the seamer where the lid is attached.

Jacksonville Chamber of
Commerce, 244

Smith & Hulsey, 245

Barnett Bank of Jacksonville,
N.A., 246-247

Independent Life, 248-249

KBJ Architects Inc., 250-251

Commander Legler Werber

Blue Cross and Blue Shield of

Florida National Bank, 265

Mathews, Osborne, McNatt &

Byron Harless, Reid &

CHAPTER 15

BUSINESS AND PROFESSIONS

Greater Jacksonville's professional community brings a wealth of service, ability, and insight to the area.

243

JACKSONVILLE CHAMBER OF COMMERCE

The Jacksonville Chamber of Commerce is one of the largest, strongest, and most active chambers in the country.

With a corporate and Committee of 100 membership of more than 8,000

Florida's First Coast is the world headquarters of Professional Golf and Tennis.

In 1986 the Jacksonville Chamber of Commerce was voted the "No. 1 Chamber in the United States." Shown here is the staff in front of the chamber headquarters.

and a staff of more than 70, the Jacksonville Chamber of Commerce consistently ranks among the top three in the nation in terms of size, budget, and program of work. The 1988 membership drive conducted in the spring set a new record by producing $766,238 in new and renewing memberships from the five previous campaigns. In 1986 the Jacksonville Chamber was voted the "No. 1 Chamber in the United States" by the nation's chambers of commerce.

A firm believer in controlled growth and the area's excellent quality of life, the chamber and its Committee of 100 leadership team work in close cooperation with Mayor Tommy Hazouri, the city council, and educational and business leaders to attract clean, prosperous industry to Jacksonville. Many new companies are moving into Jacksonville each year, representing a wide range of endeavors in such fields as finance and banking, health care, insurance, sports, information services, international development, manufacturing, shipping and distribution, retail, and others. An increasing number of corporate headquarters of national companies are choosing Jacksonville as a major base. The chamber also plays an instrumental role in the expansion of existing businesses. Florida's First Coast has also attracted the headquarters for the PGA TOUR and the Association of Tennis Professionals (ATP).

Thousands of new residents have relocated to Jacksonville as a result of chamber efforts, and a far greater number of employment opportunities have become available.

Jacksonville's energetic chamber has a long history of meeting challenges with success. It all began in 1880, when the Jacksonville Port faced economic disaster. Because the St. Johns River was silting and ships could not enter the port fully laden, commerce was rapidly declining. Businesses joined together to create the Jacksonville Board of Trade in 1884 and were successful in bringing about legislation to deepen the harbor.

The Board of Trade was also the leading force in rebuilding the city after the great fire of 1901. The group became known as the Jacksonville Chamber of Commerce in 1915, and later was instrumental in establishing the nation's first city advertising program, attracting the city's massive naval installations to Jacksonville and, in the 1960s, helping to bring about Jacksonville's streamlined, consolidated city/county government structure. The Committee of 100 and its progenitor, the Believers in Jacksonville, provide a method for individual business leaders to direct the economic development efforts. The Committee of 100 now includes about 2,000 members.

The 1980s have been a building and growing decade for the chamber. A multimillion-dollar fund-raising drive called the Jacksonville Development Fund resulted in an expanded national and international marketing program and a new three-story headquarters building at the foot of the Main Street Bridge downtown, overlooking the St. Johns River. In 1987 the scope of the chamber's efforts increased to include a new Beaches Development Department and a merger with the Jacksonville Convention and Visitors' Bureau.

The aggressive marketing efforts of the Jacksonville Chamber of Commerce to advance the city's economic growth has paid big dividends. Its residents are proud to live in one of America's outstanding cities.

SMITH & HULSEY

One of Jacksonville's oldest and largest law firms, Smith & Hulsey has a commercial practice providing counsel and legal services to local, national, and international businesses. The firm was founded in 1936 by attorneys Herbert Lamson and Lloyd Smith.

Smith & Hulsey's client base includes New York stock exchange companies, manufacturers, retailers, real estate firms, accounting firms, banks, and community and teaching hospitals.

The firm's expertise includes:

Business Law. By reason of representing many national and publicly held clients, the firm has experience unique among Jacksonville law firms in matters of corporate finance, securities law, Securities and Exchange Commission and New York Stock Exchange compliance, and general corporate and transactional law.

Environmental. Smith & Hulsey has extensive experience in Superfund, Comprehensive Environmental Response Compensation and Liability Act, and other federal and state environmental compliance and enforcement proceedings, as well as securing indemnity and defense for environmen-

Dennis L. Blackburn (left), a member of Smith & Hulsey, counsels with a client.

tal claims under general comprehensive and liability insurance policies.

Health Care. The firm provides general counsel to several leading medical centers and teaching hospitals, as well as representation in federal and state regulatory matters and liability defense.

Real Estate. The firm has many years of experience in real estate financing and title work, representing institutional lenders, developers, syndicators, and title insurers.

Litigation. Smith & Hulsey has Jacksonville's largest commercial dispute resolution practice, known for thoroughness and results obtained.

Creditors' Rights. The firm also enjoys a national reputation in reorganization, creditors' rights, and bankruptcy law, having represented many national lenders in courts throughout Florida, as well as representing private and publicly held debtors in successful Chapter 11 reorganizations of national

significance.

Tax. Smith & Hulsey also has an active commercial tax practice, as well as provides traditional trusts, estates, and probate legal services.

Smith & Hulsey takes pride in its lawyers providing creative, result-oriented legal services. Senior partner Mark Hulsey says that the firm's goal is to provide the highest-quality legal services, accomplishing the best result for the least cost to the client. "We want to provide services that will advance our clients' business interests in the most cost-efficient manner," says Hulsey.

In addition to its reputation for talented lawyers, Smith & Hulsey also places emphasis on public service. Its lawyers have served as presidents and directors of many significant charitable and civic organizations in the city, as well as local and state professional associations. Hulsey, president of the Jacksonville Chamber of Commerce for 1988-1989, explains the firm's view: "We feel a responsibility for the improvement of our community. Leadership in public service is part of our responsibility as professionals."

BARNETT BANK OF JACKSONVILLE, N.A.

For 12 consecutive years Barnett Banks, Inc., has achieved consistent, uninterrupted earnings progress, a record few banks in the country can claim. Barnett is a performance-driven company; winning is its strongest motivating force. It means setting high goals and stretching to achieve them. It means doing better every year. And most of all, it means winning the confidence of shareholders and customers.

There are a number of banking benchmarks used to measure overall performance. Earnings per share growth—consistent year-over-year improvement—is one of the most critical. Barnett has set a goal of delivering its shareholders a growth rate in earnings per share of 12 percent to 18 percent on an originally reported basis. Other financial targets include return on assets in the .9-percent to 1.1-percent range and return on equity in the 15-percent to 22-percent range.

From its earliest days Barnett Bank of Jacksonville, the Jacksonville affiliate

of Barnett Banks, Inc., has been known as the bank that cares about people.

Not long after the establishment first opened in May 1877, founder William B. Barnett was at the forefront of the fight to stop the spread of a yellow fever epidemic that had claimed the lives of many Jacksonville residents.

The following year a second and more serious yellow fever epidemic killed all his bank clerks, nearly killed

him, and left only Barnett's son, Bion, to keep the bank open. When the president and cashier of a competing bank died, Barnett cashed its customers' checks until the bank could get back on its feet.

When the great fire of 1901 destroyed every bank in Jacksonville except The Bank of Jacksonville, the original name of Barnett Bank, Barnett allowed the other banks to keep a safe in his vault while they rebuilt.

The tradition of caring has remained an integral part of the city's oldest financial institution throughout its history. The leadership of Barnett Bank of Jacksonville today follows the philosophy, begun with William Barnett, that a bank should play a larger role in the community than simply offering financial services. Today, under the leadership of chairman of the board Hugh Jones, Barnett Bank has become one of Jacksonville's foremost philanthropic leaders.

Jones initiated one of the city's first corporate employee-volunteer programs in 1982, a program in which more than 90 percent of the bank's nearly 1,000 employees have participated.

The results of the bank's efforts have drawn not only local attention but also state and national recognition. Highlighting the numerous awards the institution has received for its philanthropic efforts was the President's Volunteer Action Award presented to Jones for Barnett Bank by President Ronald Reagan in 1985.

"We believe we have the moral re-

sponsibility to be involved," says Jones. "It's part of the American tradition to help those in need. If we do well in Jacksonville, we should give part of it back to the community."

Jones believes volunteerism also has many benefits for the employees of the organization and the bank itself. "I think that by getting involved in the community, we actively develop banking business. We know of many specific instances where we've gotten accounts because of our community involvement," he explains. "It makes good business sense."

Employees of the company also benefit tremendously from the program. Departments or branches of Barnett select their own community support project and work as a team to help the group.

"We've had absolutely miraculous things happen within our departments when employees work together and get involved," Jones says. "They feel better about themselves, and they work better with each other. They come to work happier, and they are better with customers. What they get from volunteer work is immeasurable. I call it psychic income."

One of Barnett's foremost charitable projects is the Korean Heart Program founded by Jones. In collaboration with University Hospital, the bank brings indigent Korean children with congenital heart disease to Jacksonville for free, lifesaving heart surgery. The program was founded in honor of Glenn Chuck, stepson of Barnett president Roland Kennedy,

who died at age 17 of heart disease.

Education and arts have been two areas of strong involvement for Barnett. The bank has provided sponsorship for numerous local cultural events, including the Jacksonville Symphony, the Jacksonville Ballet, and the Ramses II exhibit.

Two of its newest projects are in the educational realm, being coordinated in conjunction with Florida Community College at Jacksonville. In one, women currently on public assistance are being trained in a four-month program in day-care skills so that they can operate day-care centers out of their homes, thus creating jobs for them and allowing other women the opportunity to seek employment because of readily available day care. Another educational program being offered in conjunction with the community college is a pilot program to train minorities for careers as firemen.

"We approach community service as an opportunity," says Jane Jordan, Barnett's vice-president and community affairs manager. "We tend to be more proactive than reactive. We feel a real obligation to make sure our money is well spent."

The bank believes that its greatest earnings opportunity comes from the level of convenient, quality service it provides. It is Barnett's point of distinction. It agressively pursues the available market by encouraging each bank to develop local programs and implement local ideas through its extensive office work network. This gives a tremendous advantage, especially against more centralized competitors.

In its decentralized structure each of Barnett's 33 affiliate banks has a president, management team, and local board of directors. Each bank serves a different market, and in each Barnett has deep community roots. Each bank is responsible for policy decisions af-

fecting its customers. Barnett believes the people who work in a market should shape the strategies, because they know best what their customers need and expect. This practice allows the company to keep a personal touch despite its overall size.

Barnett Bank of Jacksonville, an affiliate of the Barnett Banks, Inc., holding company, includes 33 different banks.

INDEPENDENT LIFE

The first company-owned home office was acquired in 1945.

1940s and early 1950s.

Today Independent is a billion-dollar company with more than 5,900 agents in 21 states. The largest locally owned insurance firm in Florida, it ranks among the top 7 percent of life insurance companies nationwide. The 37-story headquarters building in downtown Jacksonville stands tall as the city's most familiar and most photographed landmark.

At year-end 1987 Independent Insurance Group, the holding company that owns Independent Life and Independent Fire Company, had total assets surpassing $1.2 billion and revenues approaching $456 million.

Independent Life sells all forms of life and health insurance, annuities, and group insurance products; Independent Fire, a wholly owned subsid-

Fourth of July fireworks adorn the sky over the current Independent Life home office.

One young man thought he wanted to be a doctor until he came face-to-face with his first cadaver in medical school.

Another was a pharmacist in Minnesota who was looking for an outdoor job after years of being cooped up in a drugstore.

A third was tired of raising cotton in Georgia and came to Florida seeking his fortune.

In all, seven ambitious young men from very different backgrounds found their way into the same business in Jacksonville during the early 1900s—the insurance business.

They worked for different companies, but they had a strong common bond. They were the best in the business. Unhappy working for other firms and wanting to be their own boss, the young agents decided to break away and form their own company.

In 1920 Independent Life was born, so named because the group wanted to be known as the company truly independent from the rest of the firms in the insurance industry.

In the early days the original founders— Jacob F. Bryan II, George C. Cobourne, J. Henry Gooding, J. Arthur Howard, Harry H. Lyon, Sr., Claybourne G. Snead, and John S. Young— rode bicycles on their sales territories, working day and night to get their fledgling enterprise off the ground.

The success of the venture must have surprised even the most optimistic of them. Independent grew rapidly in its early years, and exploded in the late

iary, carries fire, home-owners, and automobile property and casualty lines.

Today the grandsons of two of the original founders lead the organization. Wilford C. Lyon, Jr., is chairman of the board of Independent, and Jacob F. Bryan IV is president. The families of the seven original founders still represent major ownership of the company.

"My grandfather was the last of the original founders to pass away," says Lyon, chairman of the board since 1984. "During his retirement years, I don't think he fully realized the scope to which the company had grown. I don't think any of the founders at that time could have conceived how large the company would become."

Jacob F. Bryan II, the founder who dropped out of medical school before going into insurance, served as president. It was his son, Jacob F. Bryan III, who saw the firm through its greatest period of growth—leading Independent for more than a quarter-century until his death in 1984. Under his leadership the Independent Life riverfront tower was opened in 1975, for many years the tallest building in Florida.

"Dad had a real belief in downtown Jacksonville and bringing the river to the forefront," says Jacob F. Bryan IV. "Situating our building in this location

A scene from Independent Life's TV commercial, winner of the prestigious Grand Sweepstakes in the International Broadcasting Awards.

was very significant to the community and spearheaded redevelopment of downtown Jacksonville. We were one of the first to recognize the river as the tremendous natural asset that it is and capitalize on it."

The impressive skyscraper, with its brilliant reflective-glass exterior, was also the first to introduce interior landscaping to the Jacksonville market. The large interior garden, complete with coral-rock formations and small waterfalls, has won a number of awards for its design.

"We believe in Jacksonville and in downtown Jacksonville. We've put our stake in the ground and dollars into our home office," Lyon says. "We're proud to make Jacksonville our home. Our company's growth and the growth of the city have paralleled each other."

Independent is one of the most active corporations in the community in terms of civic and charitable involvement. "We probably provide more contributions than just about any company in Jacksonville," Bryan states. "We believe in giving back to Jacksonville because it's our home. We have very strong feelings about the welfare of this city."

Among the benefactors of Independent's corporate generosity are Jacksonville's Children's Museum of Arts and Sciences, the Mayo Clinic, the YMCA, Big Brothers, the United Negro College Fund, the Jacksonville Symphony, Edward Waters College, Bethune Cookman College, and the

Wilford C. Lyon, Jr., chairman (left), and J.F. Bryan IV, president.

Salvation Army.

Another important area in which the organization has excelled and gained widespread attention is in its advertising. The firm's commercial "Department Store Insurance," a humorous look at the confusion of buying insurance from companies that don't specialize in it, was named World's Best Television Commercial for 1987. Directed by award-winning director Joe Sedelmaier of Federal Express and Wendy's fame, the commercial and several others in the same vein were produced by the Jacksonville firm West & Company.

"We deliberately set out to set ourselves apart from other insurance advertisers," Bryan explains. "We decided to use humor as the key to set us apart. The name recognition of our company as a result of the commercials has shown dramatic results."

The logo for the award-winning commercial reads, "Independent Life makes insurance simple," because all it sells is insurance.

KBJ ARCHITECTS INC.

The skyline of Jacksonville has been enhanced with buildings designed by KBJ Architects, such as the South Central Home Office Operations Center for Prudential Insurance Company of America. Photography by Kathleen McKenzie

KBJ Architects is a Jacksonville-based architectural and interior design firm that was founded in 1946. In more than four decades of practice, the firm has virtually sculptured the face of the downtown Jacksonville skyline, designing significant office buildings on both sides of the St. Johns River.

KBJ is well known for its design of longtime Jacksonville landmarks. Some of these include Prudential's South Central Home Office Operation Center, the Seaboard Coastline (now CSX)

The award-winning exhibition space for artifacts of Ramses II. Photography by Kathleen McKenzie

company headquarters, the Civic Auditorium, the Barnett Bank Building, the Cathedral Foundation Towers, and the Florida Publishing Company office building and newspaper plant.

The firm has to its credit recent projects such as the Atlantic National (now First Union) Bank Building, the

Independent Life Building, the Southern Bell Tower, the Federal Reserve Bank of Atlanta, the Southeast Bank Building, and the new Prudential Insurance Company Operations Complex. Another KBJ project currently under construction is the American Heritage Life Tower.

Though known primarily for corporate design, KBJ has a broad project range of size, complexity, and uniqueness. Three of KBJ's many commissions that demonstrate this diversity are the WJCT-TV broadcast studios, Vicar's Landing Retirement Community, and the award-winning Ramses II Exhibition Space.

KBJ's corporate headquarters, which was designed by famed architect Henry Klutho, reflects the firm's respect for grand inspirations of the past. In addition to its 15,000-square-foot headquarters, KBJ did the renovation of the Florida Theater, a Jacksonville historic treasure.

Committed to downtown revitalization, KBJ was selected as the designer of the Initial Action Plan/Development Program for Jacksonville's Central Business District. The program both plans the future shape of the city and recommends specific implementation actions that are required to continue its economic vitality.

In the Jacksonville educational arena, KBJ has provided its services to Florida Community College at Jacksonville for its Kent Campus and its North Campus Student Center, which is under construction. On the campus of Jacksonville University, KBJ designed the Howard Administration Building, the Gooding Urban Studies Building, the Davis College of Business, and the addition/renovation of the Wolfson Student Center. In addition to these schools, KBJ projects can be found on the campuses of Stetson University, Florida State University,

Tournament Players Clubhouse—a KBJ design.

Renovation is another facet of the firm's expertise. Shown here is the detailed restoration carried out by KBJ at the old Florida Theater. Photography by Steven Brooke

Florida A&M University, and the University of Florida.

Another area of KBJ's design expertise is in resort and recreational facilities. In the Jacksonville area, the firm's work includes the Tournament Players Club and PGA Headquarters, Marsh Landing Country Club, and the

The Davis College of Business is one of the Jacksonville University buildings designed by KBJ. Photography by Steven Brooke

Jewish Community Alliance. KBJ provided its services to other resorts located in Florida, such as Marineland, and to the Breakers Hotel in Palm Beach.

KBJ established its presence in the greater Orlando area by designing one of the nation's fastest-growing airports—the Orlando International Airport. After completing this facility in 1980, KBJ was selected by the Greater Orlando Aviation Authority to continue its vision by designing a major expansion, which more than doubles the size of the existing airport.

Recognizing that the practice of architecture is simultaneously the art, science, and business of building, KBJ's professional services have been characterized by a sensitivity to design for man in his environment, a technical knowledge of building systems, and a commitment to providing the client with comprehensive information and guidance in the decision-making process.

A high percentage of KBJ's work each year is for clients that the firm has served previously. Frequently KBJ is asked to adapt and renovate facilities

as past clients' businesses evolve. Some of KBJ's ongoing clients include Barnett Bank, Independent Life and Accident Insurance Company, the Prudential Insurance Company of America, Southern Bell Telephone & Telegraph Company, and the United States Steel Realty Company.

The firm today has a staff of more than 75, including 30 registered architects and eight interior designers. KBJ offers its clients a comprehensive range of professional services, consisting of site feasibility studies, programming, systems analysis, all aspects of building design, interiors, space planning, construction administration, graphics design, and furnishing specifications.

KBJ Architects Inc. is committed to the quality of life, not only through excellence in design, but also through community involvement. The firm's leadership and staff are active, both professionally and as individuals, in the areas of the arts, education, and civic and charitable organizations.

FIRST UNION NATIONAL BANK

Location and service have been found to be the two foremost concerns of banking customers.

Convinced that regional banking is the key to providing expanded operations and quality service to its customers, First Union National Bank of Florida has embarked on an aggressive growth plan with the goal of having a statewide presence of 300 banking offices and assets of $12 billion by 1991. The expansion would represent a more than 60-percent increase in assets and a nearly 50-percent increase in banking offices over a four-year time period.

Headquartered in the 18-story First Union tower in downtown Jacksonville, First Union National Bank of Florida would like to approach statewide what it enjoys in northeast Flor-

B.J. Walker is First Union National Bank of Florida's chairman and chief executive officer.

ida, where the banking institution has traditionally been the leader in the marketplace. First Union operates more than 20 offices in Jacksonville and more than 50 in the seven-county northeast Florida region.

Formerly the Atlantic Bancorporation—founded in Jacksonville in 1903—First Union National Bank of Florida came about as a result of a pioneer effort in 1985 in the realm of newly approved interstate banking.

Believing that the future of banking in Florida lay in regional banking with its broader institutional and capital base, Atlantic Bancorporation pres-

ident and chief executive officer B.J. Walker moved proactively to enter into a merger with First Union Corporation, one of the three largest bank holding companies in the Southeast. Head-

First Union's customer service program emphasizes employee courtesy to customers.

quartered in Charlotte, North Carolina, First Union Corporation operates more than 725 banking offices and more than 475 non-banking offices in 36 states and two foreign countries. Its assets surpass $27 billion.

Today Walker presides as chairman and chief executive officer of First Union National Bank of Florida and vice-chairman of First Union Corporation. In addition to the aggressive statewide expansion program Walker is spearheading to make First Union's banking facilities more convenient to Florida consumers, he has initiated a program to tackle the other primary concern of banking customers—service.

The Quality Customer Service (QCS) program reinforces in First Union employees the importance of providing top-level service to all customers at all times, with an emphasis on courtesy.

"The fact that the local market is so important enhances the role of the teller, the lending officer, branch manager, and operations clerk . . . and the attitude reflected by these people who come in contact with 90 percent of our public is key to the success of our bank," Walker says.

In meetings explaining the QCS program, employees learn such customer relations skills as making eye contact, smiling, introducing themselves, saying the customer's name, apologizing for delays, and thanking customers for their business.

Employees of the bank number more than 5,000 statewide, with approximately 20,000 employed throughout the entire First Union Corporation.

Automatic Teller Machines (ATMs) are another important aspect of First Union's commitment to making its banking services convenient and accessible to its customers. First Union was one of the first banking institutions in Florida to install the machines on a statewide basis, and today operates

First Union is a major sponsor of numerous community and charitable events and organizations, including the Players Championship each spring, which benefits TPC charities.

First Union National Bank of Florida is headquartered in the 18-story First Union tower in downtown Jacksonville.

more than 250 ATMs across the state for customer convenience.

Dedicated to serving the unique needs of all its customers, First Union offers specifically tailored banking services to special groups of banking customers, such as senior citizens, fixed-income families, executives, and young professionals. Other important customer services include pension plan management, trusts, and discount brokerage. The commercial operation includes commercial lending, funds management, cash and capital management, and an international banking department.

First Union is also a leading corporate citizen, both in Jacksonville and in the other communities it serves. A major supporter of the arts, First Union sponsored one of Jacksonville's biggest cultural events in years when world-renowned ballet dancer Mikhail Baryshnikov made his premier performance in northeast Florida. The bank is a regular supporter of the Jacksonville Symphony and other cultural groups.

First Union National Bank has also lent its support to numerous charitable causes, including TPC charities and St. Luke's Hospital.

PEAT MARWICK

Northeast Florida's largest accounting firm, Peat Marwick is known for its professional excellence, its dedication to client service, and its active role in community affairs.

The firm provides auditing, tax, and management consulting services to a diverse clientele that ranges from large publicly held corporations to privately owned businesses and individuals. These include retailers, manufacturers, financial institutions, health care providers, transportation concerns, and real estate companies.

Peat Marwick has been a part of Jacksonville as the city has emerged as one of the leading financial, commercial, and medical centers in the nation. With a total employment of 88, including 64 professionals and nine partners, its office is poised to meet the business and accounting needs of the corporate community. Stephen G. Butler, who serves as managing partner, expresses Peat Marwick's philosophy:

"Our goal is to be the single best resource for solving the business problems of our clients. Our professionals integrate client needs with solid business practices to achieve common

Expertise with microcomputers is essential in Peat Marwick's audit process. This automated approach speeds up the accounting process while ensuring accurate evaluation of financial data. Photo by Judy K. Jacobsen

goals, including growth, stability, and profitability. Public accounting is a multifaceted profession. The precision of numbers, the intricacies of taxes, and the advances of computerization in the business world demand expertise and a skillful grasp of complex issues. But this expertise is balanced with a commit-

Peat Marwick's commitment to Jacksonville extends beyond the work place and into the community at large. Photo by Julia B. Reid

ment to service that undergirds every business transaction. This commitment to service and professionalism is our philosophy at Peat Marwick—the cornerstone upon which we are building our practice of public accounting."

At Peat Marwick, top priority is placed on people. The firm recruits its staff primarily from Florida's universities, hiring only from among the top 25 percent of the graduating class. Emphasis is placed on individuals who have the ability to approach a client's needs from a practical as well as a technical standpoint. Other attributes, such as personality, ambition, common sense, and energy, are also considerations. While the majority of Peat Marwick's staff are Floridians, many come from other parts of the nation.

Peat Marwick established an office in Jacksonville in 1969. The firm was founded in 1897 and now includes 600 offices worldwide, employing more than 45,000 people. In 1987 accountancy income exceeded $3.25 billion. On both the national and local level, Peat Marwick's professional services are approximately 65 percent auditing, 20 percent tax work, and 15 percent management consulting.

In 1987 Peat Marwick International merged with Klynveld Main Goerdeler to form Klynveld Peat Marwick Goerdeler (KPMG). In the United States, Peat Marwick merged with KMG/Main Hurdman to form Peat Marwick Main & Co., but continues to be known as Peat Marwick.

The firm's auditing department performs services ranging from the compilation and review of financial statements for small companies to full-scope audits of middle-market and large organizations. The state's largest corporation, Winn-Dixie Stores, Inc., has been a client of Peat Marwick for many years.

The auditing department is in a continual process of developing new and increasingly sophisticated tools and techniques to better serve its clients. A leader in innovation in the auditing field internationally, Peat Marwick's offices in Jacksonville and throughout the world are fully auto-

Top priority is placed on highly responsive, personalized client service that takes Peat Marwick's professionals into the field. Photo by Judy K. Jacobsen

mated on a microcomputer-based system. Using telecommunications technology, the system allows professionals to transmit information to Peat Marwick offices from remote locations. This high-technology system enables Peat Marwick's staff to provide more accurate, efficient services, saving clients both time and money.

The tax department assists clients in achieving the most favorable tax posture, constantly keeping abreast of the continuous changes in the tax laws and their specific effect on individual businesses. Because of the importance of taxes in the day-to-day operation and management decision making of business and industry, the firm has placed increased emphasis on tax planning. On a national and statewide level, Peat Marwick takes an active role in monitoring tax legislation.

The management consulting department is an integral part of the service mix, advising clients on a wide variety of business concerns. These include compensation plans, acquisi-

tions, computer consulting, executive search, financial feasibility studies, and many more.

"We help clients with all aspects of managing a company," says David H. Busse, audit partner-in-charge. "There are very few companies for whom we just do the auditing work or just do the tax work. We work very closely with the other departments. Our client service team involves all disciplines with a focus on total service to the client in a

timely, efficient way."

Education is an area of foremost concern to the firm. The Peat Marwick professorships in the Colleges of Business of the University of Florida and Florida State University were the first to be established by a public accounting firm.

Peat Marwick also places strong emphasis on community involvement. The firm contributes to a variety of charitable and social agencies monetarily, in employee time, and in professional services. Organizations that have benefited from Peat Marwick's community focus include Big Brothers, The Players Championship, the American Cancer Society, the Jacksonville Symphony, and numerous other charitable and social agencies.

"Community involvement is a very important part of our office philosophy. Our commitment is substantial," Butler states. " All of our people are encouraged to give their time and talents back to the community. Nonprofit organizations throughout Jacksonville boast Peat Marwick professionals who are helping develop Jacksonville into a better place to live."

Peat Marwick serves a broad spectrum of clients. From a private boat builder to the corporate giants of the community, the firm's professionals are meeting the business needs of Jacksonville. Photo by Judy K. Jacobsen

PRUDENTIAL INSURANCE CO.

The Prudential South-Central complex on the St. Johns River in Jacksonville. One Prudential Plaza in the foreground is flanked by Two Prudential Plaza. Photo by Norm MacLean

When Prudential Insurance Co. first moved to Jacksonville in 1953, it marked a renaissance for the city's business community. The choice of Jacksonville as the site for the South-Central Home Office (SCHO) of the nation's largest insurance company was an incredible boon for a city that had not seen another major firm move in since 1926.

The South-Central Home Office quickly became one of Jacksonville's largest employers and a leading corporate citizen.

The company's stately 22-story office building, which took two years to construct, was the tallest building in Florida at the time—and people came from miles around to take a look at the new structure. For years afterward the building would serve as the most recognizable landmark of the city of Jacksonville.

Both Prudential and the city it had faith in have grown tremendously through the years. The original employment of 620 has increased to more than

3,000, with total policies in force handled by the South-Central Home Office surpassing $104 billion. The South-Central Home Office standing on its own would be one of the 20 largest insurance companies in the country.

The SCHO's physical facilities have more than doubled in size over the years. With the construction in the early 1980s of its new three-building, .75-million-square-foot Operations Center, Prudential played a major role in a second renaissance of the downtown area—on the south bank of the St. Johns River.

The riverfront complex, composed of two towers connected by an enclosed four-story bridge spanning San Marco Boulevard, was a major catalyst in the development of the Southbank area, which today includes the two-mile Riverwalk and some of the area's finest hotels and restaurants.

The new $90-million Southbank offices, referred to as Two Prudential Plaza, include a 20-story Operations Center, a computer center that is the second largest in the entire Prudential

organization, and a three-story parking garage. The Operations Center houses many of the line operations that were formerly located at the original building and in other locations around Jacksonville. A riverfront multilevel cafeteria, with seating for 600, is open to the public for lunch in the computer center area. With an eye to the future, Prudential constructed the building with room for expansion. Several upper floors are rental space.

The original building was given a $30-million renovation in 1987-1988, completely upgrading the electrical wiring, the life-support safety systems, the walls, the windows, the decor and furniture, and the landscaping. The original huge marble columns of the lobby are accentuated by a new ceiling, new lighting, and a grand marble stairwell. The original, or Main building, houses primarily the executive offices, medical, personnel, and marketing. Several of the upper floors of the Main building are also leased. The original building is known as One Prudential Plaza.

Prudential also has an ordinary office, a group office, and two district sales offices in the city. In 1983 the

South-Central president E. William Nash, Jr., CLU. Photo by Judith Gefter

Southeastern Regional Service Office of Prudential Property and Casualty (PRUPAC) was relocated to Jacksonville from Atlanta and is housed in One Prudential Plaza.

The Jacksonville South-Central Home Office is one of four regional home offices of Prudential Insurance Co. The others are located in Los Angeles, Minneapolis, and Philadelphia.

The South-Central facility is unique among Prudential's regional home offices because it includes nationwide administrative responsibility for the small-group insurance products. In addition to having the second-largest computer operation in the company, it has the greatest responsibility for maintenance of advanced ordinary systems.

SCHO sells insurance in 10 states and services policies in a total of 19 states nationwide. The 10-state sales territory—Alabama, Florida, Georgia, Kentucky, North Carolina, Ohio,

South Carolina, Tennessee, Virginia, and West Virginia—is the largest in the corporation in land and population. The additional states the SCHO administers include Colorado, Kansas, Missouri, New Mexico, Oklahoma, Arkansas, Mississippi, Louisiana, and Texas.

Heading the South-Central operations is E. William Nash, Jr., CLU, who took the position of president in 1981. Nash, who has been with Prudential since 1951, came to the position from the company's Southwestern Home Office, where he was president. Very active in civic affairs, Nash has served as president of the Jacksonville Chamber of Commerce, president of the United Way of Northeast Florida, and chairman of the YMCA, in addition to many other activities.

The entrance to the original Prudential building in the mid-1950s.

In its 35-year history in Jacksonville, the South-Central Home Office has had only three other presidents. Charles W. Campbell, CLU, was the original president. He was followed by John D. Buchanan, CLU, and Duncan Macfarlan, CLU, who preceded Nash.

In the 10-state area administered by the South-Central Home Office, Prudential employs nearly 9,000 people, and has a payroll of $235 million.

The mammoth Prudential Insurance Co. of America, with headquarters in Newark, New Jersey, is by far the largest insurance company in the country. With assets of $134 billion, Prudential is at least $40 billion larger than the nation's next leading contender.

Prudential's total life insurance in force surpasses $639 billion. The organization is not only the largest insurance company in the United States but also the largest non-bank corporation in the world.

Prudential's construction of its South-Central home office was the first major development in the area of the city known as the Southbank.

The company offers diverse insurance and financial services for individuals, groups, and institutions. It handles life, health, disability, automobile, home-owners, and personal liability insurance lines, as well as annuities, pension plans, individual retirement accounts, personal financial planning, mortgages, mutual funds, personal assets management, and more.

Prudential has always been a leader and an innovator in the areas of employee relations and social responsibility, both on the national and regional levels. The South-Central Home Office has carried on the company tradition by adopting new programs to help employees become happier and more productive individuals and workers, and it has always made a concerted effort to provide its employees with an attractive work environment. For example, Prudential was the first Jacksonville firm to offer its employees fitness facilities and programs. The 20th-floor fitness facility in the Main building includes Universal equipment, stationary bicycles, free weights, a treadmill, showers, and a changing area with lockers, as well as regularly scheduled exercise classes with a regular instructor.

Prudential's most innovative employee program, which involves a wide cross section of company employees, is a committee system in which employees work together to address problems, initiate new programs, and take part in volunteer activities in five different areas. Through action brought about by the Civic Affairs Committee, the Safety Committee, the Arts Committee, the Education Committee, the Volunteer Resources Committee, and the Community Services Committee, employees from throughout South-Central are involved in community activities. Each committee includes 11 to 13 members, who work as a conduit for Prudential in the community.

SCHO employees also regularly contribute their time on an individual basis to various charitable and civic events and organizations. The company as a whole is one of the city's largest contributors to United Way, the arts, and other worthy organizations.

The firm also purchases artwork from contemporary artists, both to promote the arts and to display for the enjoyment of its employees.

South-Central's first three presidents during a relaxed moment (from left) the late Charles W. Campbell, CLU (1953-1965); the late Duncan Macfarlan, CLU (1979-1981); and John D. Buchanan, Jr., CLU (1965-1979).

COOPERS & LYBRAND

Coopers & Lybrand, one of the nation's Big Eight accounting firms, emphasizes quality service, individual initiative, and teamwork in its approach to client service.

The Jacksonville office of Coopers & Lybrand, with a staff of 65, was awarded the Industry Appreciation Award as the city's Outstanding Employer in the category of 100 employees or less by the Jacksonville Chamber of Commerce.

"Our commitment to quality service, individual initiative, and teamwork, both among our people and within the community, is unique and is visible in everything we do. That's what we're all about," says Michael D. Abney, managing partner of the firm.

The local office of Coopers & Lybrand—one of the firm's seven offices in Florida and 100 nationwide—is located in a suite of offices encompassing the entire 13th floor of the First Union tower in downtown Jacksonville.

From 1983 to 1988 the size of the firm has nearly doubled, and plans call for the number of employees to double again during the next five years. The staff includes 55 accountants, the majority of whom are certified public accountants.

Coopers & Lybrand's professional staff are graduates of some of the nation's leading universities, including University of California at Berkeley, University of Nebraska, Tulane University, University of Florida, Florida State University, and University of North Florida.

"We have a very informal, very low-key approach. We encourage our staff to feel comfortable while doing business," Abney says. "We place a big emphasis on the individual."

The Jacksonville office handles a diverse list of clients in the geographic area bounded by Savannah, to the north, Tallahassee to the west, and Ocala to the south. Some 85 percent of the firm's clients are located in the Jacksonville area.

Insurance companies, health care institutions, and manufacturers figure prominently in Coopers & Lybrand's client base, which includes a wide cross section of business and industry.

"We consider ourselves forward-thinking advisers to business, not just accountants and auditors of historic data," concludes Abney.

Coopers & Lybrand is committed to the community and is involved in contributing both financially and in employee volunteer time to such organizations as Junior Achievement, the Jacksonville Zoo, the United Way, the Jacksonville Symphony, and a number of area educational and medical institutions.

Coopers & Lybrand employs more than 14,000 people in its 100 U.S. offices. The firm has offices in more than 100 countries.

Derrek Dewan, tax PIC, and Byron Thompson, audit partner, discussing client problems.

Don Withers, audit partner, relays information to Michael Abney, office managing partner, on phone with client.

ROBERT M. ANGAS ASSOCIATES

Robert M. Angas Associates (RMA) is one of Jacksonville's oldest continuously operating planning, engineering, and surveying companies.

Founded in 1924 by Robert M. Angas, the firm has handled planning, surveying, and site engineering for many of Jacksonville's best-known residential areas, largest office buildings, and office parks.

During World War II the firm served as consultant on site selection and as surveyor for numerous military facilities from Key West to Brunswick, Georgia, including the comprehensive land surveys for Jacksonville's three Navy bases—Mayport, Jax NAS, and Cecil Field. RMA also performed early surveying and site engineering for Cape Canaveral Space Center (Cape Kennedy).

RMA's planning and design capabilities include single- and multifamily residential, as well as industrial and commercial developments. The firm's civil engineering services include water treatment and distribution; sanitary sewage collection, transmission, and treatment; paving and drainage; and storm-water collection and treatment. Surveying capabilities include boundary, topographic, hydrographic, and construction layout.

"The product of our design is not the glamorous part of a development.

The RMA home office in Deerwood Center.

But it's an essential part, the part that serves the structure—like the circulatory system in your body. Our work is frequently buried beneath the ground. You never see it."

From its earliest years the company has served as consultant and surveyor with some of northeast Florida's largest developers. Through association with Stockton, Whatley, Davin & Company, The Bryant Skinner Company, and Gate Lands Company, RMA has

served in the continuing development of the Ponte Vedra and Deerwood residential communities. As planning consultant and engineer, the firm is assisting Florida Title Group in the development of Pace Island, a 997-acre, 1,100-unit exclusive single-family residential community in Clay County. Other area developments utilizing Angas planning, design, and surveying services include Ortega, Ortega Forest, Empire Point, St. Nicholas, San Marco, and Arlingwood.

The firm has been involved in numerous area commercial developments. RMA was surveyor and engineer for Deerwood Center Office and Industrial Park, and performed site design and surveying services for many individual projects developed in the park. The company has been similarly involved in other area office and industrial parks, including Imeson Industrial Park, Southpoint, Interstate South, and Belfort Park.

Additional commercial project involvement by RMA includes the Independent Life Building, the Southern Bell Tower, the Federal Reserve Bank, Sheraton at St. Johns Place, the Jacksonville Marriott, Deerwood Village, Enterprise Center, and Jacksonville

Thorough research and planning are essential for efficient service and quality product.

Center.

Participation in governmental and institutional facilities development includes support services to Federal Reserve Bank, Mayo Clinic, First Baptist Church, The Bolles School, Crystal Springs Elementary and other area schools, and numerous military site developments.

In business since 1924, the partnership of Robert M. Angas and Associates was formed in 1950 with Russell DeGrove and Richard Lampp, longtime employees. After the deaths of Angas in 1955 and DeGrove in 1964, Lampp became the managing partner and, along with Wesley Sweat, who joined the firm in 1965 and was active through the early 1970s, operated the company until 1981, when T.T. Wilson, associated with the firm since 1964 as design engineer, project manager, and senior planner, and David Lampp joined the partnership, forming Robert M. Angas Associates.

Through the years the firm has retained the "Angas" name because of its identity and the history of the company in the community. "Mr. Angas was so well thought of by both his clients and his employees that we wanted to keep the name," says Richard Lampp, who began his career with Angas in 1937 as a draftsman. "The name in the community has always been associated with quality. We have always insisted on maintaining the highest integrity and delivering a quality product."

Subsequent to his retirement from the partnership in 1984, Richard Lampp has remained as senior consultant and continues to be active in the daily operation of the firm.

Growth of the partnership through the years has been controlled and deliberate, reflecting the belief that high quality is maintained through personal involvement in each phase of a project's development.

The company operated for nearly 50 years from its offices on the fourth

The professionals at RMA have provided planning, surveying, and site engineering for residential, commercial, and industrial projects in northeastern Florida since 1924.

floor of the Hildebrant Building (First Federal Building, downtown). In 1976 the firm moved to the San Marco area and, in 1987, doubled its office size with a move to its current location in Deerwood Center, the office park it helped develop.

For 65 years Robert M. Angas Associates has offered quality planning,

Land surveying capability also complements full-spectrum planning and civil engineering design services.

engineering, and land surveying services through a highly dedicated team of qualified professionals, skilled technicians, and support staff.

COMMANDER LEGLER WERBER DAWES SADLER & HOWELL

Corporate and banking partners (left to right) Nancy Bowen, John Welch, Luther Sadler, Charles Hedrick, and Mitchell Legler.

Founded in 1976, Commander Legler Werber Dawes Sadler & Howell has grown dramatically during the past decade to become one of Jacksonville's largest law firms.

Specializing in business law and litigation, the full-service firm presently includes 16 partners and 23 associate attorneys. Lawyers in the firm have an average age of 40, one of the youngest average ages of any firm in Jacksonville.

"We've always considered ourselves to be a young, aggressive group," says partner Luther Sadler. "We're able to bring efficiency and flexibility to our clients, as well as experience and expertise. We have a very broad-based pool of lawyers."

The firm has consistently attracted and retained the highest-quality lawyers from leading universities and law schools around the country, including Yale, University of Virginia, Duke, Boston College, University of Florida, and University of Pittsburgh.

Charles E. Commander III, Mitch-

ell W. Legler, Steven A. Werber, and Luther F. Sadler, Jr., senior partners in the firm, were four of only 160 Florida lawyers named in the *Best Lawyers in America,* a book by Naifeh and Smith, which represents the most attorneys selected from any one Jacksonville law firm.

The firm primarily represents major corporations, including financial institutions, construction companies, real estate developers, insurance companies, general manufacturers, securities and syndication firms, governmental entities, maritime concerns, and the retail industry in diverse areas of business law.

Approximately one-half of the firm's clients are Jacksonville-based companies, including some of the city's

Real estate and tax partners (left to right, from top) Emerson Lotzia, Robert Heekin, David Peek, Gresham Stoneburner, Michael Dawes, and Charles Commander.

leading corporations and financial institutions. The firm also represents a number of regional, national, and international clients.

"We don't take our clients for granted. We work very hard to keep them happy," says Commander, one of the organization's founders. "We have good lawyers in all fields of business law. That's one of our main strengths, and we've built on it."

Established in 1976 when four attorneys from different Jacksonville firms formed a partnership, Commander Legler Werber Dawes Sadler & Howell experienced steady growth until 1982, when it doubled in size through a merger with eight attorneys from one of Florida's largest commercial law firms.

The firm is departmentalized into four areas of expertise to best handle the complexities of the legal needs of its client base: real estate, litigation, taxation and estate planning, and corporate, securities, and banking.

"Our approach to law emphasizes practicality and teamwork in seeking to

render the highest-quality services at a cost-effective price," says managing partner Mitchell Legler.

Steven Werber heads the Litigation Department, which was strengthened significantly in 1985 with the addition of experienced litigator Charles Cook Howell III. The Litigation Department regularly handles cases in such commercial areas as bankruptcy, contract disputes, construction, landlord and tenant, probate and trust, securities, and antitrust, as well as insurance defense and personal injury areas, including automobile, medical negligence, and product liability.

The Taxation and Estate Planning Department, headed by Gresham Stoneburner, deals extensively with taxation of individuals, corporations, partnerships, estates, and trusts. Clients are counseled in a broad range of tax matters and are represented in such tax proceedings as audits, tax collection actions, and asserted tax deficiencies. The department specializes in corporate and partnership tax matters.

Headed by Luther Sadler, the Cor-

Litigation partners (left to right) Michael O'Neal, Douglas Chunn, Charles Howell, and Steven Werber.

porate, Securities, and Banking Department represents corporations, banks and other financial institutions, as well as individuals and partnerships, in a broad range of commercial, financial, and securities law matters. Clients are also represented in connection with business combinations involving mergers, consolidations, sales and purchases of stock and assets, and other contract matters.

The Real Estate Department, headed by Charles Commander, has attracted regional, national, and international clients in the acquisition, development, management, financing, and sale of both residential and commercial projects. The department's lawyers have experience with state and federal agencies in connection with application for governmental approvals such as zoning, platting, and environmental permits.

The firm moved into a new headquarters building in 1985 after purchasing and completely renovating the historic 12-story Greenleaf Building. Located in the heart of Jacksonville's central business district, the Greenleaf Building was built in 1927 and has been designated as a historic landmark by the Jacksonville Historic Landmarks Commission. A dramatic glass wall along the building's northern face provides a panoramic view of the heart of downtown Jacksonville. The law firm currently occupies six stories of the building and leases other floors.

"We have a real belief in Jacksonville and the downtown area," says Commander. "Our purchase of the Greenleaf Building expresses that belief in a very tangible way."

In 1985 the firm purchased, renovated, and occupied the historic Greenleaf Building in downtown Jacksonville.

BLUE CROSS AND BLUE SHIELD OF FLORIDA

Since 1944, when its original office opened with a staff of four, Blue Cross and Blue Shield of Florida has grown to more than 4,000 employees statewide.

From a small beginning in 1944, Blue Cross and Blue Shield of Florida is now the state's leading provider of health insurance and Jacksonville's eighth-largest corporation, servicing more than 3 million Floridians and processing more than 140,000 claims each day.

The Florida Plan has grown dramatically in expertise and in size to more than 4,000 employees statewide. However, the purpose of the company remains unchanged—to provide quality health care coverage and excellent service to each policyholder.

As public demand for affordable hospital care grew, the Florida Hospital Service Corporation opened a four-person office in Jacksonville, Florida, in 1944. The fledgling company offered groups a prepayment plan to cover hospital care. Two years later a division of Florida Medical Service Corporation developed a similar group plan to cover the cost of physicians' services.

In 1951 the hospital care plan adopted the name of Blue Cross of Florida, and the physicians' care plan became Blue Shield of Florida. With that change, the companies began offering individual enrollment on a statewide basis.

During the mid-1950s the two Florida companies began administering various government programs until 1966, when they became the primary administrators of the newly created Medicare program. The firm continues serving Medicare beneficiaries today on behalf of the federal government.

The two separate companies merged into Blue Cross and Blue Shield of Florida, Inc., in 1980. This merger streamlined administration and enabled the company to establish new and varied health financing programs such as preferred provider organizations (PPOs).

In 1982 Blue Cross and Blue Shield of Florida became a mutual insurance company and policyholders were given voting rights. Members of the board of directors come from primarily non-health care fields to ensure the organization remains publicly responsive and accountable.

Health Options, Inc., is Blue Cross and Blue Shield of Florida's health maintenance organization. Incorporated in February 1984, it now has the state's largest HMO membership.

The corporation works continuously with physicians, hospitals, employers, and government agencies to provide the best service possible and control rising health care costs.

The Florida Plan has played an active role as the health insurance sponsor of the 1988 U.S. Olympic Team, holding fund-raising community events statewide. Blue Cross and Blue Shield plans nationwide pledged to raise at least $2.5 million to support the athletes.

Blue Cross and Blue Shield of Florida has administered the government's Medicare program for Floridians since the national health care program began in 1966.

FLORIDA NATIONAL BANK

The Florida National Bank Tower, headquarters for Florida National Bank and Florida National Bank/Jacksonville, was opened in May 1986 and is the first phase of Enterprise Center in downtown Jacksonville.

Florida National Bank, currently celebrating its 100th anniversary of service, began in Jacksonville in 1888 as Southern Savings and Trust Company. The founder and first president, Samuel B. Hubbard, was a successful hardware entrepreneur who initiated the establishment of the bank when Jacksonville was struggling to recover from the Civil War. Factors such as the outstanding river economy, the new concentration of northern tourists after the war, and burgeoning industrialization worked in Hubbard's favor. He capitalized on the positive business climate by founding the bank and several other businesses.

Still under the leadership of Hubbard, Southern Savings changed its name in 1900 to Mercantile Exchange. Only one year later Jacksonville experienced its darkest hour—the great fire of 1901. Mercantile Exchange was completely destroyed except for its fireproof vault. The *Florida Times Union* reported at the time that the vault was found intact with "not even the paint of the interior wall scorched." The bank quickly recovered, and in 1906 acquired a national bank charter and was sold to the newly formed Flor-

ida Bank and Trust Company, which then became Florida National Bank of Jacksonville.

In the late 1920s Alfred I. duPont, internationally known financier and philanthropist, invested in Florida National Bank and served as its president in the Jacksonville location from 1930 to 1933. Under his leadership many banks were added to the growing group throughout the state. DuPont continued his involvement with the bank through his brother-in-law, Ed Ball, who served as president and member of the board of directors from 1942 until 1971.

DuPont, his wife, Jessie Ball duPont, and her brother, Ed Ball, made their distinguished mark on the City of Jacksonville. The Jessie Ball duPont Religious, Education, and Charitable Trust and the Nemours Children's Clinic are only two examples of their philanthropic activities that continue to benefit the city today.

In 1971 the Florida National Group of Banks reorganized into Florida National Banks of Florida, Inc., a bank holding company, and in 1983 the banks were merged into one statewide organization. Today Florida National Banks of Florida, Inc., is a public

company and its holdings include Florida National Bank, Kingsley Bank, and other financial service subsidiaries.

Now the third-largest, state-based bank, Florida National is a growing financial services organization dedicated to excellence and to achieving the financial goals of its customers. Professional bankers, a broad range of products and services, and state-of-the-art technology mean that Florida National can provide its customers with superior resources for their financial needs.

One of the major lenders in the city, FNB has helped Jacksonville grow by financing some of the most prestigious corporate, residential, and industrial developments. Florida National's commitment to its local communities is demonstrated by the dedication of a portion of the bank's earnings to a variety of civic, medical, cultural, and educational causes. One of the bank's most visible contributions is the Florida National Jazz Festival/Jacksonville, held under the Florida National Pavilion on the banks of the St. Johns River each fall. Another important community effort spearheaded by the bank was the recent Florida National Cancer Challenge, which raised more than $3 million.

The Florida National Pavilion during an event at Metropolitan Park. Starting in 1988 the Florida National Jazz Festival/Jacksonville will be the name of the annual jazz festivities, thanks to the bank's title sponsorship.

MATHEWS, OSBORNE, McNATT & COBB

The management committee (from left): Floyd L. Matthews, Jr., Harris Brown, and John M. McNatt., Jr.

Mathews, Osborne, McNatt & Cobb is one of Jacksonville's oldest and largest law firms. The partnership, which has roots in Jacksonville reaching back to 1882, has a tradition rich in excellence in the legal profession. It is one of the top civil trial litigation firms in Jacksonville.

Throughout its history it has produced lawyers who have distinguished themselves in leadership roles in both government and the legal profession. These include presidents of local and state bar associations and members of the state judiciary, including the Supreme Court of Florida. John E. Mathews, Jr., a founding partner of the modern-day firm, served as president of the Florida Senate and was a candidate for governor of the State of Florida.

The firm's litigation practice focuses on trial, appellate, and administrative law, including constitutional issues. The practice also encompasses numerous areas of insurance defense, including professional malpractice, products liability, workers' compensation, and claims for extra-contractual damages.

The earliest beginnings of what today has become the city's third-oldest and fifth-largest law firm date back to 1882, when John P. Cooper joined his father, Charles P. Cooper, in the practice of law. The elder Cooper became attorney general of Florida during the mid-1880s, and his son was elected mayor of Jacksonville in 1891 but de-

clined the office.

The firm expanded through the years, and in the 1920s changed its name to Cooper, Cooper & Osborne with the addition of John Cooper's son-in-law, H.P. Osborne, to the firm. Osborne's son, H.P. Osborne, Jr., now retired, is a founding partner of the modern-day firm.

In 1959 the modern-day foundation of the firm was established with the merger of Osborne, Copp, Markham and Ehrlich with McNatt & Mathews.

John M. McNatt, Jr., senior partner with Mathews, Osborne, McNatt & Cobb today, is a founding partner of the modern-day firm. McNatt is the second generation of his family to practice law in the McNatt & Mathews firm, as was John E. Mathews, Jr.

Mathews, who died in 1988, followed his father into the legal profession as well as into the political arena.

Partners of the firm (from left, seated): Floyd L. Matthews, Jr., Frank W. Hession, J. Stephen O'Hara, Jr., John M. McNatt, Jr., Michael J. Obringer, Harris Brown, and James P. Wolf. Standing on the left is Jack W. Shaw, Jr., and James E. Cobb is standing on the right.

His father, John E. Mathews, Sr., served as a state senator and later became chief justice of the Supreme Court of Florida. John E. Mathews III, who began his practice of law with the firm, today is a county judge. Raymond Ehrlich, another founding partner, today sits as chief justice of the Supreme Court of Florida.

The firm currently has members who have served in leadership positions in local, state, and national bar associations. Several current partners are fellows of the American College of Trial Lawyers.

The firm's offices have been located in the American Heritage Life

Building in downtown Jacksonville since 1959. This reflects the long-standing tradition of the firm. "We're a long-term law firm with a lot of tradition," says Cobb. "People regard us as such."

Currently with more than 20 lawyers, Mathews, Osborne, McNatt & Cobb has a varied practice with emphasis on trial litigation. Clients include financial institutions, property and casualty insurance companies, health insurers, medical providers, product manufacturers, and other corporate institutions.

"We have a very diverse group of clients," says McNatt. "As Jacksonville's economic base has diversified, so has our client base, and we expect that trend to continue. The growth of our firm has paralleled the growth of Jacksonville, and we also expect that trend to continue."

BYRON HARLESS, REID & ASSOCIATES

The professional staff at the Jacksonville office of Byron Harless, Reid & Associates, Inc. Left to right: Reid, Hartman, Reynolds, and Lister.

Morale and productivity are down at a manufacturing plant, and management wants to know why.

An employer has a supervisory position to fill and wants to find out which of his employees has the most potential for promotion.

A company is going through a merger and needs help in responding to employee concerns.

These are typical of the many cases in which businesses have found the need for the services of a consulting psychologist.

Jacksonville's first and largest private firm that provides psychological services to individuals, business, industry, and government is Byron Harless, Reid & Associates.

"We have been able to increase the morale, productivity, and efficiency in the companies we've worked with, all of which lead to an increase in profitability," says the organization's president, Melvin P. Reid, Ph.D., who has been with the firm since he opened the Jacksonville office in 1962. "We help good companies get better. We help them be more responsive to their em-

ployees, and we show them how to use people more efficiently."

The firm was founded in Tampa in 1946 by Byron Harless, who later became an executive with the Knight-Ridder newspaper chain but remains a stockholder in Byron Harless, Reid & Associates. The company's Tampa and Jacksonville offices have served more than 3,000 clients in 42 states and several foreign countries. Currently about 500 local companies use the firm's services.

The company's client base includes organizations in the fields of communications, finance, transportation, manufacturing, retail, construction, professional services, and government.

The most frequent service Byron Harless, Reid & Associates is called on to perform is in-depth evaluation of managerial and supervisory candidates for employment or promotion. The

company performs more than 2,000 such evaluations each year.

"We help the employer to make more objective decisions about the people in their organization. We help them assess individual strengths and developmental needs, as well as helping them to enhance development," says William D. Buel, Ph.D., of the firm's Tampa office.

Attitude and opinion surveys and developmental studies are a major service of the firm, used by some 80 clients per year. Such surveys explore employee opinions on working conditions, compensation, and benefits; attitudes toward management; communication; and other aspects of organizational effectiveness.

Byron Harless, Reid & Associates remains flexible to address a wide range of organizational needs. Included among the firm's services are supervisory and managerial training, team building, and specialized training in negotiations, human relations skills, and time management. The firm also provides consultation with top management, offers special studies for partnerships and small businesses, directs consumer opinion surveys, and develops specialized assessment programs for employee selection and turnover reduction.

Among the company's many clinical and individual services is a full range of counseling and psychological assessment in the areas of personal, marital/family, sexual, and stress-related problems. The firm's offerings also extend to neuropsychological evaluations, forensic consultation, biofeedback-assisted stress management therapy, career counseling, and outplacement services.

Headquartered at 2426 Phillips Highway, Byron Harless, Reid & Associates has a staff of 23 in the Jacksonville and Tampa offices. All of the professional staff are licensed psychologists and include Melvin P. Reid, Ph.D., president; William D. Buel, Ph.D., vice-president; Harry Goldsmith, Ph.D.; James L. Lister, Ed.D.; Gerald E. Reynolds, Ph.D.; and Joseph H. Hartman, Ph.D.

LAW ENGINEERING

As a specialty consultant to Jacksonville's leading architects, building contractors, and industries, Law Engineering has been involved in most of the major building projects in the city for the past 30 years.

Independent Square, the Southern Bell tower, the original and new Prudential Insurance Company buildings, Jacksonville Landing, the Riverwalk, the Jacksonville Shipyards, Deerwood Center, and the Dames Point Bridge lead the list of nearly 11,000 local projects the company has completed.

Law Engineering's role is in testing construction materials and providing geotechnical engineering services—the soil testing, site evaluation, and foundation quality control during construction.

"Because of our unique involvement in the engineering community we've had the opportunity to be involved in a greater number of projects than traditional design firms. We've

grown with the city, and we want to be a continued part of Jacksonville's growth," says James Horton, a senior geotechnical engineer and branch manager of the Jacksonville office.

Founded in Atlanta in 1946, Law Engineering has evolved to become one of the 30 largest engineering companies in the country. The firm has more than 30 branch and project offices around the country, with approximately 1,900 employees nationwide. Five of the offices are located in Florida.

The Florida Division of Law Engineering is headed by Woody Lingo, based in Jacksonville. Horton leads the Jacksonville branch, which employs a staff of 75. The staff includes a drilling group, materials testing technicians, and the engineering group.

The Jacksonville office of Law Engineering was opened in 1956. Located at 3901 Carmichael Avenue for nearly 20 years, it covers a territory that extends north to Savannah, west to Tallahassee, and south to Gainesville.

The Jacksonville offices include four drill rigs and a complete laboratory for testing of soils and construction materials. There are 16 experienced soils and materials engineers, nine of whom are registered professionals.

The firm's engineers are recruited from leading engineering schools throughout the country. The staff has extensive experience and in-depth knowledge in geotechnical, materials, asbestos, and environmental engineering services, as well as construction materials engineering, testing, and inspection services.

"The quality of our organization is based solely on the quality of our people," Horton says. "Our people are our product. We have a highly qualified staff."

Law Engineering is an employee-owned company with no outside stockholders.

AT&T AMERICAN TRANSTECH

AT&T American Transtech was formed as a wholly owned subsidiary of AT&T to manage shareowner services for AT&T's divestiture—the largest in history.

When American Telephone & Telegraph Company was divested in 1983 into AT&T and seven regional companies, American Transtech's mission was to manage the 22 million AT&T and regional holding companies' shareowner accounts.

Today the organization that has

Located on a park-like 27-acre campus in Deerwood Center, the AT&T American Transtech five-building, lakefront complex features a mauve-paneled, reflective-glass exterior. Photography by Richard Payne, AIA

become one of Jacksonville's major employers is the largest stock transfer agent in the United States and has diversified to include a direct marketing arm, which in a few years has grown to become the nation's fifth-largest tele-

marketing service bureau.

AT&T chose Jacksonville as the site for American Transtech after considering a total of 60 U.S. cities. Jacksonville was selected because of its quality of life, the availability of full-time and part-time employees, and the opportunity for AT&T to make a significant impact on the city. Indeed, the choice of Jacksonville by an international company that is one of the world's largest corporations made a major impact on the city's economic development efforts, as well as its existing economic environment.

The suburban Deerwood Center was chosen as the site of AT&T American Transtech's five-building complex. Located on a park-like 27-acre campus complete with a lake and waterfall, the lovely complex with reflective-glass and mauve-paneled exteriors was built in a record 11 months by The Haskell Company, a Jacksonville-based firm. The American Transtech offices are what they were intended to be, a showcase for the community.

The high-tech, high-volume information-management firm provides a full range of services to shareowners, including transfer, payment processing, proxy, dividend reinvestment programs, and shareowner contact. The company also provides shareholder services for other corporate customers, such as Charles Schwab Company and COMSAT.

American Transtech's wide range of services includes the capability to conduct an entire program for corporate reorganization. The firm has provided corporate reorganization management and implementation to tender offers, odd-lot programs, mergers and acquisitions, divestitures and spinoffs, initial public offerings, and solicitations for clients ranging in size from only a few investors to as many as 1.9 million investors.

Artwork by Florida artists, such as this mural in American Transtech's lobby, is exhibited throughout the complex to create a pleasant working environment. Photography by Richard Payne, AIA

Overall, each year American Transtech's financial services process more than 60 million shareowner transactions, 4 million written and telephone inquiries, and 6 million stock transfers, as well as print and mail 35 million dividend checks.

Direct Marketing Services was introduced by American Transtech in 1984, making use of the communications capabilities developed during divestiture. The marketing services include inbound and outbound telemarketing, direct mail, fulfillment, and list and data base management services.

More than 50 major corporations use American Transtech to perform their telemarketing needs, including Sears, Johnson & Johnson, Goodyear, Pan Am, Blue Cross and Blue Shield of Florida, and General Motors Insurance Corporation.

In a year's time the company manages more than 10 million inbound and outbound telephone calls, 100 million pieces of mail, and 150 million computer transactions performed by three mainframe computers.

In addition to its financial and marketing services, American Transtech in 1988 became the first site where AT&T's newest technologies are showcased for AT&T customers. American Transtech was selected as the premiere "Profiles" site because of its advanced AT&T telecommunications equipment and telemarketing software.

American Transtech maintains more than 1,200 permanent employees, and contracts up to 800 more for special projects. It is led by president and chief executive officer William Hightower.

Hightower leads the company in an innovative organizational style that is based on teamwork. The management structure was streamlined from five tiers to three, thus increasing communication between employees and executives. Instead of having separate departments for each processing function, employees are grouped into teams, each handling AT&T, one of the seven regional companies, or corporate customers, so that the team becomes well

AT&T American Transtech communicators handle a total of 10 million inbound and outbound phone calls each year.

acquainted with the particular group's needs.

American Transtech's first president, Larry Lemasters, instituted the Corporate Culture team approach, and Hightower has expanded and refined it. "I'm convinced that the single-greatest factor relative to the performance of a business is its people and the way responsibility is vested within the firm," Hightower says.

Obviously the team concept is working. Productivity has increased 100 percent, and some groups have been able to cut costs by up to 40 percent. The system is also popular with employees—the annual turnover rate has been reduced to less than 4 percent.

The interior layout of the three-story, nearly half-million-square-foot office complex is also designed with the team approach in mind. Cluster-style work places suit both team and individual needs.

The entire complex was built with people in mind. In addition to the natural campus-like exterior setting, the outdoors is brought indoors by extensive use of windows and skylights. Most employees are within a few steps of a view of the company's beautifully landscaped lawns or lake.

Another element added to the

complex' interiors to create a pleasant working environment is the display of more than 75 pieces of original artwork by leading Florida artists. Each piece was specially selected with consideration to the building's lighting and design.

AT&T American Transtech has a very serious commitment to the city of Jacksonville, and its executives and other employees are actively involved in numerous civic and charitable organizations. Hightower is the 1988 president of the University of North Florida Foundation, and has served as chairman of the Jacksonville Chamber of Commerce's Committee of 100. He also led the city's effort to acquire a National Football League franchise.

The firm's mailing operation sends out more than 100 million pieces of mail each year.

ROGERS, TOWERS, BAILEY, JONES & GAY

The members of Rogers, Towers, Bailey, Jones & Gay are pictured clockwise (left to right). Seated are John B. Chandler, Jr., Clyde A. Reese, Jr., James M. McLean, C.D. Towers, Jr., Fred M. Ringel, David M. Foster, Allan T. Geiger, and C. William Reiney. Standing are Alexandra K. Hedrick, Irvin M. Weinstein, Douglas A. Ward, Paul P. Sanford, Joseph O. Stroud, Jr., Michael J. Dewberry, Frank X. Friedmann, Jr., Samuel L. LePrell, Robert T. Hyde, Jr., H. Joseph O'Shields, Donald C. Wright, G. Kenneth Norrie, and Michael A. Wodrich.

The firm of Rogers, Towers, Bailey, Jones & Gay is one of the oldest and most prestigious law firms in the city of Jacksonville, reflecting more than 80 years of outstanding legal services.

The firm was founded in 1902 by Colonel William Toomer and Judge J.C. Reynolds. At that time it was known as Toomer & Reynolds, and remained so until 1913, when Colonel Toomer retired and was replaced by William Harlowe Rogers. The firm then became known as Reynolds & Rogers.

In the early 1920s a young associate, C. Daughtry Towers, became a partner, and the firm's name was changed to Reynolds, Rogers & Towers. After the death of Reynolds in 1926, the firm was known as Rogers & Towers. Partners Cecil Bailey, Taylor Jones, and Ed Gay arrived in 1937, 1954, and 1962, respectively, reflecting the firm name as it appears today.

The firm's offices were originally located at 116-126 East Bay Street in the Consolidated Building, one of the first structures to be erected after the Jacksonville fire of 1901. The all-wood building was then considered to be a skyscraper, towering to a full height of seven stories.

Decor at the original offices was simple. Founder Reynolds was known to have said that a law firm should have sawdust on the floor in case a client missed the spittoon. And so it was at Rogers, Towers in the early years. Appearances gradually changed to a more modern look. Carpeting replaced the sawdust, wooden panels replaced the plaster walls, and French antiques replaced austere furnishings. But even among the elegance that replaced the sawdust, each office possessed its own brass spittoon as late as 1950.

Since its inception the firm has expanded in size to keep pace with Jacksonville's growth and the success and expansion of the firm's clients. It presently consists of more than 40 lawyers.

Rogers, Towers is known for its stability among the city's larger firms. There have been no mergers of any sort in its history, and no partner at Rogers, Towers has ever left the firm and remained in the practice of law.

Rogers, Towers engages in a broad civil practice, acting as a full-service firm to companies of all sizes doing business in Jacksonville and elsewhere in Florida. The firm's clients include individuals and companies in diverse industries, from real estate developers to contractors, from insurance companies to manufacturers and distributors, and from financial institutions to hospitals. Because of the firm's stability and diversified practice, long-standing relationships have continued with many of the firm's clients, with several of these close relationships continuing for more than 40 years.

In addition to its expertise in real estate law, corporate and finance law, trusts and estates, bankruptcy, taxation, health care law, employment relations, administrative law, and all aspects of civil litigation and appellate practice, the firm has gained a significant reputation, particularly in the past decade, in newer and more specialized areas of law.

One of the fastest growing areas of the firm's practice is its environmental and land use department. There, attorneys who have gained invaluable experience by serving on appointed boards and working as staff members of state and federal agencies have come together to form a unique environmental team that understands both sides of current environmental and land use issues. As such, the department has been privileged to work on the cutting edge of most major recent real estate developments in Jacksonville and surrounding areas.

Although several members of the firm were born in Jacksonville, the attorneys practicing with Rogers, Towers were attracted to the firm from diverse geographic and educational backgrounds. Law schools that are represented by the lawyers are Harvard University, Columbia University, Duke University, Vanderbilt University, University of Virginia, University of North Carolina, University of Georgia, University of Florida, Florida State University, and Mercer University. Several attorneys are admitted to practice in more than one state, including Florida, Georgia, New York, the District of Columbia, and Kentucky.

Public service is vitally important to the firm and its attorneys. In addition to participation in nonprofit organizations and community affairs by most of its lawyers, five Rogers, Towers attorneys have served as president of the Jacksonville Bar Association and one as president of the Florida Bar. Many of the attorneys provide legal services to those who cannot otherwise afford them through the Jacksonville Area Legal Aid.

The home office of Rogers, Towers is now on the top two floors of the 1300 Building, which is located on the south bank of the St. Johns River. In 1988 the firm opened an office at J. Turner Butler Boulevard and I-95 to provide more convenient service to its real estate and financial institution clients. Rogers, Towers also has a branch office next door to the state capitol in Tallahassee.

NASSAU COUNTY COMMITTEE OF 100

Port facilities, manufacturing, and the fishing industry all join hands at Nassau County's new deep-water harbor. Photo by David Burghardt

Visitors enjoy the Annual Isle of 8 Flags Shrimp Boat Festival in historic downtown Fernandina Beach.

In 1983 members of the board of directors of the Amelia Island-Fernandina Beach Chamber of Commerce collectively realized the need for placing greater emphasis on the creation of new jobs in Nassau County.

The concept that developed out of that realization and an effort to act on it was called The Committee of 100. A natural outward growth of the industrial development committee of the chamber, The Committee of 100 was originally formed with representatives from 100 major businesses in the area.

Serving as first chairman of the committee was Tommy Tate, who was instrumental in organizing bylaws, overseeing their institution, and creating a statement of purpose that would provide the new endeavor with strong direction toward creating new jobs.

With the buildup of the Kings Bay Submarine Station in neighboring St. Mary's, Georgia, 1986 chairman Joel Embry expanded that initial direction of the committee by establishing target markets for the program and holding strategic planning sessions with other committee members. It was through such meetings that the Nassau County video, funded largely by a grant from Container Corporation, was produced to aid in reaching prospective new businesses and industries visually. The video since has become an invaluable tool of the committee.

The year 1986 also marked the beginning of The Committee of 100's participation in the Florida Department of Commerce Blue Chip Community Program. The Blue Chip Program is implemented by the Economic Development Division of the State Department of Commerce, and is designed to certify or "stamp with approval" those communities in the state that are adequately prepared for the influx of new business and industry. The Committee of 100 received such certification that same year.

Later in 1986 Susan P. McCranie was made the first executive director of the committee, and through her leadership the marketing program was expanded to include advertising in major economic development publications.

An indication of the success of the committee's marketing efforts occurred in 1987, under the new leadership of chairman Anthony Leggio, when Nassau County was placed on the list of proposed sites for the Superconducting Super Collider project, a proposed $4-billion federal project of NASA and the Department of Energy. Although the county was not ultimately chosen as the site, the qualities that placed it among top choices made it a prospective site for future industry in the minds of many major developers.

With its abundance of available land, excellent port facilities, extensive highway systems, uncongested beaches, world-class resorts, and quiet, rural living, Nassau County has a great deal to offer any potential new business.

The Committee of 100, encouraged by the past and challenged by the future, is working closely with economic development groups in the Jacksonville area to build a healthy, diverse economy through prospective new businesses and industries. Currently Kristey Nielsen and Jeanne Layland staff committee efforts. Orville Harrell serves as volunteer chair, and Bruce Jasinsky is chair elect.

AMELIA ISLAND PLANTATION

One-third of the 13.5-mile-long lush Amelia Island is occupied by the plantation.

Amelia Island, given its name after the daughter of King George II during a period of English rule, is the southernmost island in the chain of Golden Isles that begins off the coast of North Carolina. A place rich with both North American and Florida history, the island was first discovered in 1562 by French explorers and is the only land mass in the United States to have been under eight flags of domination—French, Spanish, English, Patriots, Green Cross of Florida, Mexican, Confederate States, and the United States—spanning a time period of nearly five centuries.

The island today houses one of the most outstanding resorts and residential communities in the Southeast—Amelia Island Plantation. The plantation occupies nearly 1,250 acres at the southern end of Amelia Island, roughly one-third of its 13.5-mile length. The land of the plantation was owned in the 1960s by Union Carbide and was slated to be strip-mined for minerals.

Before the process began, however,

Amelia Island Plantation is the perfect combination of beauty and nature and five centuries of history.

the area was sold to Charles Fraser of the Sea Pines Company of Hilton Head Island, South Carolina. Sea Pines opened the land area in 1972 and the resort two years later. Shortly thereafter, in 1978, the plantation was sold to Cleveland businessman and current owner Richard L. Cooper.

Development of Amelia Island Plantation was begun with an exceptional goal. The Sea Pines Company contracted the firm of Wallace, McHarg, Roberts & Todd of Los Angeles to conduct a land-use study of the 3,000 newly acquired acres—2,000 above high tide and 1,000 of tidal marsh. The objective of the study was

to find an optimum fit between the habitat required by man in a resort community and the physical conditions and animal and plant ecology that existed there.

As a result of such ecological and environmental concern during development, residents and visitors can now enjoy a resort that respects all aspects of the natural resources surrounding it. Amelia Island Plantation is a very diversified resort and residential community. Tennis camps are a specialty, supervised by All American Sports Academy, one of the leading sports academies in the United States. Golf, swimming, horseback riding, fishing, youth programs, and other activities are also available.

The plantation also serves as a site for business conferences, offering both an eight-acre Racquet Park Conference Center and a 22,500-square-foot Executive Meeting Center with state-of-the-art facilities for achieving business-related goals amidst accommodations, dining, and recreational opportunities that are among the best on the plantation.

Amelia Island Plantation has been described as the perfect combination of nature, beauty, championship sports, resort accommodations, and executive conference centers. But, above all else, it is a development built from a concern for the beauty of an island rich with five centuries of history.

All manner of sports can be enjoyed including golf on this course that blends into the natural surroundings.

C H A P T E R   1 6

BUILDING GREATER JACKSONVILLE

From concept to completion,
Jacksonville's building industry
shapes tomorrow's skyline.

279

Photo by Kelly LaDuke

WATSON REALTY CORP., REALTORS®

William A. Watson, Jr., president, who founded the realty firm in Jacksonville in 1965.

Watson Realty is people who are committed to making Jacksonville a better place to live.

Watson Realty is Jacksonville's number-one Real Estate firm, handling more than 30 percent of the sales in the Jacksonville, Clay County, and Beaches Multiple Listing Service—more than double that of any other firm.

The growth and expansion of Watson Realty to its present position is one of Jacksonville's true success stories. Bill Watson, the company's president and founder, opened a small office on Atlantic Boulevard in 1965, sharing space with an insurance company. A graduate of Stetson University with a major in Real Estate, he dreamed of a people-oriented company sensitive to the needs, wants, and desires of its customers and clients.

The firm has been built on the con-

Watson Realty is Jacksonville's number-one Real Estate firm, and is a major REALTOR in 50 offices from St. Marys, Georgia, to St. Petersburg, Florida. Pictured is the headquarters building at 11226-1 San Jose Boulevard, Jacksonville.

cept of excellence by going the extra mile, putting forth extra effort, and a commitment to making buying a home a most enjoyable experience. Watson Realty is known for its Home Advantage, which is centered around 400 highly people-oriented sales persons in the Jacksonville area, 27 committed managers, and an unequaled support staff.

Watson Realty is more than just Jacksonville, with 50 offices located from St. Marys, Georgia, to St. Petersburg, Florida, including Orlando, Tampa, Clearwater, Gainesville, Daytona, DeLand, New Smyrna Beach, Keystone Heights, Orange Park, the Beaches and St. Augustine.

Watson Realty's neighborhood concept offers the Home Advantage to its customers and clients with 21 sales offices located conveniently to all price ranges, styles, and areas of Duval and Clay counties.

The Home Advantage also includes an award-winning Commercial Division that handles office buildings, industrial and retail sites, and hotels and apartment buildings. It was also involved in site selection for several major commercial developments.

The Commercial Division has also developed special syndications and limited partnerships of a medical building, a manufactured home community, and single-family rental homes. The Commercial Division works in conjunction with four property management offices, located in Jacksonville, Jacksonville Beach, Orange Park, and Ponte Vedra.

To complete the Home Advantage, Watson Realty offers relocation services through its Corporate Relocation Division, one of the largest full-service corporate-transfer offices in Florida. The relocation office is dedicated to the needs of people being transferred in to and out of the North Florida area, with 10 people committed

Sue Fonda and Diana Kilman are part of the Corporate Relocation Division, one of the largest full-service corporate transfer offices in Florida.

Harvey Stringer, executive vice-president of the Commercial/Investment Division.

to helping the newcomer to the city. This office offers extra service and support through separate relocation centers in Tampa, Orlando, Gainesville, and Daytona.

Watson Realty also offers career counseling, a Real Estate School Division, and complete Real Estate train-

ing, all providing counseling on the ingredients for a successful Real Estate career and the necessary licensing requirements for securing a Real Estate license.

Watson Realty is a people company, committed to helping people with their Real Estate needs, desires, and wants—a company built around integrity and dedication to meeting your needs and desires.

MILLER ELECTRIC COMPANY

At nighttime in Jacksonville the glowing lights of the city's skyline reflect across the shimmering waters of the St. Johns. The vision must give even the most indifferent of residents a little shiver down the spine and a boost of pride in their city. No one should feel more pride than the people at Miller Electric Company. They are responsible for many of the electrical systems producing those lights. A driver cannot go many blocks in Jacksonville without passing a structure with an electrical system installed and/or maintained by Miller Electric.

Blue Cross/Blue Shield, Barnett Bank Building, Florida National Bank Building, Federal Office Building, Florida Theatre, Ivey's department stores, University of North Florida, FCCJ South Campus, and numerous area hospitals, hotels, and residential complexes have had their electrical contracting work performed by Miller Electric.

H.E. "Buck" Autrey, president and general manager of the company, says, "It makes me feel very proud—I

Miller Electric has done the electrical contracting work on a number of educational institutions, including the University of North Florida.

can drive a customer anywhere in the city and show him many jobs we've done."

Celebrating its 60th birthday in 1988, Miller Electric was founded in Jacksonville in 1928 by Henry G. Miller. His daughter, Jane Miller Wynn, serves as executive vice-president and secretary/treasurer of the firm today. She and Autrey are the two major stockholders of the corporation.

Miller Electric, which began as a residential electrical company, has grown to become one of the largest electrical contractors in the nation. Its annual sales volume surpasses $50 million.

Today the main thrust of the business is in the industrial sector, including nuclear waste management. Industrial contracting accounts for up to 70 percent of the firm's business. "We do more in pulp and paper and power production than any other area except nuclear," Autrey says. "We got heavily involved in the pulp and paper industry in the 1970s, both new and expanding plants, not only in Jacksonville, but throughout Florida and the Southeast."

Since the early 1970s Miller Electric has done the electrical work on nearly 75 major pulp and paper industry

Barnett Bank and other leading financial institutions have been longtime Miller customers.

projects, including Jefferson Smurfit Corporation's two mills in the Jacksonville area (Alton Packaging and Container Corporation of America), Seminole Kraft, Georgia Pacific, Gilman Paper Company, and St. Joe Paper Company. The largest such project was the major plant expansion for the Weyerhaeuser Company in Plymouth, North Carolina, in 1974, which required more than one million man-hours to complete.

Miller Electric's largest endeavor, one it began in 1951 and continues to this day, is the original construction and continuous expansion and maintenance of the Savannah River Nuclear Facility in Aiken, South Carolina. Thus far contract work there for the federal government has surpassed $200 million. "We have the longest-running federal contract with a single contractor in history. It's been ongoing for 37 years," says Autrey.

In addition to the Savannah River Plant, Miller Electric has performed electrical work for many municipal power companies in Florida, including the Jacksonville Electric Authority, Seminole Electric Cooperative, Lake Worth Utilities, and the City of Tallahassee.

Through the years the firm has had some interesting assignments, such as building launch complexes at Cape Ca-

Miller Electric's installation lights up the renovated Florida Theatre.

Riverside Hospital is one of many medical institutions that has benefited from Miller's high-tech sophisticated systems.

naveral and the underground distribution system for EPCOT Center at Walt Disney World.

More than 1,000 people are employed throughout the Southeast by Miller Electric, with approximately 250 of those in Jacksonville. More than 700 work at the Savannah River Plant. The corporation also has offices in Newport News, Virginia, and Orlando, Florida.

"Most of our management people began as electricians. This assures that the men in the office know just what the men in the field are going through," explains Autrey, who was an electrician with the company for 15 years before becoming president in 1966. He has also voluntarily served the electrical industry in various capacities, from the local level to serving as national president of the National Electrical Contractors Association from 1980 to 1986. He feels this "giving back" to the industry is most important and very rewarding personally.

Miller's business is divided equally between new installations and long-term service maintenance, including extensive renovation work for many

customers. Miller prides itself on its quick response to emergency situations. Says Autrey, "I don't remember ever losing a customer. We continue to do service work for people we installed for, and we also have a lot of service work-only customers. Customer Satisfaction Comes First is our motto.

"Our local service operation is one of the largest in the Southeast. Our cus-

The industrial sector accounts for the major part of Miller's business. The Jacksonville Shipyards has been a customer for many years.

tomers know they can call us and count on having qualified people on board to take care of their problems in a timely manner.

"Our company's greatest asset is our people. We have many employees who have been with us ever since they came electricians. They have an attitude toward quality and workmanship that is irreplaceable."

Miller Electric Company employees are also active in many community and charitable activities, and the corporation is a regular supporter of such organizations as the USO, YMCA, Boy Scouts, Prevent Blindness, numerous hospitals, and other charities.

SUMMERHOMES INCORPORATED

Charley Brown was one of those kids you couldn't leave alone for long.

The moment his mother would turn her back, Charley would start taking apart the alarm clock, dismantling the family radio, or disassembling some other household appliance. He was always fascinated with the way things worked, and built forts, boats, planes— anything he could think of.

Unlike his comic strip counterpart, Charley knew no fear. At age seven he was about to see if he could fly with a pair of wings he had built, when his mother caught him just in time at a second-story window.

Today, a half-century later, Charley Brown is still building, and he's still taking chances. One of Jacksonville's most prolific home builders, he is known for his unique designs, his concern for the environment, and his innovative use of computers in designing homes.

Brown's company, Summerhomes Incorporated, has built nearly 2,000 houses since its formation in 1975, and has grown to become one of the top 500 home builders in the country. During 1989 Brown expects to sell more than 350 homes, with sales surpassing $25 million.

Brown's homes run the gamut from attached townhomes to courtyard

Charley Brown, owner and president of Summerhomes Incorporated.

homes to single-family homes. They range in price from $50,000 to nearly $400,000 at the oceanfront Turtle Shores in South Ponte Vedra.

Following his natural instinct for building, Brown enrolled in the Massachusetts Institute of Technology (MIT) where he earned a degree in mechanical engineering design. After graduation he worked as a design engineer for Lockheed Aircraft, and later built aircraft and ship test facilities in the Navy involving the UNIVAC computer. He became interested in home building through a friend who built houses, and Charley "couldn't believe you got paid for doing something that was so much fun."

Brown gained experience working with U.S. Homes in Clearwater and later Fletcher Properties in Jacksonville. When he decided to start building on his own, he knew he wanted to create a different, and memorable, product.

"Most of the houses I had seen in Jacksonville were really northern houses, the kind of houses with long dark halls that totally shut out the outside," says Brown. "We design houses for this area of Florida, which has such a beautiful outdoors. In all of our homes we try to bring the outdoors inside by using a lot of light, vaulted ceilings, angled walls, and wooden decks.

"We try to produce homes that are more than just a box to keep the rain off. We build houses that are fun to live in, that a person can be proud of."

During his first year Brown constructed five homes. The next year he built 20. His company hasn't stopped growing since.

Today Summerhomes Incorporated has completed 22 communities in the Jacksonville area, and has another nine in various stages of construction. In recent years the firm has expanded from designing and building individual homes to designing and building entire communities.

"We feel very strongly that it's not just the home that is important, but the total neighborhood environment—the street layout, the entry, the drainage system, the recreational facilities, the

Business is facilitated with a Computer Aided Design system (CAD) with a hot line hookup to all sales offices.

The RiverWoods community in Arlington captures the natural elegance and rolling terrain of northern Florida.

entire concept, should all make it a wonderful place to live," Brown says.

Brown has earned a well-deserved reputation as an environmentalist. In his communities any tree that can possibly be saved is saved.

"Our feeling about the environment is very deep-seated. Building can be done in harmony with the environment. You don't have to go in and knock down all the trees and end up with a desert," he explains. "We spend a tremendous amount of effort on preserving the environment. We try to work with Mother Nature, rather than fighting her."

Brown has also won the respect of state historians for preserving archaeological artifacts found while clearing homesites. The first intact outline of a Timucuan Indian house was discovered in a Fort Caroline community that Brown was developing in 1987. Rather than bulldozing the site, as many developers legally might have done, Brown contacted a local archaeologist and set the site apart as a mini-park in the community. A few months later a 1,000-year-old Indian burial ground was unearthed in another community. Brown took three $25,000 lots off the market, and even paid for the archaeological work.

For his efforts Brown was presented a state award by the Florida Archaeological Society. He has won numerous other environmental and design awards, including being named one of the top five home builders in the country by the National Association of Homebuilders.

However, it is innovation in the field of computers that has brought him the most national acclaim. Presented with a prestigious Professional Achievement Award by *Professional Builder Magazine* for computer innovation, Brown has emerged as a national leader in the application of computers to home building. Summerhomes' Computer Aided Design (CAD) sys-

Beach Pavilion at Turtle Shores—a premier community in South Ponte Vedra.

tem allows the entire home to be designed on the computer, with alterations to the plan accomplished as easily as the push of a button.

"The computer virtually eliminates pencils, erasers, and drawing boards in our design department," Brown says. "It allows us to be more creative and to produce a lot more accurate, error-free drawings. The computer allows us to show much more detail, and redesign extremely fast."

Summerhomes uses computer design on a much larger scale than any other builder. Builders from around the country visit Summerhomes Mandarin offices to observe how the system works.

"We want people to have the homes they want, not the homes we want. The computer gives us the flexibility to give them what they want. We can make custom changes that used to take days in just a few minutes," Brown states.

In addition to being the first builder to introduce computer design

to northeast Florida, Brown also introduced one-bedroom homes and "mingle" homes to the community. Mingle homes have two master bedroom suites.

"Everyone has different needs, and we want to build homes that fit the buyer's specific needs. A retired couple isn't going to want the same kind of house as the young guy who drives a Corvette," he explains.

Brown sees himself as the "coach" of his company, with his more than 50 employees making up his team. "We believe home building is extremely important because it has a dramatic effect on people's lives. We have a tremendous responsibility to do it right," he says. "But we also have a lot of fun building houses. If you walk through our halls, you'll hear the laughter of people enjoying what they do."

On the chart of his company's structure, Brown places himself at the bottom and the customer at the top, with those employees who deal more closely with the customer nearer the top. "The bottom line," he says, "is happy home buyers."

Brown concludes, "We believe that good guys can finish first."

PAXSON ELECTRIC COMPANY

From Disney World's thrilling Space Mountain to EPCOT's majestic sphere to the statuesque Independent Life Building to the dazzling Jacksonville Landing, Paxson Electric Co. has installed the power systems that bring them all to life.

Those projects, along with dozens of high-rise office buildings, medical complexes, hotels and motels, shopping malls, and industrial plants, have established Paxson Electric as one of the leading electrical contracting firms

Jacksonville Convention Center. Photo by Judy K. Jacobsen

in the Southeast. Annual sales average $20 million to $25 million.

Wesley C. Paxson founded the company in 1957. He had become interested in electrical work from his stepfather, Henry Miller, founder of Miller Electric. Paxson went to Georgia Tech and graduated with a degree in electrical engineering. Tragically, Miller was killed in an automobile accident, so Paxson decided to start his own business.

Paxson began his venture out of the back of a garage, doing warehouse and other commercial work. By the end of the first year, his business was thriv-

ing. Its first major project, Jacksonville City Hall, cemented Paxson's place in the field. The firm grew rapidly thereafter.

"Jacksonville was growing, and we grew with Jacksonville," Paxson says. "We're a homegrown Jacksonville company, and we're proud to have been a part of Jacksonville's growth."

Projects that followed spanned every area of the commercial sector. "We cover a broad spectrum," says Paxson. "We like to think of ourselves as able to do the difficult, highly technical projects such as powerhouses, hospitals, and coal-handling plants. We have become more heavy industrial, high tech through the years."

Paxson Electric has been involved with multimillion-dollar installations at a number of pulp and paper companies, including Alton Box Board Company, Container Corporation, Georgia Pacific Corporation, and ITT Rayonier. The firm did much of the installation work at the Westinghouse-subsidiary Offshore Power Systems (OPS) during the 1970s, including the mammoth OPS crane, which was the largest crane in the world at the time.

Paxson's other industrial clients run the gamut of local manufacturers and distributors. The corporation continues to service its clients after completing the initial electrical work.

"We sent a man to Maxwell House 30 years ago, and he's still there," Paxson says. "The key to our success has been repeat business. We work hard to keep happy, satisfied customers."

The company also has wide experience in the field of power and energy plants, from complete utility power plants to total energy plants to substations to peaking units. Projects have included the Jacksonville Electric Authority's Northside and Southside stations, the Florida Power & Light Company's Sanford Station, and the coal-handling equipment, the precipitators, and flue gas equipment at St. Johns Power Park.

Office buildings the firm has

The Jacksonville Landing

Spaceship Earth—EPCOT Center

served as electrical contractor shape Jacksonville's skyline—Independent Life, Southern Bell Tower, First Union, Gulf Life, and the new American Heritage Jacksonville Center. Major suburban office buildings include State Farm regional headquarters, First Boston, and the state HRS headquarters. Hospitals for which Paxson was the electrical contractor include Baptist Medical Center, St. Luke's, St. Vincent's, University, and Methodist.

Approximately 90 percent of Paxson's projects are in the Jacksonville area, but the company has had major out-of-town contracts. Perhaps the largest of these was the $30 million in work completed at Disney World's Magic Kingdom and EPCOT Center. As one of the most dominant electrical contractors at Disney World, Paxson performed the electrical contracting for Space Mountain, Pirates of the Caribbean, Empress Lilly, World Telephone & Computer Building, and the Vista Communications Building in the Magic Kingdom.

At EPCOT Center, Paxson Electric's endeavors included Spaceship Earth, Communicore, the American Adventure, Mexico Pavilion, the East restaurant complex, the main entrance, and the central energy plant.

"Working for Disney is a very different experience. You're working more with the design than the engineering. The types of rides and visual presenta-

tions are much different than what we usually handle," Paxson notes.

At Disney World, Paxson was also the electrical contractor for the Royal Buena Vista Palace hotel and for the expansion work on the Polynesian Village hotel. The company's hotel projects have spanned the state, and include some of Florida's most exclusive accommodations, such as The Breakers expansion in Palm Beach, Omni International in Miami, the Ponce de Leon in St. Augustine, and the Hilton, Turtle Inn, and Thunderbird in Jacksonville.

The electrical work on the expansion of the Lake Buena Vista Shopping Village was also handled by Paxson, as were numerous other shopping and retail projects. Regency Square, Orange Park Mall, Roosevelt Mall's expansion, and a number of centers of comparable size in other Florida cities were Paxson

endeavors. Individual retail clients have included Ivey's of Florida, May-Cohens, Jordan Marsh, Kmart, Burdines, Maas Brothers, Neiman Marcus, JCPenney, Sears, Saks Fifth Avenue, Publix, Sav-A-Stop, and others.

The firm today has 50 permanent employees, with field employees running as high as 400, depending on what jobs are under contract. It maintains a staff of service personnel with a fleet of equipped and stocked trucks who are on call 24 hours a day to provide emergency service and repair as well as ongoing maintenance. Collectively, the staff has more than 400 years of electrical contracting experience.

Paxson serves as president of the company, and his son Wesley C. Paxson, Jr., is vice-president. Elbert Scott, Robert Lasseter, and Doris W. Loeke serve as officers and have been with the firm for many years.

A longtime civic leader in Jacksonville, Paxson was chairman of the Jacksonville Transportation Authority for eight years during the 1970s, being appointed to the board by Governor Claude Kirk and reappointed by Governor Reubin Askew. During his tenure J. Turner Butler Boulevard was built, and original planning work was completed for the Dames Point Bridge.

Paxson is also a past president of the Gator Bowl Association and the Jacksonville Museum of Arts and Sciences, and is past chairman of the Tournament of Players Championship golf tournament.

The Dames Point Bridge

FLORIDA ASPHALT CONTRACTING INC.

The idea for Florida Asphalt Contracting Inc. came to J. Richard Baker in the early 1970s, when he was hauling limestone to Jacksonville for his father's trucking company.

The limestone Rock Haulers Inc. was bringing from Gainesville was used as the base material in the roadbeds of Jacksonville's streets and highways. The question Baker kept hearing from the developers was, "Do you know any companies who do good paving work?'

Baker decided to create one. In 1974 he purchased equipment and hired the staff of a small contracting firm. Today the venture that began with sales of $400,000 a year earns $14 million annually and has become one of the largest paving companies in northeast Florida.

"It was tough going for awhile," says Baker. "Right off the bat, the recession caught us. But we weathered it, and grew slowly until 1980."

That year one of the largest paving companies in Jacksonville—Houdaille Duval Wright—closed down its state-wide operations, and Florida Asphalt hired many of the employees from that firm. "In one year we went from 30 employees to 130 employees," says Baker. "Then our real growth began."

Headquartered on five acres in Middleburg, Florida Asphalt Contracting Inc. specializes in residential, industrial, and commercial work. The company performs the entire turnkey job in paving projects, something that few firms do. The total road job includes the clearing and excavation work, the water and sewage drainage system, as well as the actual asphalt paving work. The corporation owns a wide array of heavy earth-moving machines.

Owned by Baker Enterprises, Inc., a holding company, Florida Asphalt Contracting Inc. is situated on this five-acre site. All of the companies under the Baker Enterprises umbrella are based in Middleburg.

Representative projects for which the company has performed the site work, paving, and drainage include the Florida Community College at Jacksonville Downtown Campus, Merchant's Walk Shopping Center in Mandarin, the Mike Shad Ford dealership, a number of office complexes in Southpoint office park, and a variety of warehouses, apartment complexes, restaurants, and commercial businesses in northeast Florida.

Building the roads in new residential subdivisions is a major component of the firm's business. Florida Asphalt has performed the road work in dozens of subdivisions throughout the Jack-

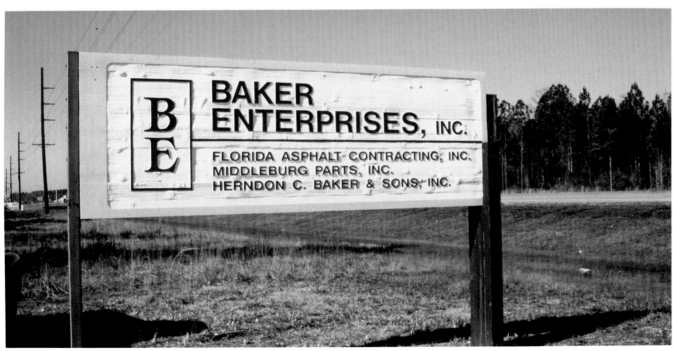

Florida Asphalt performed the site work, paving, and drainage for the Reynolds Smith & Hill offices (above) among others at Southpoint, and the Merchant's Walk Shopping Center in Mandarin (right).

In partnership with C. Finley Knight, Baker Enterprises has formed K&B Properties. One of its initial projects is the 89-unit subdivision Lake Woodbourne off Old King's Road in the Baymeadows area.

sonville area, including Mandarin, Baymeadows, the Jacksonville beaches, Orange Park, and the Monument Road area. In all, the company builds approximately 30 miles of roadway each year.

Florida Asphalt Contracting Inc. is owned by the holding company Baker Enterprises, Inc., which was formed in 1977. The corporation also includes Middleburg Parts Inc., which is a NAPA store, as well as Herndon C. Baker & Sons, Inc., which currently operates as a dredging company.

Richard Baker serves as president of the corporation; his younger brother, J. Daniel Baker, is the secretary/treasurer. Their father, Herndon C. Baker, no longer takes an active role in the organization, but remains chairman of the board. Rock Haulers Inc., the original company founded by Herndon Baker, continued to operate under the corporation until 1984, when it was sold.

The firm's newest venture is in the field of home building. In a partnership with builder C. Finley Knight, Baker Enterprises has formed K&B Properties. The company built the 89-unit subdivision Lake Woodbourne off Old King's Road in the Baymeadows area.

The Lake Woodbourne project consists of single-family homes in the $70,000 to $75,000 price range. The firm has plans for future development in a similar price range. Baker's son, J. Richard Baker, Jr., is heavily involved

in the home building company and serves as vice-president of J.R. Baker & Sons, Inc.

All of the companies that comprise Baker Enterprises are based in Middleburg. Florida Asphalt is by far the largest, with 130 employees, including heavy-equipment operators, laborers, pipe layers, and concrete finishers in addition to the full administrative staff. "The success of our business is the result of the people we have," says J. Richard Baker. "Without them, we wouldn't have anything."

The Baker family is heavily involved in local and state politics, as well as in community and charitable organizations. J. Daniel Baker is on the board of directors of the local Multiple Sclerosis Society, as well as being a member of the National Advisory

Council. He is an alumnus of Leadership Jacksonville Class of 1985 and has been a committee chairman at the Players Championship for the past several years.

J. Richard Baker serves on the board of trustees of Florida Informed Parents, Bolles School, the Southeast Jacksonville Rotary Club, and the Northeast Florida Builders Association. Baker Enterprises has lent its support to numerous worthy causes, including the Just Say No anti-drug campaign and leukemia research.

AUCHTER COMPANY

Auchter Company president William O. Mims remembers getting a phone call in 1987 from a newcomer to Jacksonville. The potential client asked, "Have you built anything in town I can look at?" Mims smiles to himself at the familiar question.

"I told him to go to his window, look to the left, then look to the right, and tell me what he saw," says Mims. "When he got halfway down Jacksonville's skyline, he said, 'That's enough.' We got his plans the next day."

One of the city's oldest construction firms, Auchter Company has virtually built downtown Jacksonville. However, the low-key organization has never been one to toot its own horn. Instead, Auchter has let the quality of the buildings it has constructed speak for itself.

Auchter's project list reads like a walking tour of the downtown area's most prominent structures: Independent Life, Southern Bell, First Union, Jacksonville City Hall, Duval County Courthouse, and Jacksonville Landing. Across the river at Southbank, Auchter erected the Gulf Life Tower, the Jacksonville Hotel, the new Prudential (joint venture) complex, Southeast Bank, and the Baptist Medical Center Pavilion. Auchter remains at the forefront of new high-rise construction downtown. It is constructing the new 23-story first phase of Jacksonville Center for Rouse and Associates.

In an age where the average life of a building contracting firm is six years, Auchter Company celebrates its 60th anniversary in 1989. Founded by George D. Auchter in 1929, the Auchter name has been synonymous with quality since the organization's beginnings.

"Mr. Auchter Sr.'s philosophy was to never take on any more work than you can properly handle," Mims says. "It was a successful philosophy then, and it's one we've always lived by. People are happy with the quality of our work. We get a tremendous amount of repeat business."

The organization also breeds loyalty in its employees. Many Auchter employees came to the company right

out of school and have never left. Two, and even three, generations of families have stayed with the firm.

There are no longer any members of the Auchter family involved with the company, but the son and grandson of one of the founders, James T. Monahan, are still with the firm. James T. Monahan, Jr., serves as senior vice-president and general superinten-

Auchter Company has had a decided impact on the Jacksonville skyline. The inset identifies Auchter projects in rendering period.

William O. Mims (left), president, and Donald Robinson, chairman of the board, of Auchter Company, one of Jacksonville's oldest construction firms.

dent. Wilbur H. Glass, Jr., executive vice-president, is the son of former Auchter president Wilbur Glass, who headed the corporation during the time the Gulf Life Tower and Independent Life Building were built.

"We have enjoyed a very favorable low-turnover rate, and that's a real plus in this industry. We have building superintendents whose fathers were superintendents with us," says Mims,

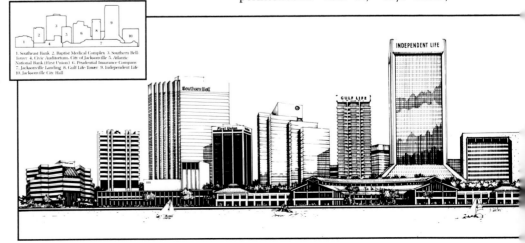

1. Southeast Bank 2. Baptist Medical Complex 3. Southern Bell Tower 4. Civic Auditorium, City of Jacksonville 5. Atlantic National Bank (First Union) 6. Prudential Insurance Company 7. Jacksonville Landing 8. Gulf Life Tower 9. Independent Life 10. Jacksonville City Hall

who has been with the company since 1949. He became president in January 1988 at the retirement of longtime president Arthur William Avent.

"A lot of contractors hire people for a specific job, and then let them go when the job's over. But if we find somebody who's good, we utilize them in other areas when the job is over until another job comes along," Mims says.

The contracting firm has a full-time salaried staff of nearly 60 employees, but total employment of the firm varies, running as high as 300 during major projects. The company's administration offices have been located at 1021 Oak Street in Five Points since 1957. Auchter's heavy equipment is kept at a four-acre facility at the foot of the Mathews Bridge off Talleyrand Avenue.

Originally a bridge builder, Auchter Company has through the years expanded its client base to include virtually every kind of commercial and industrial construction. In its early years the firm built numerous bridges throughout Florida, including the McCormick Bridge over the Intracoastal Waterway on Beach Boulevard, and a portion of the bridge piers for the Mathews Bridge. Auchter was one of the major contractors for Jacksonville's expressway system, and performed much of the original construction at the Jacksonville and Mayport naval air stations.

In the 1940s and 1950s Auchter expanded widely in the heavy-industrial sector, erecting a large number of power plants and paper mills, both in northeast Florida and statewide. In the Jacksonville area, Auchter served as building contractor for the Northside Generating Station Main Plant, and the Container Corporation of America, ITT Rayonier, Hudson, and Seminole (formerly St. Regis) paper mills.

Auchter began building hospitals in the 1950s, and today remains the area's number-one building contractor in the highly specialized health care field. The corporation has performed contracting work for and has an ongoing relationship with St. Vincent's Medical Center, Baptist Medical Center, St. Luke's Hospital, Riverside Hospital, and St. Augustine General Hospital.

Among landmark structures the company has constructed through the years are the Cummer Art Gallery, the Florida Publishing Company, the Jacksonville International Airport terminal building, and the Civic Auditorium in Jacksonville. Statewide, unique projects include the Palm Beach Breakers Hotel addition; the Florida State Museum in Gainesville; University of Florida classroom, dormitory, and law buildings; Century Tower; and the Marineland Hotel south of St. Augustine.

Auchter, although licensed in most southeastern states, builds primarily in northeast Florida, maintaining a yearly sales volume in the $40-million to $60-million range. Specializing primarily today in high-rise office structures, the company has had a heavy presence in the construction of suburban office parks. One major recent project is the BancBoston office complex in Cypress Plaza.

Setting Auchter apart from many other contracting firms is the fact that it has the capabilities of performing a wide range of construction services, including pile driving, concrete, excavating, carpentry, mill work, masonry, and iron work. Capabilities also include construction management services.

Because of the important role it has played in the creation of so much of Jacksonville's skyline, the firm feels a deep commitment to the community. A leading corporate citizen, Auchter Company takes an active role in numerous community activities and organizations, including the Boy Scouts, the Say No to Drugs campaign, Prevention of Blindness, the Jacksonville Wolfson Children's Hospital, and the United Way.

One of Auchter Company's more recent projects, the imposing Independent Life Building (right), contrasts with the historic Western Union Building (below), circa 1933, one of Auchter's first projects in Jacksonville.

HIDDEN HILLS GOLF AND COUNTRY CLUB

Hidden Hills Country Club is a family-oriented residential community of luxurious homes built by some of Jacksonville's most respected custom builders.

"Hidden Hills Country Club is a very family-oriented, residential community. We're definitely not a resort or second-home community," Newkirk says. "About 70 percent of our home buyers are under 49 years of age, and two-thirds of them have children."

A protected community with 24-hour guard service, Hidden Hills Country Club offers all the amenities of country club living. In addition to the 18-hole championship golf course, Hidden Hills offers its residents a new Olympic-size swimming pool, eight

Hidden Hills Golf and Country Club has been one of Jacksonville's most popular golf courses for two decades. Located on one of the most unusual pieces of property in Florida, the club's undulating hills and varied elevation have presented a distinct challenge to golfers found nowhere else in northeast Florida.

With the addition of 250 surrounding acres in 1985, Hidden Hills Country Club today is developing one of Jacksonville's most luxurious residential communities amidst the hills and valleys of the club's completely revamped golf course—designed by famed golfer Arnold Palmer. The course is the only Arnold Palmer-signature golf course within the city.

"Our property is unique to most of Florida," says Larry Newkirk, vice-president of Hidden Hills Golf Club and president of Hidden Hills Realty. "We have 50 feet of rolling elevation. Our lowest point is 30 feet above sea level, and our highest point is 80 feet above sea level. We have fabulous high lots that look down onto the golf course with lots of lakes scattered around the course."

During the next few years nearly 400 luxurious homes, priced between $175,000 and $700,000, will be built at Hidden Hills Country Club. Nearly half of the homes will be located directly on the golf course. Lots are

The clubhouse facilities have undergone a $3-million renovation, doubling its size and offering elaborate dining and lounge facilities, private conference rooms for business meetings, and an expanded golf pro shop.

priced from $50,000 to $150,000.

The elegant homes in the Hidden Hills community are being built by some of the city's most respected custom builders. Home buyers may choose to have any builder construct their home, but plans must be approved by an architectural review committee.

All homes in the community are single-family dwellings on one-third-acre lots, plus they offer 45 detached patio homes that begin in the $175,000 range. The Masters Ridge patio home development offers four elaborate models from which to choose, each with a variety of floor plans and lavish extras.

rubico clay tennis courts, complete locker room facilities, and a health club that includes whirlpools, steam rooms, and full Nautilus and aerobics programs. Initiation fees for the club are included in the purchase of a home.

In addition to the renovation and expansion of the golf course, the clubhouse facilities have also undergone $3 million of massive improvements. The clubhouse has doubled in size to 36,000 square feet and includes elaborate dining and lounge facilities, private conference rooms for business meetings, and an expanded golf pro shop.

The strongly supported tennis program at Hidden Hills includes a new pro shop, lounge, and observation deck. Both the tennis and golf programs are led by well-respected professionals in the community.

The golf course, which remained

playable throughout the transition, was designed by Arnold Palmer with the everyday country club golfer in mind but with enough challenge to captivate the most seasoned professionals. To complement all levels of play, he added multiple tee markers on each hole. Palmer's restructuring lengthened the course to 6,850 yards, widened fairways substantially, and expanded the greens. A player may expect to use every club in the bag during a round.

Palmer's signature hole on the course is the exciting Number 11, a 630-yard dazzler that ends with an island green. Golfers may choose from one of seven different tee boxes for their approach to the hole.

"Arnold Palmer was personally involved in the design of the course and has come here several times to personally inspect the course. It's a fabulous

The golf course was designed by famed professional golfer Arnold Palmer (inset) with the everyday golfer in mind. In a round a player may expect to use every club in the bag. Golf course photo by Linda Mathews; photo of Arnold Palmer courtesy, TPC

golf course made more interesting by the rolling elevation and the talents of Arnold Palmer."

Hidden Hills Country Club is located near the intersection of Monument Road and Fort Caroline Road in one of the most rapidly growing sections of Jacksonville. The centralized location is 11 miles to the Atlantic Ocean, 10 miles to downtown, and 5 miles to Regency Square Mall. With the opening of the Dames Point Bridge, the Jacksonville International Airport will be just a 15-minute drive from Hidden Hills.

"Some of our buyers have told us they're moving to Hidden Hills from the beach in anticipation of the Dames Point Bridge opening, because they do a lot of traveling and are tired of the long drive to the airport," Newkirk says. The widening of Monument Road to four lanes and the construction of a nearby elementary school are also big pluses for the community, he adds.

Owned by partners James E. Putnal and Wayland T. "Tommy" Coppedge III, Hidden Hills Country Club was opened in 1967. The club hosted the Greater Jacksonville Open, the predecessor to the Tournament Players Championship, from 1970 to 1972, as well as other tour events. The new golf course homesites, and related facilities are the finest in the area. Hidden Hills Golf and Country Club offers incomparable living standards.

WALTER DICKINSON INC.

Baymeadows, Regency Square, and Orange Park are three of Jacksonville's largest boom areas of the 1980s and the fastest and most convenient places for a majority of city residents to do a little shopping, get a bite to eat, or take in a movie.

Perhaps no one in Jacksonville has played a greater role in the development of these and other commercial properties in Jacksonville than the Walter Dickinson Inc. commercial real estate firm.

With total annual sales in the $50-million range, the organization has sold property for hotels, office buildings, shopping centers, industrial centers, and restaurants to many of the nation's leading corporations, including Pizza Hut, McDonald's, Taco Bell, Kinney Shoes, Shell Oil, Church's Chicken, Red Roof Inn, La Quinta Inn, Bennigan's, Hardee's, and many more.

A full-service real estate company, Walter Dickinson Inc. provides corporations looking to expand or relocate in Jacksonville with assistance in site selection, leasing, property management, and multifamily and investment properties, as well as the mainstay of its business—helping clients find the most profitable locations for their operations.

Since Walter Dickinson, Jr., opened his venture more than two decades ago, the company has grown to include 18 full-time realtors in the Jacksonville office, which is headquartered in a suite of offices in the Independent Life Building.

Because half of its business is in out-of-town markets, the firm has expanded to include a branch in Tampa, headed by Dickinson's son Eddie, and plans call for the opening of an Orlando office.

"We purposely grow slowly as the need arises. We want to continue to give good service and quality," says Dickinson, a Jacksonville native and graduate of Emory University who once served on Jacksonville's City Council. "We look for team players. Our business is geared toward cooperation. We have very little turnover here. That's one of our strong points."

All of the company's sales staff have a formal education as well as years of experience in the field. It is the people he has working for him, according to Dickinson, that have given his organization a national reputation for quality among some of the country's corporate giants.

Dickinson says his firm has a tremendous volume of repeat and referral business from satisfied customers, and through the years it has developed a sprawling referral network with large independent brokers nationwide. "They prefer to call us rather than a national real estate company," he adds. "We've been told by many large national companies we've worked with that we're one of the most professional companies in Florida."

Walter Dickinson Inc.'s office maintains information on areas of growth and development both in Jacksonville and in other parts of the state and Southeast, and provides clients with assistance in analyzing properties that have investment potential.

The specialist in commercial industrial real estate.

Courtesy, David Dobbs

Memorial Medical Center, 298-299   *Baptist Medical Center, 303*

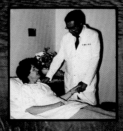

Riverside Hospital, 310-311   *St. Luke's Hospital, 312*

QUALITY OF LIFE

Medical and educational institutions
contribute to the quality of life of
Jacksonville area residents.

297

MEMORIAL MEDICAL CENTER

Memorial Medical Center has become one of the city's most progressive, highly diversified health care facilities since opening its doors in 1969 as a private, nonprofit hospital.

Located in the heart of Jacksonville's Southside, near the intersection of University and Beach boulevards, Memorial Medical Center places special emphasis on personalized care and providing state-of-the-art services and equipment for diagnosis and treatment of illnesses.

Nearly 600 physicians representing all major specialties and subspecialties have privileges at Memorial. The hospital employs a total staff of 1,500.

The 353-bed medical center offers emergency treatment, a critical care center, and six Centers of Excellence, which are areas that provide special expertise and service as fine as any in the region.

Women's Services
A comprehensive array of services is available to women at Memorial Medical Center. The perinatal center includes birthing rooms, primary care nursing where the nurse takes care of both mother and baby, individual nurseries beside each mother's room, neo-

Located at the intersection of University and Beach boulevards, Memorial Medical Center is one of the city's most rapidly growing health care facilities.

natologists, and a complete offering of childbirth and sibling preparation classes.

For couples having trouble conceiving, Memorial has the region's only In Vitro Fertilization Clinic. Treatment is offered for male and female infertility. During the center's first two years of operation, there were three successful IVF births.

Three different modalities for detecting breast disease in women are available at the Breast Imaging Center.

The center has mammography, as well as multispectral transillumination and ultrasonography.

Rounding out the comprehensive array of services for women is the dual photon densitometry device, used in the detection of osteoporosis. In a surprisingly simple, 45-minute procedure similar to X ray, hospital staff can determine the progressive calcium loss in the bone structure, which is largely responsible for osteoporosis.

The Center for Heart Disease
Memorial Medical Center has developed one of the finest heart disease facilities in the area. The center offers the most sophisticated diagnostic testing equipment available today, including PET (Positron Emission Tomography), thalium treadmill tests, CAT Scans, and S.P.E.C.T., which provides a three-dimensional view of the heart. Services also include heart catheterization, angioplasty, and open-heart surgery.

Oncology
The Oncology Unit at Memorial Medical Center is made up of several different teams of health care professionals offering chemotherapy, radiotherapy, and surgery. The oncology staff operates its own pharmacy, outpatient treatment room, and tumor registry, and is involved in the testing of new drugs and treatments.

As part of an extensive guest relations program, Memorial's Courtesy Car transports hundreds of visitors a day from the parking lot to the medical center.

The Joslin Diabetes Clinic

The Joslin Diabetes Clinic at Memorial is the only satellite of the internationally known Boston Diabetes Center and offers a full range of services for diabetic patients. Attracting patients from throughout Florida and the Southeast, the Joslin Diabetes Clinic has the benefit of calling on Boston-done research that aggressively examines the potential causes of diabetes, and better methods of treatment. Studies involving the testing of new drugs and treatments are often available to patients at the Jacksonville Clinic.

Memorial Regional Rehabilitation Center

Memorial Regional Rehabilitation Center is the largest rehabilitation hospital in the region, serving up to 128 inpatients and 200 outpatients on a daily basis. The hospital treats disabled

The mammography screening at the Imaging Center is an important part of the many services available to women at Memorial Medical Center.

Memorial Regional Rehabilitation Center, which helps physically disabled adults and children, is the largest facility of its kind in the state.

adults and children suffering from spinal cord injuries, cerebrovascular accidents, brain injuries, amputations, and other illnesses and accident-related disabilities.

Outpatient Services

For those patients who do not require hospitalization, Memorial Medical Center offers one of the most beautiful and comprehensive outpatient centers in the country. In 1987 more than 30,000 patients had outpatient procedures performed, ranging from cataract surgery to hernia operations.

The Imaging Center provides all imaging modalities in one central location. The center houses an eight-ton MRI, CAT Scan, Nuclear Medicine, and X ray.

Other Services

Working in conjuction with the Memorial Rehabilitation Center is Memorial's Pain Management Center, which provides a comprehensive program of treatment for people suffering with chronic or terminal pain. During an intensive outpatient program, a medical team analyzes the source of pain and prescribes a method to treat pain, or gives the patient guidelines to follow to live with the pain in a way that does not make it the focal point of his life.

Another special center operated by Memorial is the Health Care Center, which acts as an occupational walk-in facility for local businesses. Services in-

clude physical examinations, workers' compensation, work-release exams, drug and alcohol screening, X ray, and laboratory services.

H.E.A.R.T.—The Center for Health and Fitness—is an ultramodern facility with 17 Nautilus machines, stationary bikes, treadmills, rowing machines, whirlpool, wet and dry saunas, locker rooms, and showers. A full range of exercise classes, including aerobics and stretch, are offered throughout the day and evening. Programs are available for pregnant women and seniors.

Guest Relations

To help ensure that visitor and patient stays at Memorial Medical Center are as pleasant and comfortable as possible, Memorial has instituted a guest relations program. It includes a Courtesy Car that picks them up in the parking lot and takes them to and from the medical center. A guest relations specialist is available in the medical center lobby to provide directions and information as needed. Another guest relations specialist visits patients in their rooms and answers any questions they might have.

For the Community

Memorial Medical Center offers extensive community services, including education classes, seminars, a speakers' bureau, newcomers program, tours, health screenings, and special events. The medical center also maintains a physician referral and information service, which allows callers to obtain the names of physicians who have access to the many services at Memorial Medical Center.

BAPTIST MEDICAL CENTER

Baptist Medical Center, the largest hospital in northeast Florida, has earned a reputation for excellence in health care through its technological advances and innovative health services.

From modest beginnings as a 125-bed hospital in 1955, Baptist has grown to a 579-bed regional medical center that is one of the most sophisticated diagnostic and treatment facilities in the nation. Baptist Medical Center (BMC) is a recognized community leader in such areas as cancer, cardiac care, pediatrics, obstetrics, pulmonary disease, outpatient surgery, sleep disorders, women's services, urology, radiology, and many others.

BMC is one of the city's leading employers, with a staff of 2,400. Its 860 physicians, many of whom are known worldwide, represent all major medical specialties and subspecialties.

William C. Mason, FACHE, president and chief executive officer of Baptist, leads a progressive management team that continually seeks new and better ways to meet the health needs of the community. Because of a flexible management approach and adherence to a well-defined strategic plan, members of Baptist's medical staff are able to achieve individual and professional goals, which in turn benefit patients and the community at large.

BMC's riverfront campus on Jacksonville's Southbank spans nearly 16 acres and includes the new multifunctional, 17-story Baptist Medical

The Baptist Medical Center complex continues to expand with the recent opening of the 17-story Baptist Medical Pavilion. This multifaceted structure encompasses the Wolfson Center for Mothers and Infants, the Baptist Health and Fitness Center, The Pavilion Inn (a 48-room hotel), other hospital services, physicians' offices, and commercial businesses.

Pavilion, and the area's preeminent pediatric facility, Jacksonville Wolfson Children's Hospital. Nemours Children's Clinic, under construction just across Interstate 95, will be linked to BMC by an automated skyway express. The affiliation between Wolfson Children's Hospital and Nemours will create a "pediatric center of excellence" of national scope.

Wolfson Children's Hospital cares for more than 25,000 children each year. The 125-bed, full-service, acute care hospital is the largest pediatric specialty medical center in northeast Florida and the second-largest in the state. The hospital emphasizes that children are special patients requiring special care.

The special care is provided through a team approach, which extends beyond physicians and nurses to include physician assistants, therapists, social workers, chaplains, and volunteers. Education, play therapy, and entertainment programs help make the children's stay a little easier. Specialized health care facilities in the Wolfson Children's Hospital include a neonatal intensive care unit, a pediatric emergency care center, a pediatric intensive care unit, pediatric radiology, and a pediatric outpatient surgical unit.

BMC president and chief executive officer William C. Mason, FACHE, visits one of the playrooms at Jacksonville Wolfson Children's Hospital. These fun-filled rooms provide a welcome diversion for children requiring medical care at JWCH.

The Cogeneration Energy Complex saved Baptist Medical Center more than $1.4 million in energy costs during 1987. This complex, which made BMC the first fully energy-independent hospital in the nation in 1982, serves as a model for hospitals and other industries throughout the United States.

The new, $30-million Nemours Children's Clinic will operate in a cooperative joint effort with Wolfson's Children's Hospital, serving as a major outpatient diagnostic center for children. The clinic will house facilities for physical, respiratory, and occupational therapy. Treatment programs are provided for children with scoliosis, spina bifida, muscular dystrophy, rheumatoid arthritis, open wounds, and burns. Sports medicine, general orthopedics, genetic counseling, and numerous other services are available.

The Wolfson Center for Mothers and Infants—located on the second and third floors of the new Pavilion—specializes in high-risk obstetrics and emphasizes family-centered childbirth, offering a variety of options. Six birthing rooms allow women the opportunity to experience labor, delivery, bonding, and recovery in a homelike setting with family members present.

The neonatal intensive care unit is located immediately adjacent to the de-

livery area, and a postpartum unit offers individual care to new mothers and their families. A term nursery provides "rooming in" parenting education.

The Wolfson Center also houses the Women's Resource Center, which includes a library, educational programs, support services, and a comprehensive health care program for women

New mothers and their babies enjoy the recently opened Wolfson Center for Mothers and Infants located in the Pavilion at Baptist Medical Center. The center provides ultramodern delivery facilities and homelike birthing rooms, as well as a nursery and a neonatal intensive care unit.

who undergo procedures that do not require hospitalization. The professional staff of the Baptist Health and Fitness Center prescribes comprehensive, individualized health programs. Facilities include Nautilus exercise equipment and an indoor jogging track.

Adjacent to the fitness center is the Cardiac Rehabilitation Center, an integral part of the Baptist Heart Center. The Physical Therapy Department includes outpatient orthopedic services, the Back School, and The Jacksonville Sports Medicine Program, the only one of its kind in the country that focuses on the health and safety of student athletes.

The remainder of the Pavilion

Minutes count when serious illness or injury occurs. Life Flight provides 24-hour air-ambulance service to the ill and injured of Jacksonville, northeast Florida, and southeast Georgia. Staffed by specially trained nurses and technicians, this BMC service is indeed an asset to the community.

of all ages. For the early detection of breast cancer, the Northeast Florida Breast Care Center provides diagnostic mammography and ultrasonographic testing.

In addition to the Wolfson Center, the Pavilion is also the home of the medical center's Outpatient Lab and Ambulatory Surgical Unit for patients

complex houses physician offices and a unique, 48-room hotel designed for patients and their families. Especially convenient for out-of-town patients, The Pavilion Inn allows family members to be close by during a loved one's hospital stay. High-risk obstetrics patients who are confined to bed sometimes stay in the hotel during the

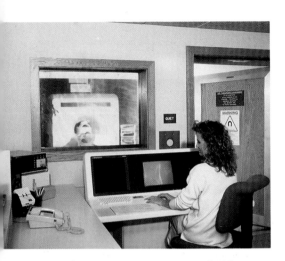

The magnetic resonance imager (MRI) is provided by Nemours Children's Clinic and located at BMC. This machine uses a magnetic field to diagnose abnormalities in the central nervous system. This state-of-the-art technology does not use X rays; rather, it yields high-resolution pictures with far less risk to the patient.

weeks preceding their delivery.

Two primary areas of specialization and expertise at BMC are in cardiac care, through the Baptist Heart Center, and in the treatment of cancer, through the Malone Cancer Institute which includes the Williams Cancer Treatment Center.

The Baptist Heart Center, home of the Heart Emergency Network, provides comprehensive heart services, including catheterization, angioplasty, open-heart surgery, and cardiac rehabilitation. The center's physicians and surgeons have also established a comprehensive educational program to help the public understand the risks of heart disease and take steps toward reducing those risks.

Regular medical seminars, community workshops, and special events help patients understand the cause, diagnosis, and treatment of cardiovascular disease, and physicians conduct in-depth research and hold regular seminars and cardiovascular conferences to stay abreast of the most recent health care developments. Such renowned heart surgeons as Drs. Christiaan Barnard and Michael DeBakey have been part of Baptist's educational series.

The Malone Cancer Institute cre-ated the first comprehensive cancer program in the community. The center employs all known methods of detecting and treating cancer and performs ongoing research into finding new ways of fighting the disease. The oncology department is designed to meet the diagnostic, therapeutic, nutritional, rehabilitative, psychosocial, and spiritual needs of both the patient and the family, and the Williams Cancer Treatment Center, the community's foremost radiology center, is the only cancer facility in northeast Florida that uses radiation therapy, hyperthermia, and radioactive implants.

BMC is also a leader in the field of urology. The Southern Kidney Stone Center of Jacksonville—a joint venture between Baptist, St. Vincent's Medical Center, Memorial Medical Center, and Humana-Orange Park Hospital—is located on the BMC campus, and offers one of the region's lithotripter facilities, which uses sound waves to nonsurgically treat kidney stones. Noninvasive procedures such as this one are the wave of the future in health care, and BMC is at the forefront.

Baptist is the home of the city's first Alzheimer's center, offering medical, diagnostic, and treatment services for those suffering from the progressive, organic brain disorder. There, a team approach is used, in which the patient, family, physician, behavioral scientist, and representatives of social services, nursing, and rehabilitation, work together in an atmosphere of pastoral care.

A comprehensive program of services and activities for all senior adults is available through BMC's 55+ Connection. Services provided through the program include health and fitness, medical assistance, education, leisure activities, and other special services.

In the area of emergency care, the Johnston Emergency Center is open 24 hours a day, seven days a week, to handle both routine emergencies and major trauma cases. The center includes 17 examination and treatment rooms, and separate pediatric areas. Baptist's Life Flight, the first 24-hour emergency helicopter service in Jacksonville, makes approximately 1,000 flights per year, transporting emergency patients to the medical center for treatment.

One of the most common causes of stroke is the narrowing of the carotid arteries with the buildup of plaque. BMC now has the Quantum, a device used in the noninvasive procedure called Angio-Dynography. With this procedure disturbances in the flow of blood to the brain can be identified.

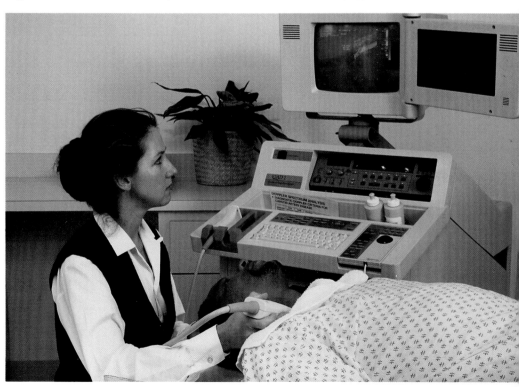

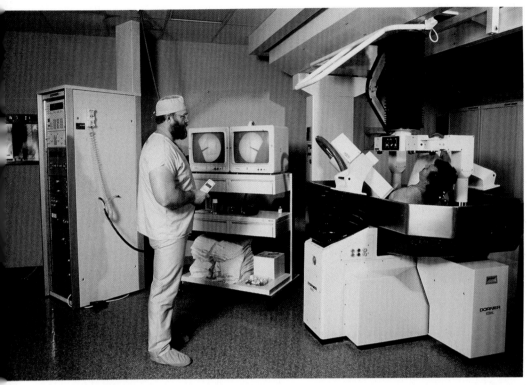

BMC also has specialists who deal with psychological problems. The Psychiatric Unit, Jacksonville's largest, provides a comprehensive, individualized diagnostic and treatment approach, carefully planning activities and therapy to assist in recovery.

BMC is regarded in the medical community as a leader in health education, sponsoring in excess of 1,500 programs annually for continuing medical education, staff training and development, and community health education at the 220-seat Jessie Ball duPont Center for Continuing Health Education.

The medical center is affiliated with the Jacksonville Health Education Program (JHEP), a division of the University of Florida College of Medicine. The Baptist Medical Center-Jacksonville University School of Nursing graduated its first class of nurses in 1986.

As Baptist continues to provide excellence in education, professionals coordinate the on-site operations of the BMC School of Radiologic Technology, BMC School of Phlebotomy, and the School of Medical Technology.

Community education is offered through a number of seminars and spe-

Baptist Medical Center, Memorial Medical Center, Humana-Orange Park Hospital, and St. Vincent's Medical Center jointly purchased a $2-million lithotripter. This equipment is used for the noninvasive crushing of kidney stones. The procedure uses shock waves transmitted through water, which in turn crumble kidney stones into particles the size of grains of sand. These particles are then passed painlessly through the body's normal elimination system.

cial events in such areas as smoking cessation, marriage, parenting, confronting grief, and coping with chronic illness, to name a few. The medical center supports numerous community, civic, and charitable events, including River City Kids' Day and other major health events.

Conversely, hundreds of members

of the community become involved in Baptist Medical Center each year through its volunteer programs. Three organizations—BMC Auxiliary, the Jacksonville Wolfson Children's Hospital Auxiliary, and the Women's Board—have a combined membership of more than 1,000 volunteers who generously donate their time to service and fund-raising activities.

In its effort to deliver the most efficient, high-quality care possible at the lowest cost possible, Baptist has made several significant strides at conserving resources to provide affordable health care. The medical center's Total Energy Center, opened in 1982, provides BMC with 100 percent of its energy needs. The first hospital in the country to be completely energy independent, BMC has saved its patients more than $7 million. Other savings are realized through shared services—such as laundry—and purchasing arrangements with other hospitals.

In every aspect of providing quality health care services to the community, Baptist Medical Center strives for excellence through sound management practices and bold innovation. Following its creed that "To be good is not enough. To be the best is the constant challenge," Baptist Medical Center is drawing the blueprints today for the highest-quality health care of tomorrow.

The Williams Cancer Treatment Center at Baptist Medical Center was the first comprehensive cancer center in North Florida and continues to stand alone as it utilizes radiation therapy, hyperthermia, and radioactive implants. The center houses the latest equipment and state-of-the-art technology, including the 20 MEV Linear Accelerator.

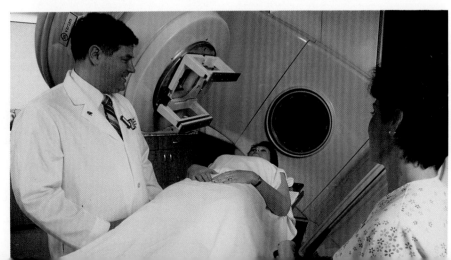

UNIVERSITY HOSPITAL

One of the foremost teaching hospitals in the Southeast, University Hospital is an innovator in health care, offering numerous special services unique to the Jacksonville medical community.

As Jacksonville's only major teaching hospital, University has successfully accomplished the perfect blend of progressive education, in-depth medical research, and high-quality patient care.

The hospital is a major affiliated teaching hospital of the University of Florida Health Science Center, offering graduate medical residency programs in 15 specialties to 250 residents from around the country. All of the 135 full-time attending physicians on staff are University of Florida faculty members.

Serving northeast Florida and southeast Georgia since 1870, University Hospital was a public institution until 1982, when it became a private, not-for-profit facility. A longtime provider of medical care for the city's indi-

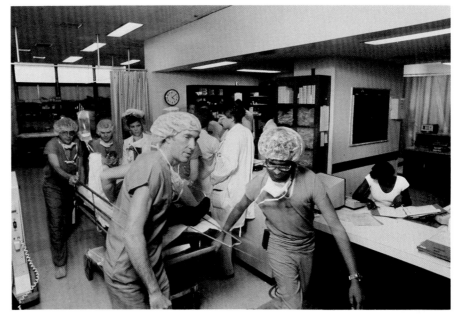

Doctors and nurses transport a gunshot wound victim from the trauma center to the operating room where highly trained trauma surgeons operate to save lives every day.

gent population, University continues to hold the sole contract with the city to render medical care to the poor, and remains committed to this service.

The 485-bed hospital provides comprehensive programs in diagnosis, treatment, mental health, and rehabilitation on an inpatient and outpatient basis. A five-story outpatient clinic houses care centers for 97 subspecialties, such as sickle cell anemia, spinal

cord injuries, and pediatric diabetes.

At the forefront of special services offered only by University Hospital of Jacksonville is the level one trauma center, TraumaOne, which provides highly specialized and immediate care for people who are critically injured.

TraumaOne is the only level one trauma center in North Florida, and one of only four in the state. Named one of the top 20 trauma centers in the country by *Reader's Digest* magazine, it is ready with a fully staffed professional team 24 hours a day, 365 days a year. TraumaOne recently opened a new state-of-the-art trauma center.

The unit's TraumaOne helicopter rushes specially trained staff to the scene of accidents, saving critical time for accident victims. The TraumaOne helicopter is a twin-engine BK-117 and the most advanced emergency medical services aircraft available. The helicopter also is specially equipped to give cardiac care to heart attack victims.

TraumaOne is a critical part of University's emergency department, which is by far the busiest emergency department in North Florida, seeing more than 90,000 patients each year.

The TraumaOne helicopter, a BK-117, is the most advanced aeromedical spaceship available and transports critically ill patients to University's level one trauma center 24 hours a day.

University is also the home of the area's only state-designated highest-level neonatal intensive care unit. The unit treats nearly 500 high-risk newborns each year, accepting transfers of newborn babies from Florida and South Georgia. A team of specially trained nurses and respiratory therapists is on call 24 hours a day, every day of the year. A new 33-bed addition to the unit is under construction as part of a six-floor clinic expansion.

The city's only pediatric cardiovascular surgery program is housed at University Hospital, and is one of only four such programs in the state. In 1985 University initiated the Korean Heart Program, giving free lifesaving heart surgery to eight Korean children each year.

University's overall cardiovascular services are the most comprehensive in the city, including patient care and rehabilitation, teaching, and research.

The only pediatric kidney dialysis clinic in Jacksonville is located at University, as well as the city's first adult dialysis clinic. The hospital has the only program in the city offering home dialysis training, and has one of only two chronic peritoneal dialysis units in Jacksonville.

The prenatal diagnostic program specializes in early detection of chromosomal and structural defects in the unborn child, and treats all local high-risk mothers either directly or through referrals.

University Hospital has always

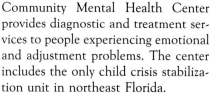

These two smiling children are part of University's Korean Heart Program in which eight Korean children each year are given free lifesaving heart surgery.

More than 500 newborn critically ill babies are treated each year in University's sophisticated level three neonatal intensive care unit.

been a leader in the treatment and care of cancer patients. The first facility in Jacksonville to offer radiotherapy, University offers the most sophisticated and technically advanced equipment in the area in its ultramodern radiation oncology center.

The institution specializes in the care and treatment of uterine and cervical cancer, and has the only two board-certified gynecological oncologists in the city on staff. It is also the only center in the city offering MOHS surgery, an advanced method for treating skin cancer.

Mental health is an area of major concern and service at University. The Community Mental Health Center provides diagnostic and treatment services to people experiencing emotional and adjustment problems. The center includes the only child crisis stabilization unit in northeast Florida.

Residents at University further their education by working closely with staff physicians and hundreds of volunteer physicians in general areas of medicine as well as in their particular field of specialization. Residency programs are offered in the specialties of anesthesiology, emergency medicine, family practice, internal medicine, obstetrics/gynecology, ophthalmology, oral and maxillofacial surgery, orthopedics, pathology, pediatrics, pharmacy, plastic surgery, radiology, surgery, and general dentistry. Dental students rotate through the University of Florida College of Dentistry in Jacksonville, a multichair clinic that treats a wide variety of local patients at minimal cost. University of Florida nursing students also gain experience through the affiliation with University Hospital as part of their training.

With more than 2,000 employees on staff, University is a multibuilding complex located on a several-block campus near the intersection of Eighth Street and I-95. Constantly in the process of expanding its services and facilities, the hospital currently has a number of construction projects under way, including a large new faculty clinic building and parking garage.

Playing a vital part in the operation of the institution is a large staff of volunteers. The University Hospital Auxiliary has rendered both time and monetary aid since 1952. Another important volunteer group is University Hospital Development Council, which is dedicated to both monetary and community support for the hospital through work with civic and business leaders.

A major fund-raising effort of the hospital is the year-round Children's Miracle Network project, which culminates in a telethon held each spring. Proceeds directly benefit University Hospital's children's medical programs.

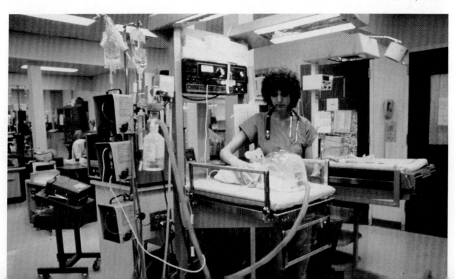

ST. VINCENT'S MEDICAL CENTER

St. Vincent's Medical Center, Jacksonville.

St. Vincent's Medical Center has provided the Jacksonville community with quality health care for more than 70 years, establishing itself as a leader in many areas including cardiac, pulmonary care, orthopedics, and neurosurgery.

Through its Heart and Lung Institute, St. Vincent's is at the forefront of research, technology, diagnosis, treatment, patient care, and physician and community education in the battle to reduce the number of deaths attributed to cardiovascular and pulmonary problems.

A pioneer in open-heart surgery in the Southeast, St. Vincent's performs more of the lifesaving procedures than any other medical institution in the area, and its program has emerged as one of the best in the nation. The hospital's heart team is composed of highly respected cardiologists and surgeons from around the country, supported by a highly skilled nursing staff.

Cardiac care at St. Vincent's includes cardiac catheterization, balloon angioplasty, cardiac rehabilitation, and noninvasive diagnostic procedures such as stress testing, nuclear cardiology, Holter monitoring, and echocardiography. St. Vincent's physicians perform more than 1,500 cardiac cath-

eterizations each year in the medical center's new catheterization lab. In all, more than 10,000 heart procedures have been performed at St. Vincent's during the past five years.

The medical center's pulmonary staff provides all aspects of pulmonary care, including intensive care, sleep studies, respiratory therapy, and pul-

monary rehabilitation. Because of the high rate of lung cancer in Duval County, St. Vincent's is focusing on the research and treatment of the disease, using laser technology as one treatment method.

St. Vincent's is a state-designated acute care spinal cord injury center. An entire nursing unit with a specially trained staff is devoted to the care of neurosurgery and neurology patients. A separate 40-bed unit is dedicated to the treatment and care of orthopedic patients.

St. Vincent's was founded in 1916 when, at the request of physicians and community leaders, Daughters of Charity representatives came to Jacksonville to take over the operation of a small institution called DeSoto Sanitorium. The name was soon changed to St. Vincent's Hospital, and the Sisters turned it into an efficient, well-respected institution.

St. Vincent's has experienced steady growth through the years. The private not-for-profit institution that maintained 42 beds to treat 622 patients during its first year has grown to

Both diagnosis and treatment of heart disease are performed in the heart catheterization lab. Here a team performs balloon angioplasty, an alternative to surgery for some patients.

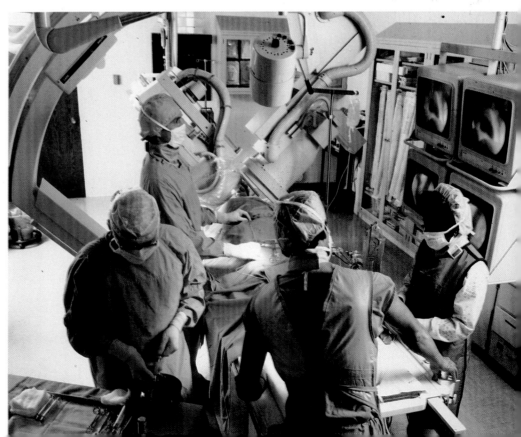

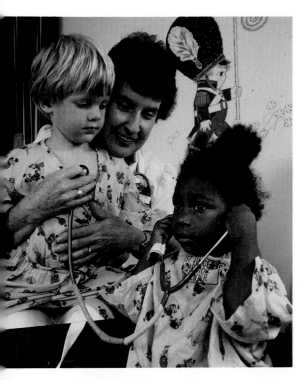

Children on the pediatric unit receive quality care and loving attention from the nursing staff at St. Vincent's Medical Center.

Generating an intense, sharply focused beam of electromagnetic energy, lasers are unique tools for many medical and surgical applications. State-of-the-art laser techniques permit surgeons to destroy cancer cells while leaving normal cells intact.

ter's Heart and Lung Institute, the St. Vincent's Imaging Center, along with other areas, to be housed in the building.

In addition to the strong leadership role St. Vincent's has taken in the areas of cardiac and pulmonary care, the medical center's oncology department is among the best in the Southeast. St. Vincent's team of highly skilled professionals includes specialists in every facet of cancer prevention, diagnosis, treatment, nursing care, and psychological and emotional support. St. Vincent's is one of the few cancer treatment centers in northeast Florida that is approved by both the American College of Radiology and the American College of Surgeons. It's the first hospital in northeast Florida to operate an American Cancer Society office within the medical center to offer patients educational information and support.

Another of St. Vincent's major departments is the Department of Obstetrics/Gynecology, which has shared in the birth of thousands of children during the years. Special family-related classes are offered through the Diocesan Center for Family Life. St. Vincent's childbirth unit provides the latest procedures in fetal monitoring, "rooming in" with the newborn, and sibling visitation. A 10-bed Level II Special Care unit serves babies who have critical care problems. St. Vincent's Bereavement Program offers counseling support to parents who have lost a baby during pregnancy or shortly after birth.

For older children, the medical center has a 29-bed pediatric center. Smaller children are prepared for their hospital stay through a special Pediatric Orientation Program (POP), which includes a puppet show and slide and videotape programs.

Ophthalmology is another area of expertise and leadership at St. Vincent's. With three surgical suites equipped with the most sophisticated technologies available, the medical center is capable of performing a broad range of eye-care services and surgeries. Its nine active ophthalmologists perform more than 1,800 eye surgeries per year, including 1,500 cataract surgeries.

St. Vincent's broad range of services includes critical care units to provide optimal care to the critically ill and 24-hour emergency services to treat a variety of immediate medical and surgical needs. The emergency room is designated a Level II Trauma Center. St. Vincent's also is the home of the area's only Poison Control Center, with a specially trained pharmacist on duty 24 hours a day to respond to poisonings or suspected poisonings.

The medical center's Home Care service was one of the first hospital-based home health agencies in Florida, and provides nursing care; physical, occupational, and speech therapy; and nutrition information to home-bound patients.

Educational classes offered by St. Vincent's include diabetes education, early pregnancy, childbirth, sibling classes, cardiac education, smoking cessation, and numerous others. The medical center sponsors two television programs, "Health Matters" and "Health Live," to help educate the public about medical concerns.

St. Vincent's Medical Center also plays an active role in community and charitable events, including the Players Championship, the River Run, the Jacksonville Marathon, and the Bausch and Lomb Tennis Tournament.

become northeast Florida's second-largest medical center, with 518 beds, treating nearly 25,000 patients each year.

Today St. Vincent's employs more than 2,200 individuals, with 250 physicians on active staff. The full staff of physicians approaches 800. The medical center is led by Sister Mary Clare Hughes, who has been president since 1986.

The only Catholic hospital in the northeast Florida area, St. Vincent's provides millions of dollars worth of charitable medical care each year to the city's indigent and needy.

The medical center's facilities span several acres on the banks of the St. Johns River in Jacksonville's Riverside section. Renovations to the medical center include the addition of the 300-seat Bryan Auditorium, a radiation oncology department, and the renovation of a majority of patient rooms. The nine-story DePaul Office Building, which includes physicians' offices and a 482-parking-space garage, opened in 1988. Plans call for the medical cen-

McIVER UROLOGICAL CLINIC

The professional staff at McIver Urological Clinic.

At the forefront of innovation in the field of urological care for more than 50 years, the McIver Urological Clinic is the oldest urological group practice in the state of Florida. The clinic was founded by Dr. Robert Boyd McIver, an internationally known pioneer in urology who was one of the first board-certified urologists.

Today the clinic is composed of seven board-certified urologists who provide full patient care in the diagnosis, care, and treatment of the diseases of the male and female urinary and reproductive organs. The urologists utilize both medical and surgical treatment of diseases involved in the kidneys, bladder, ureters, urethra, male genitalia, and prostate.

The clinic is affiliated with most major hospitals in the area. A regional practice, the McIver Urological Clinic treats patients throughout northeast Florida and southeast Georgia. Through the years the clinic has provided a leadership role in the innovation of the newest medical technology in the field of urological care. Located at 710 Lomax Street in the Riverside

area of Jacksonville, the clinic is a full-service, state-of-the-art diagnostic and treatment facility.

The clinic physicians are Dr. Joseph B. Stokes, Jr., Dr. Jack L. Sapolsky, Dr. James N. Burt, Dr. John R. Whittaker, Dr. Paul M. Crum, Dr. James A. Baldock, and Dr. Richard H. Lewis. All are Fellows of the American College of Surgery and are certified by the American Board of Urology.

The physicians are also active in lo-

cal, state, and national affairs, as well as serving in leadership roles in local hospitals and the medical societies. In addition to the seven physicians, the clinic employs a full complement of medical support personnel to assist in all areas of expertise.

The growth of McIver Urological Clinic has paralleled the growth of the community, bringing the latest technology in urological care to the area.

Affiliated with most major hospitals in the area, the McIver Clinic, at 710 Lomax Street, provides the latest medical technology in the field of urological care.

JACKSONVILLE UNIVERSITY

Rugg's Recommendations on the Colleges ranks Jacksonville University among the top 14 percent of colleges and universities in the country, particularly noting its biology, marine science, and music programs.

A private, independent, coeducational institution founded in 1934, Jacksonville University has an enrollment of more than 2,300. Approximately half of the students are from Florida; the others come from 40 states and 40 foreign countries and live in eight on-campus dormitories.

Students are enrolled in one of three colleges—the College of Arts and Sciences, the College of Business, or the College of Fine Arts. Degrees are offered in 60 undergraduate and 14 graduate fields of study.

Specialized programs offered by the university include nursing, mechanical engineering, aviation management, marine science, education, and pre-professional preparation in medicine, dentistry, veterinary science, law, and engineering. Particularly popular programs are the executive master of business administration (EMBA), which draws many of the nation's top executives as guest lecturers, and the College of Weekend Studies, which enables nontraditional students to earn a college degree while maintaining full-time jobs.

The faculty is composed of more than 100 full-time scholars, teachers, and artists, 70 percent of whom hold doctorate degrees, a percentage above the national average. While JU professors regularly engage in research projects and author articles for professional journals, they place high priority on teaching and share a deep commitment to excellence and the liberal arts.

Serving as president of Jacksonville University since 1979 is Dr. Frances Bartlett Kinne, Florida's first female university president. A familiar face on campus with faculty and students alike, Dr. Kinne knows many students on a first-name basis and sets the tone for the close relationship between students and faculty. The average class size is kept small—17—to ensure close student-professor interaction.

JU's beautiful 214-acre campus, overlooking the St. Johns River in Arlington, is composed of 27 modern buildings nestled among native magnolias, stately palms, and ancient moss-draped oaks. The Phillips Fine Arts Building is the home of the Alexander Brest Museum, which contains one of the finest private collections of Oriental and European ivories in the nation. The Swisher Auditorium seats 540 and is fully equipped for staging theatrical productions. Housing the university's library collection of 350,000 volumes is the Carl S. Swisher library. One of the newest and most modern buildings on campus is the striking, $3-million Davis College of Business.

Athletic facilities include the Swisher Gymnasium, baseball and soft-

Students relax and study on the Student Center patio with one of the university's newest additions, the striking $3-million Davis College of Business, in the background.

The Gooding Building, one of 27 modern structures on the beautiful JU campus, is a two-story structure with classrooms and offices connected by a walkway to an auditorium seating 255 people.

ball diamonds, a soccer field, tennis and racquetball courts, a nine-hole golf course, an archery range, a track, the Lonnie Wurn swimming pool, and a boathouse.

JU fields strong intercollegiate teams in a number of sports, and has found particular success in basketball, baseball, soccer, and crew. The Dolphin basketball team reached the NCAA finals in 1970 and was the Sun Belt Conference champion in 1986. Crew also holds a strong national reputation and has competed in such interesting locales as the Nile River in Egypt.

Jacksonville University's small classes, dedicated faculty, friendly campus, and superb location present unlimited opportunities for students to prepare for outstanding futures.

METHODIST HOSPITAL

Called "The Miracle On Eighth Street" by president Marcus E. Drewa, FACHE, Methodist Hospital has undergone a dramatic transformation since it was founded in 1967 in the turn-of-the-century former Brewster Hospital building.

The opening of the hospital's new seven-story medical center in late 1988 signifies the completion of an ambitious master plan set in action in the early 1970s. The institution's growth during the past two decades includes the construction of twin medical towers and the $40-million expansion and renovation of the former St. Luke's Hospital property.

Today the 244-bed hospital and all its facilities span five city blocks on Eighth Street in Northside and include a full employment of more than 1,000. A nonprofit community hospital offering comprehensive medical care, Methodist is known throughout the community for its hospice unit for the terminally ill and its center for the treatment of alcohol and drug abuse.

Patient comfort is a primary concern at Methodist.

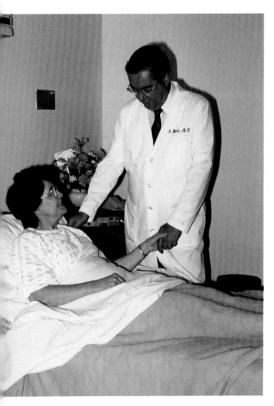

An artist's rendering of the new Methodist Medical Center.

Drewa, president of the hospital since its founding and former administrator of Brewster Hospital, organized the original effort to open Methodist with a group of civic leaders headed by Jacob F. Bryan III, then chairman of the board of Independent Life and Accident Insurance Company. With property leased from the Women's Division of the Board of Missions of the United Methodist Church, the hospital became the first Methodist hospital established in Florida. Methodist also was the state's first all private-room, private-bath hospital.

In 1975 the first of two medical plazas opened, followed by an adjacent twin tower five years later. The 10-story buildings house doctors' offices, support services, and such health care programs as Hospice, Pathway, the Ambulatory Center for Surgical and Diagnostic Services, and other community-related services.

In 1984 Methodist purchased the adjacent St. Luke's property, and initiated a building and renovation program that produced the Methodist Pavilion, which houses surgical and emergency services.

The new Methodist Medical Center, also located on the restored property, will be the home of three patient bed floors, an intensive care unit, and ancillary services. It will also include a pharmacy, cafeteria, gift shop, and chapel, as well as admitting, social services, medical records, and other offices. Physical therapy, respiratory therapy, and cardiopulmonary therapy services will also be located in the building.

The hospital's active and courtesy staff of 440 physicians represent virtually every medical specialty. The hospital offers medical care in all specialties except obstetrics and pediatrics.

Methodist established the city's first comprehensive hospice program in 1980. Methodist Hospital Hospice provides a full program of physical, psychological, social, and spiritual care for the terminally ill and their families. Members of the hospice staff work together as a team to identify the individual needs of each patient and family member. The team members work together to give compassionate, efficient care in both the inpatient unit and in the patient's home.

Methodist Pathway Center, located in the Methodist Plaza, offers a comprehensive treatment program to individuals and their families who suffer from alcohol and/or drug dependencies. Care includes primary treatment, inpatient and outpatient treatment, after-care, and a family program. The program maintains contact with the patient and family over a two-year period to increase chances of recovery. In addition, the center provides intervention services, in which family and friends of a substance abuser meet with the troubled individual to encourage him or her to seek treatment.

Methodist is also widely known for the Diabetes Treatment Center. One of only 21 centers in the country recognized by the American Diabetes Association for quality patient education programs, it provides an individual treatment plan for each patient, developed and monitored to assure close control of blood-sugar levels. The center approaches patient care through a team approach led by the patient's physician. Each patient participates in an extensive education and training curriculum that includes such topics as diet, urine and blood-sugar testing, insulin administration, skin care, exercise, complications, and research.

The hospital provides emergency medical care 24 hours a day, seven days a week in the new 12-bed emergency room. The Level II Trauma Center includes a specially equipped cast room, X-ray room, two resuscitation rooms, and a major trauma room with direct access from the ambulance entrance. The center also includes a decontamination chamber for burn and chemical-spill victims.

Doctor/nurse interaction is essential to provide well-rounded, quality care to each patient.

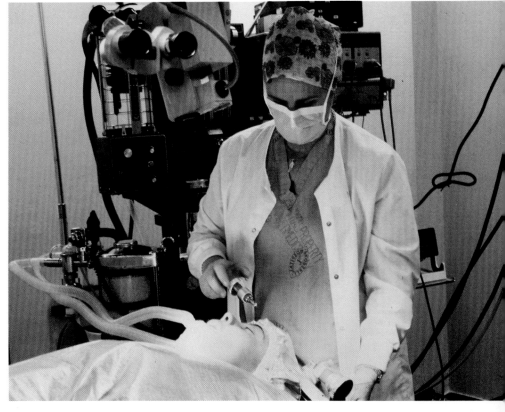

Expert care is given to each patient.

To better serve patients who can be treated on an outpatient basis, Methodist operates the Ambulatory Center for Surgical and Diagnostic Services. The center offers a wide range of diagnostic services and surgical procedures that can be performed on an outpatient basis.

For patient recovery at home, the

ABC Home Health Services provides a complete network of health professionals who perform medical, social, and support services in the patient's home. An affiliate of Methodist Health System, ABC Home Health Services offers such home services as skilled nursing, physical therapy, occupational therapy, speech therapy, home health aide services, and social services. Highly responsive to patients on an individualized basis, the program allows patients to function within their families and in the community while recovering from illness.

A leader in health education in the community, Methodist's Charter Center for Health Education offers complete facilities for medical seminars, training sessions, and educational programs. Methodist's Center for Wellness and Disease Prevention provides instruction in such areas as nutrition, smoking cessation, stress management, and exercise, as well as offers a wide range of programs to promote wellness and reduce life-style risk factors.

ST. LUKE'S HOSPITAL

St. Luke's Hospital holds the distinction of being Jacksonville's oldest—and newest—hospital.

Founded in 1873 as Florida's first private hospital, St. Luke's today is one of the city's newest, most modern hospitals headquartered in a facility that opened in December 1984. Located in Southpoint off J. Turner Butler Boulevard, the 289-bed, state-of-the-art medical complex is part of a 52-acre "complete campus of care" that includes two physicians' office buildings housing doctors representing virtually every medical specialty.

In 1987 St. Luke's became a Mayo-affiliated hospital. As part of the Mayo Medical Network, St. Luke's works closely with Mayo Clinic Jacksonville, which is situated nine miles east of the hospital. Nearly 100 Mayo physicians have privileges on the medical staff, and virtually all Mayo patients requiring hospitalization are admitted to St. Luke's. At the same time St. Luke's has maintained an open medical staff, with some 400 community physicians practicing medicine at the hospital.

A not-for-profit hospital, St. Luke's operates as a general acute care facility, providing services on an inpatient basis in every specialty except obstetrics, pediatrics, and psychiatry. In addition, outpatient services, including same-day surgery, are available, and comprehensive emergency medical

Founded in 1873, St. Luke's Hospital holds the distinction of being Jacksonville's oldest and newest health care facility. The new 289-bed hospital, opened in 1984, is part of a 52-acre "complete campus of care."

treatment and urgent-care services are offered through the hospital's 24-hour emergency center.

Orthopedics is a field of particular specialization at St. Luke's. The hospital provides a broad spectrum of orthopedic services, including microsurgery, arthroscopy, and total joint replacement, many of which are performed in the hospital's specially designed operating suite featuring the city's only complete-wall Laminar Flow air-purification system.

Led by a team of hand and microvascular surgeons, St. Luke's Hand Services offers reconstruction, replantation, and rehabilitation in the treatment of all hand disorders, deformities, and potentially crippling diseases such as arthritis.

St. Luke's cardiology services are extensive, featuring a state-of-the-art heart catheterization lab and specially designed open-heart surgery suites. The hospital also takes a leadership role in cancer treatment and research. The program at St. Luke's Hospital offers a multidisciplinary approach to both the treatment and clinical research of can-

cer. The unit, which is staffed by both community and Mayo Clinic physicians, offers the city's only autologous bone marrow transplants and, through its access to the Mayo Comprehensive Cancer Center in Rochester, Minnesota, will provide future treatments for patients not currently available at any area hospitals.

A leader in diagnostics, St. Luke's was the area's first health care facility to offer Magnetic Resonance Imaging (MRI) and features the nation's only "cassetteless" radiography system.

Throughout its long history St. Luke's has always been a leading resource for health education and information. A series of Health Events provide the community with seminars, classes, and publications to increase public awareness of health issues.

St. Luke's is also one of a handful of hospitals nationwide, that participate in the Johnson & Johnson Live For Life health promotion program. Through this wellness program the hospital currently offers a full range of health and fitness activities to its employees, as well as to area businesses.

A Mayo-affiliated hospital since 1987, St. Luke's is a general acute care facility providing services in every specialty except obstetrics and pediatrics.

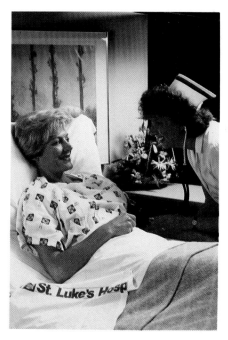

Courtesy, Wendell Metzen

C H A P T E R   1 8

THE
MARKETPLACE

Jacksonville's retail establishments,
service industries, and products are
enjoyed by residents and visitors
to the area.

315

BURGER KING®
(SOUTHERN INDUSTRIAL CORPORATION)

The second-largest fast-food hamburger restaurant chain in the world started right here in Jacksonville in 1954 with a small unit on Beach Boulevard.

The rest is fast-food history, with Burger King® Restaurants now located worldwide with more than 5,000 units and providing in excess of 250,000 jobs.

It all started when the Stein family developed an attractive business that became one of the front-runners of the fast-food industry. Under the direction of David Stein, president and chairman of the board for Southern Industrial Corporation, the parent company of the Jacksonville-area Burger King® franchise, the restaurants experienced tremendous growth.

In 1967 the Burger King® trademarks were sold to two Miami businessmen, and then sold to the Pillsbury Corporation.

Stein retained the franchise rights to all restaurants located in Duval, Clay, and St. Johns counties. Today

Jacksonville's newest Burger King® Restaurant, located at 210 State Street.

Stein oversees 19 Burger King® Restaurants in Jacksonville, two at the beaches, one in St. Augustine, and one in Orange Park.

Each restaurant averages more than one million dollars in sales annually. The company employs more than 1,000 people in the tri-county area, making it one of Jacksonville's largest employers.

Always on the lookout for growth opportunities, Stein established King Provision Corporation, a full-line independent distribution company that presently provides Burger King® Restaurants throughout the South with food items, paper products, cleaning supplies, and uniforms. Stein recently opened satellite distribution centers in Tampa, Florida; Louisville, Kentucky; and Atlanta, Georgia, to further accommodate the company's rapid business growth.

With David Stein holding the reins, the firm has been a successful family operation. David's father, Ben Stein, was an investor in the early years of the company, while brothers Albert and Martin serve on the board. David has even brought his daughter, Tracey, on board to head up sales and market-

David A. Stein, president of Southern Industrial Corporation.

ing for the distribution company.

Ever since the first Burger King® Restaurant opened on Beach Boulevard, the firm has taken an active part in civic and community activities. While Stein himself serves on the boards of such organizations as the March of Dimes, the Jacksonville Chamber of Commerce's Committee of 100, the United Way, and the Jewish Community Alliance, his company's officers and employees are involved in more than 30 local civic and charitable projects.

The history of Stein's business is that of success and pride, but Stein has no intention of resting on his laurels. In the Jacksonville area, Stein is continually planning on future restaurant locations for "The Home Of The Whopper®."

SHERATON AT ST. JOHNS PLACE

Wooden planks stretch for blocks underfoot, moored boats rock gently in the water, and alluring restaurants with seafood specialties tempt the taste buds.

There is definitely a mood reminiscent of Fisherman's Wharf at the Sheraton at St. Johns Place on Jacksonville's Riverwalk. The riverfront complex, which opened to much fanfare in 1980, was modeled after a similar one at the San Francisco waterfront.

The opening of the Sheraton at St. Johns Place—and the 1.2-mile Riverwalk five years later—brought about a total transformation of the entire Southbank area across the St. Johns River from downtown Jacksonville. What once was an area of overgrown lots and broken-down buildings today is one of the primary focal points and entertainment spots of the city.

The entire complex includes the 350-room Sheraton at St. Johns Place hotel, its two restaurants, and two separate riverfront dining establishments—Crawdaddy's and The Chart House—as well as a strip of riverside offices.

Popular with tourists and business travelers alike, the Sheraton at St. Johns Place is also the largest convention hotel in the city of Jacksonville. The hotel's 20 meeting rooms vary in size from 360 to 10,000 square feet, with total exhibition area encompassing 20,000 square feet. Banquets can accommodate up to 1,000 people, while theater-style seating is available for 1,400.

More than 40 major conventions

The 350-room Sheraton at St. Johns Place is the largest convention hotel in the city of Jacksonville.

The Sheraton at St. Johns Place overlooks the 1.2-mile Riverwalk, a popular gathering place in Jacksonville.

each year are held at the Sheraton at St. Johns Place, ranging from meetings of pharmacists to public relations professionals to military engineers. Large foyers outside the meeting rooms are suitable for exhibit space and are well used during trade shows held at the hotel. A popular appeal of the five-story establishment is that all the meeting space is located on the first floor, with meeting rooms side by side.

Priding itself on the hotel's reputation for good service, the Sheraton management employs a staff of 300—nearly one employee per guest room.

The interior of the structure's lobby and meeting room area is designed with a nautical motif resembling the interior of a ship, with exposed piping in the ceiling and nautical artwork throughout.

The Sheraton's Admiralty Restaurant is a favorite among local connois-

seurs, and is the winner of numerous statewide Golden Spoon awards for its gourmet dining. The Watergarden Cafe is the hotel's casual dining spot, featuring breakfast and lunch fare. The Cameo Bar in the lobby area is a pleasant place to relax.

A swimming pool and two lighted tennis courts are available for guest convenience, and taking a stroll or jogging along the Riverwalk are also popular pastimes of hotel guests. River taxis will take Sheraton guests and other Riverwalk visitors across the St. Johns River to the city's new Jacksonville Landing festival marketplace and other downtown sites. Also, the river can be crossed easily by car or on foot at the nearby Main Street Bridge.

The Sheraton has an outside catering service that caters such events as weddings, corporate dinners, and other occasions at various Jacksonville locations, including aboard yachts.

Sheraton Hotels, Resorts & Inns Worldwide operates more than 500 hotels worldwide. The Sheraton at St. Johns Place is owned by Wharfside II Limited Inc.

SCOTT-McRAE GROUP

Walter A. McRae, Jr., chairman and chief executive officer.

Woodrow Wilson was president, Prohibition was right around the corner, and the country was abuzz about a new invention called the telephone. The year was 1916. And another not-so-old invention was beginning to make its presence felt throughout the United States.

Henry Ford was selling Model T automobiles as fast as his assembly line could produce them, and Ford dealerships were beginning to appear around the country to sell the popular cars. In Jacksonville, the Duval Motor Company was opened downtown, becoming one of the very first Ford dealerships in the state.

Today, nearly 75 years later, Duval Ford is the oldest continuously owned Ford dealership in Florida and one of the largest Ford dealers in the nation. Located for many years at the corner of

Lee and Forsyth streets downtown, the dealership expanded to the point that it outgrew that facility, and in 1968 moved to its present 16-acre location at 1616 Cassat Avenue.

Today Duval Ford is the flagship company of the Scott-McRae Group, which consists of six automobile dealerships, a leasing company, an advertising company, a fleet sales company, a real estate firm, and a vehicle preparation service. The group realizes annual sales in excess of $144 million, has more than $47 million in assets, and employs 500-plus people.

Walter A. McRae, Jr., and Jack L. Scott began a partnership in 1947 that

still exists today. McRae is the son of Walter McRae, Sr., who joined the Duval Motor Co. in 1922 and took over ownership a few years later. From that point on, the company grew steadily in sales and service, surviving the lean years of the Depression and World War II, in which many dealerships fell by the wayside.

In 1982 the partners formed the Scott-McRae Group as a holding company under which all the businesses were placed. It was in 1984 that Henry H. Graham, Jr., was promoted to the position of president and chief operating officer and began further company expansion. In addition to Duval Ford, which is by far the largest of the companies, the organization owns Duval Honda, Duval Isuzu, Duval Hyundai, Duval Acura, All Fleet, Scott-McRae Advertising, Scott-McRae Properties, and Spectrum Services in Jacksonville, as well as Tampa Hondaland in Tampa and Autolease in Jacksonville and Tampa.

Duval Ford is one of the largest used car dealers in northeast Florida and regularly leads all Ford business in the Jacksonville area. Duval Ford carries all the models of cars, vans, and light trucks produced by Ford Motor Company, including Crown Victoria, Thunderbird, Taurus, Mustang, Tempo, Escort, Festiva, Aerostar, Econoline vans and conversion vans, Bronco and Bronco II, Ranger, and F-150 and F-250 pickups.

The parts department at Duval Ford is one of the largest and best stocked in the Southeast. Composed of 17,000 square feet of space, the department has more than one million dollars in inventory on hand.

Duval Honda was the second Honda franchise in Florida, and among the first 100 in the nation. As the popularity of this line of imports grew rapidly, the Honda sales department became Duval Honda in 1978. Since then increased sales have brought about two expansions, and the dealership is located in a newly renovated facility at 1290 Cassat Avenue. Duval Honda operates the largest exclusively Honda parts warehouse in Florida and is the

Jack L. Scott, vice-chairman.

Henry H. Graham, Jr., president and chief operating officer.

leader in wholesale parts in the Honda Group. A sister company, Hondaland, has operated in Tampa since 1981.

Duval Isuzu was created in 1980, offering a wide assortment of cars and trucks, including the Impulse, PUP, heavy-duty KS-22 truck, I-Mark, and the Trooper II. Located at 1810 Cassat Avenue, Duval Isuzu operates a full-service department and truck shop, and has a wide inventory of factory parts.

Not far away, at 7233 Blanding Boulevard, is Duval Hyundai, the company's third quality import car dealership, which was opened in 1986. Duval Hyundai markets the Excel, including the GLS four-door sedan and five-door hatchback. The city's first Hyundai dealership, it has met with phenomenal success.

In 1986, on the other side of the city on Atlantic Boulevard, Duval Acura was opened, the first Acura dealership established between Atlanta and Orlando. The prestigious, luxury automobile is designed for the discriminating customer. Duval Acura has the largest exclusive Acura parts inventory in the Southeast.

Scott-McRae's Autolease firm has operated since 1952 and currently has a leasing fleet in excess of 1,100 automobiles and trucks in its two southeastern locations. All Fleet, located on the Duval Ford lot, provides small and large fleets of cars to an expanding list of customers. Spectrum Services prepares new and used vehicles for sale, installing various accessories and reconditioning used vehicles. Located at 5201 Waterside Drive in Jacksonville, Spectrum was founded in 1985.

Outside of the automobile industry, Scott-McRae also includes Scott-McRae Advertising and Scott-McRae Properties, a real estate firm. Operating for more than 25 years, the advertising agency originally came into being to promote the automobile operations, but has since branched out to serve a diverse group of clients throughout the community. The real estate company was founded in 1985 to coordinate existing real estate investments for the group and to locate properties for future dealerships and investments.

Scott-McRae Group supports a wide variety of community and charitable organizations, including the Muscular Dystrophy Association, the Gator Bowl Association, Jacksonville University, Edward Waters College, and the United Way.

Members of the group actively participate in the Jacksonville Chamber of Commerce, with Walter A. McRea, Jr., a past president; Jack Scott, a former member of the board of governors; and Henry Graham, Jr., currently a member of the board of governors.

RING POWER CORPORATION

Founded in 1961 by L.C. "Ring" Ringhaver, the company was first appointed an engine dealer for Caterpillar, with headquarters located in St. Augustine. In 1962 the company acquired the entire Caterpillar line, and headquarters were moved to Jacksonville.

Today, with L.C. Ringhaver's son, Randal Ringhaver, as president, Ring Power employs more than 500 people in six branches throughout North Florida. In addition to the corporate headquarters in Jacksonville, which is located on 30 acres with more than 214,000 square feet of building space, the company has full-service facilities in Ocala, Tallahassee, Perry, Lake City, and Gainesville.

As well as handling Caterpillar products, Ring Power is also a dealer for several other manufacturers, including Raymond Corporation and Generac. To support these numerous products, Ring Power offers complete parts and service backup. The company main-

For more than a quarter-century Ring Power Corporation has been a prime contributor to the growth of Jacksonville and North Florida.

A full-line dealer for Caterpillar Inc. since 1962, the company handles a diversified line of equipment for construction, earth moving, logging, and other applications, as well as engines for truck, marine, and industrial uses; generators; and material-handling equipment. In addition to new, the company has quality used, rebuilt, and reconditioned machines for purchase, lease, or rent from the largest inventory in the southeastern United States. Additionally, the company actively exports equipment, principally in Central and South America, through its International Division.

Ring Power Corporation's corporate headquarters is located on 30 acres at the corner of Phillips Highway and Baymeadows Road.

Three Caterpillar generator sets supply all the electrical power cooling and heating for most of the Jacksonville facility. Excess electrical power produced is sold to the Jacksonville Electrical Authority.

build buckets, attachments, and other items to support its equipment sales.

The company places strong emphasis on preventive maintenance. Programs such as Scheduled Oil Sampling (SOS) spot potential trouble before breakdowns occur; Technical Analysis service vehicles perform complete diagnostic evaluations of job-site equipment; and Custom Track Inspection Service helps keep track-type equipment running at the lowest-possible cost per hour.

Ring Power showcases its advanced technological capabilities in its Energy Center, a 4,000-square-foot cogeneration facility located at the company's Jacksonville complex. The facility provides all the electrical power cooling and heating for most of the Jacksonville offices.

Through this advanced technology and a sincere dedication to the development of new and improved products, Ring Power Corporation's strong commitment to customer service and excellence will continue to be a driving force in the growth of Jacksonville and North Florida.

tains a parts inventory of more than 70,000 items, providing a parts availability unequaled in the industry. An on-line computer processes parts orders and also networks with Caterpillar parts depots and other dealers. This helps provide emergency parts service 24 hours a day, seven days a week.

In addition to parts availability, Ring Power offers complete service programs that are second to none. With more than 300 mechanics, 123 service bays, and radio-dispatched field service trucks that are equipped with state-of-the-art technology, customers are assured of receiving the finest workmanship available in the industry.

Engines, transmissions, undercarriage, and other components can be rebuilt at Ring Power's in-shop service facilities. And the company's specialization repair areas allow technicians to test these components under simulated operating conditions.

In addition to the product support activities, the company has recently established a manufacturing division to

Caterpillar equipment ranges from large track-type tractors to front end loaders, engines, generators, lift trucks, and more.

ATLANTIC MARINE, INC.

Huge aircraft carriers such as the Forrestal *are repaired by Atlantic Marine's Mayport Division on the Navy base.*

From huge passenger ferries to oceanographic research vessels to crab trawlers and shrimp boats to space shuttle booster-recovery ships, Atlantic Marine, Inc., has built them all.

From Navy minesweepers to vast aircraft carriers to luxurious cruise ships to patrol boats and tugs, Atlantic Dry Dock Corporation and Atlantic Marine's Mayport Division have repaired them all.

An overview of the shipyards of Atlantic Marine and Atlantic Dry Dock, located on Hecksher Drive where the Intracoastal Waterway meets the St. Johns River. Photo by Dale K. Bulock

The two sister corporations make up one of the largest shipyard concerns in Florida and are known throughout the industry for their quality workmanship and state-of-the-art repair and construction technology.

Located on the St. Johns River just two miles from the ocean, Atlantic Marine and Atlantic Dry Dock have undergone tremendous expansion during recent years—with sales volume today topping $60 million, a sixfold increase over a decade ago. Both companies are governed under the same management team, headed by George W. Gibbs III, who founded Atlantic Marine, Inc., in 1964.

Gibbs, whose family has a long history in the shipyard business in Jacksonville, began the business at the site of a small marina not long after attending Georgia Tech. During its early years the company primarily built fishing and shrimp boats, and other relatively small vessels such as tugboats.

Two years after opening Atlantic Marine, Gibbs opened Atlantic Dry Dock on adjacent land to repair seagoing vessels. Both businesses underwent extensive growth during the 1970s as both the commercial business and the Navy business from the nearby Mayport Naval Base grew.

In the early 1970s Atlantic Marine opened its Mayport Division on base to repair huge naval vessels such as aircraft carriers and frigates on site. The Mayport service facility has grown to become a leader in the rapid turnaround of vital equipment on the Navy's complex combatant ships.

Major growth was made possible at Atlantic Marine and Atlantic Dry Dock in the 1980s by numerous improvements and additions to the facilities. To allow the handling of larger vessels, the pier was lengthened, water depth was increased at berthing areas, new construction launchways were built, and a 4,000-ton dry dock was constructed.

Today the 36-acre waterfront site includes 735 feet of continuous bulkhead; a 455-foot pier; the 4,000-ton dry dock and marine railway; another 1,500-ton railway; complete shops for

The USS Perry *was the first of many frigates that have docked for repairs at Atlantic Dry Dock.*

carpentry, rigging, paint, and labor, and steel crafts; a full-service machine shop; numerous cranes with up to 150-ton capacity; and a modern administration building.

Together the companies have an average employment of more than 500, with peak employment sometimes reaching as high as 800. Workers have special expertise in such fields as welding, shipfitting, pipe fitting, electronics, mechanics, carpentry, rigging, sandblasting, and others.

Gibbs serves as chairman of the board of both firms and president of Atlantic Dry Dock. Edward P. Doherty serves as president of Atlantic Marine, Inc.

Throughout the years Atlantic Marine has built more than 200 vessels, which have been sold to individuals and organizations worldwide. Today the company has the capacity to build ships up to 400 feet in length.

The construction of passenger vehicle ferries is a major part of the firm's market. Atlantic Marine ferries transport millions of passengers and vehicles across waterways each year in such locales as Maine, Virginia, Florida, and the Virgin Islands.

Always at the forefront of innovation, Atlantic Marine acquired the exclusive U.S. license to build the "Rolls-Royce" of passenger ferries, the Swedish Marinjet Catamaran. Popularly used in Europe, Marinjets are high-speed, low-weight craft that are also used for fire fighting, rescue, and patrol, as well as passenger transportation.

Shrimp, scallop, and crab trawlers, as well as other fishing boats that are built at the Jacksonville company sail the seas of the world in search of their catch. Atlantic Marine-produced research boats travel the oceans in search of another bounty: scientific information. Such vessels as the *Seward Johnson*, built for the Harbor Branch Foundation in Fort Pierce, Florida, have earned a reputation as some of the finest in the world.

Perhaps the most unusual vessels produced by Atlantic Marine are the *Freedom Star* and the *Liberty Star*, which are used in the recovery of space shuttle booster rockets after launches at Cape Canaveral.

In both its original construction and repair work, Atlantic Marine and Atlantic Dry Dock are known for getting the job done on, or ahead of, schedule.

On the local scene Atlantic Marine is heavily involved in community activities and is a supporter of numerous business, civic, military, and charitable service organizations, including the Greater Jacksonville USO Council, the Navy Relief Society, the Florida Theatre, the Jacksonville Symphony, the YMCA, St. Luke's Hospital, Baptist Medical Center, Jacksonville University, and the Propeller Club.

The Liberty Star, *built by Atlantic Marine, is used to recover space shuttle booster rockets after launches at Cape Canaveral.*

MAZDA MOTOR OF AMERICA, INC.

What began in 1970 as a small automobile distributorship employing only 22 people has grown to become a billion-dollar-per-year business with a major investment in Jacksonville.

Mazda Motor of America, Inc., today maintains a Southeast Regional headquarters, which for 1988 will have brought in 66,000 cars through the Port of Jacksonville, led by sales of the popular Mazda 323 and Mazda 626.

Known for their high quality and craftsmanship, the full line of Mazda automobiles and trucks is shipped directly to the Port of Jacksonville from Mazda factories in Japan, with the exception of the sporty Mazda MX-6, which is built in Flat Rock, Michigan. The automobiles are distributed to more than 126 Mazda dealers in seven states. Jacksonville cars and trucks are shipped as far away as West Virginia; another port in the North serves the Northeast.

The fourth-largest automobile manufacturer in Japan, Mazda began shipping its cars to Jacksonville in 1970, when Mazda Motors of Florida, Inc., opened a small distributorship on Phillips Highway, originally serving 14 dealers. Ownership of the venture changed a few times during those first years; however, the company weathered the recession, and Mazda Motors of America (East) Inc. was born February 1975 as a distributor-importer. (In July

Mazda Southeast Region, located in the Deerwood Center office park, imports and distributes more than 66,000 cars and trucks each year.

1988 the company became part of Mazda Motor of America, Inc., a new company consolidating into one of the import, distribution, and technical facilities in the United States.)

In the spring of 1977 the economy

Mazda GLC was introduced, followed closely by the first RX-7 sports car, and the popularity of Mazda automobiles in the United States exploded.

One of the original tenants of the Deerwood Center office park, the company purchased a 10-acre site in 1974 and erected an administrative building, large warehouse, and service training center.

An expanded new headquarters building opened in early 1987 at the same site, containing more than 250,000 square feet of floor space. The centerpiece of the modern structure is a unique, high-ceilinged interior atrium, often used to showcase new automobiles. The headquarters building also houses a 350-seat auditorium, a large computer center, 11 conference rooms, and a full fitness center. The executive suite includes a 32-seat boardroom with full audiovisual capabilities and a separate hospitality room.

A quality-assurance laboratory uses state-of-the-art equipment to test every aspect of randomly selected new imports to ensure that Mazda's high

New autos are showcased in the unique interior atrium.

standards of quality are met.

The entire rear portion of the building houses the primary parts warehouse for the southeastern United States. The warehouse services seven states in that area with every type of current Mazda part made. Another warehouse contains slow-moving parts.

At the Port of Jacksonville, a Mazda facility cleans automobiles of a special covering used to protect them on their long sea voyage. Some equipment, such as stripes or air-conditioning, may be installed at the port.

Led by William D. Goetze, southeast regional manager, Mazda works in concert with five other regions throughout the United States to execute corporate strategy.

As part of Mazda's long-term promotional plan and community involvement program, the company has become heavily involved in supporting major amateur and professional sporting events. In Jacksonville, Mazda sponsors two of the city's biggest ath-

The dynomometer room in the quality-assurance area.

letic events of the year—the Mazda Gator Bowl and Mazda Seniors Tournament Players Championship.

The Mazda Gator Bowl, held New Year's night, is perennially one of the great college football games of the season, and is televised to a national market. Mazda Gator Bowl activities last for more than a month and encompass such events as a basketball tournament, a junior tennis tournament, a 5,000-

meter run, yachting, and a parade. Of more lasting importance are the $5,000 scholarships Mazda presents to the schools in the name of a player on each team.

The Mazda Seniors Tournament Players Championship in nearby Ponte Vedra is a nationally televised event that brings many of the legends of the game together in a battle where experience can create classic golf. Nationally, Mazda sponsors a number of other professional golf events.

Through the years Mazda also has been heavily involved in major league automobile racing competition. Mazda has won eight straight IMSA Grand Touring Under-Three-Liter Class championships with the Mazda RX-7 sports car.

In addition to the sports arena, Mazda has been a leader in community involvement in its work with a number of charitable organizations and social agencies. The Mazda Course on driving under the influence of alcohol or drugs won a president's commendation and a national award from the nation's police chiefs. It is now on its way to becoming the most successful program of its kind in the nation's schools.

The warehouse services seven states in the southeastern United States with every type of current Mazda part.

HUNTLEY'S JIFFY STORES, INC.

Huntley's Jiffy Stores, Inc., a privately owned corporation, is one of the largest convenience store chains in the country. The company is managed by brothers Louis and Bill Huntley, president and secretary/treasurer, respectively. What began as a small family business, opening its first store in 1966, has grown to 325 stores in Florida and South Georgia with sales surpassing $200 million a year.

Huntley's Jiffy's mission, to provide high-demand products and services to its customers, has resulted in many additions to the company. Starting with the introduction of self-service gasoline in the mid-1970s, the firm has added game machines, on-premise fresh food service, video movie rentals, FleetShare, and, recently, the Florida Lottery. The company constantly tests and evaluates new products and services while recognizing the limitations of the business. Convenience means quick service—like the name "Jiffy"— and the goal is to offer fast, friendly service to its customers.

Huntley's Jiffy is appreciative of their success and demonstrates this by participating in numerous civic and charitable events and organizations— many of them youth oriented. Through employee activities and store promotions the firm raises funds for youth charities, such as Rodeheaver Boy's Ranch in Palatka, Youth Estate in Brunswick, and Children's Haven in Orange Park. Huntley Jiffy has also been a charter supporter of Safe Place throughout the state and the annual Just Say No campaign.

Attracting and retaining quality employees is one of the biggest challenges facing the company, and the industry, today and in the future. Huntley Jiffy offers its employees opportunities to grow personally and professionally through various programs such as management training and tuition assistance. Huntley Jiffy conducts training in safety and security in order to provide a safer, more secure environment for its customers and employees. The firm provides good benefits to employees and rewards service with part-ownership in the company through

its Employee Stock Ownership Plan. Huntley Jiffy's Mission Statement assures a productive environment for its employees through fair and equal treatment.

The company's strategic goals are to maintain market share, to strive for market domination, to enter new markets by acquisition, and to seek out appropriate vertical integration opportunities. Its active Real Estate and Development Department has structured site criteria and acquisition methods using studies compiled on each location, including market demographics, traffic studies, customer spotting, and computer modeling to ensure it acquires only the best-possible locations. The firm's Construction and Site Prep-

W.T. Huntley, Ward Huntley, and Louis L. Huntley were present for the grand opening of the Huntley Jiffy store at U.S. 1 and Sunbeam Road, Jacksonville. It is one of the largest convenience store chains in the country with 20 to 30 new facilities added every year.

aration Division is kept busy building 20 to 30 new stores a year, with about the same number of jobs remodeling existing stores, to meet current and future customer needs.

The Huntleys, the management team, and the firm's 2,200-plus employees look forward to the future growth of the company. Plans are under way for a new headquarters building. An electronic-store-reporting system is in the implementation stage. Innovative marketing plans are continuing— to provide high-demand products and services to the customers. Through a structured Business Plan, long-range goals have been developed to ensure continued growth.

Attracting and retaining quality employees is important to Huntley's Jiffy, and growth opportunities are offered through training programs for new store managers as shown here.

BRADBURY SUITES HOTEL

A stay at the Bradbury Suites Hotel provides a uniquely memorable experience, from the European-style bed and breakfast ambience to the unforgettable theme suites.

Designed to create a homey, comfortable atmosphere for corporate travelers, Bradbury Suites offers its visitors a generous array of complimentary amenities found at few hotels.

Among free services of the establishment are a breakfast buffet each morning, an after-work cocktail hour each evening, transportation to city restaurants, evening movies, *USA Today* newspapers, and access to a comfort chest stocked full of toiletries, work materials, and other necessities. Three meeting rooms with a total capacity of 75 are available for use free of charge to business groups staying at the hotel. After work, guests can enjoy the facility's large swimming pool and fully equipped exercise suite.

"We offer an alternative to business travelers from the dull, drab routine of regular hotels," says Sharon Whipple, manager of the Baymeadows establishment since it opened in June 1987. "We've taken a European tradition and made it part of our experience. During our breakfasts and cocktail hours, our guests can relax and get to

The Bradbury Suites Hotel offers its guests complimentary amenities such as a lavish breakfast buffet each morning or an after-work cocktail hour every evening.

know each other, something that so often is lost in larger hotels. We pride ourselves on our amenities."

Each of the hostelry's 114 tastefully decorated suites includes a separate living room and bedroom, a large desk, two telephones, and the unconventional extra of a second television set in the bathroom.

Despite the large suites and ample amenity package, Bradbury Suites is a mid-price hotel, offering considerably lower rates than other suite hotels. "There is a part of corporate America that doesn't want to pay $90 to $100 a night, but does want the extra room and extra amenities that go with suite products," Whipple explains. "That is who our hotel is directed toward."

Employees undergo an intensive two-week training program in which cleanliness, friendliness, and professional efficiency are stressed. "Our employees are taught to take care of our guests' every want. When our guests ask for something, we want the answer from our employee to be 'I can do that',"

Whipple says of the hotel's staff of 30.

Located at 8277 Western Way, off Baymeadows Road, the Jacksonville facility is Bradbury's only presence in Florida. Nine other Bradbury Suites operate in the Southeast and Midwest.

Owned by the Hillmark Corporation, which is headquartered in Atlanta, Bradbury Suites may be best known for its specialty theme suites. The Jacksonville Bradbury has nine theme suites, each distinctively—and in some cases lavishly—decorated around a specific motif. They are especially popular for honeymoons and with local weekend business.

"Out of Africa" features a rhino's head on the wall, bamboo wallpaper, mosquito netting around the bed, and other decorations reminiscent of the bush. The "5,000 B.C." characterizes a cavelike dwelling of prehistoric times. For a reminder of the not-so-distant past, the "Hollywood Cafe" is a step back into the 1950s, complete with a jukebox, soda-fountain stools, and art deco decor.

Other theme rooms include "Safe Harbor" with a nautical motif, the beachy "Surf's Up," the oriental "Pagoda Suite," and the rustic "Mountainside."

All theme suites include a refrigerator and wet bar in addition to standard suite features, and cost $10 more per night. Specially deodorized nonsmoking suites are also available.

The Jacksonville Bradbury has nine theme suites such as this unique "Out of Africa" motif, complete with a rhino's head on the wall.

JACKSONVILLE MARRIOTT

From the moment you alight from your car under the theatrically lit porte cochere and are guided through the French doors of the entryway by a friendly doorman, it is apparent that the Jacksonville Marriott is something special.

Located adjacent to the rapidly growing Southpoint office park off I-95 in Jacksonville's Southside, the 256-room hotel is specifically tailored to meet the needs of the corporate traveler. Among executive extras that the Jacksonville Marriott introduced to the local market are two telephone lines into each guest room, along with a full-size desk.

The Marriott also offers complete recreation and physical fitness facilities for visiting business persons, including whirlpool, sauna, and exercise room.

The brass ceiling and theatrical lighting of the Marriott's porte cochere make a memorable impression.

The hotel is the only one in Jacksonville that boasts both an indoor and outdoor pool.

The guest rooms and the hotel's 10,000 square feet of meeting and banquet space exude a kind of homey elegance, designed to make business travelers feel comfortable in their home away from home.

"We did a lot with accessories to give that residential feeling—such as skirted table coverings and throw pillows on the couches," says Nancy Nodler, the Houston-based interior designer who developed the hotel's interiors. "The furnishings are a transitional mix to appeal to all tastes. There are

contemporary, oriental, and antique pieces mixed in. It's decorated the way you would decorate a home—with pieces collected over time. That gives the hotel more character."

Particularly appealing are three smaller boardrooms, two of which have adjoining sitting rooms. A fireplace, built-in bookcases, and lovely antique furniture adorn the sitting rooms, making them attractive for a variety of uses from executive board meetings to wedding rehearsal dinners. Both sitting rooms overlook the garden pool terrace.

The Southpoint Ballroom can accommodate up to 500 guests for banquets, or can seat 800 people theater-style. The ballroom also can be divided into four completely private rooms. Groups ranging from insurance salesmen to cloggers to chamber of commerce members have made use of the Marriott's convention facilities. The hotel's staff tries to make each meeting an individual and memorable experience.

"We try to be unique," says Timothy Brennan, a Marriott Corporation executive for more than 15 years and the Jacksonville Marriott's general manager since its opening in October 1986. "For a meeting of Prudential Insurance Co.'s top salesmen we built a general store and our staff dressed in overalls to do something different on their coffee breaks. We wanted something to break up the monotony of the meetings and something that our guests would remember." The hotel's catering staff will plan theme parties, receptions, or banquets for daytime meetings or evening functions. An in-house audiovisual service is also available to complement company presentations.

The 144-seat Banyans restaurant is as pleasing to the taste buds as it is to the eye. As bright and airy as it is for breakfast, Banyans transforms to an elegant dining room at dinnertime. Full breakfast and lunch buffets are served, as well as a complete array of menu selections. The artwork of a variety of southern artists decorates the walls of the restaurant.

At cocktail time Beau's is a pop-

Guests often enjoy poolside dining. The Marriott is Jacksonville's only hotel to have both an outdoor and indoor pool.

The maître d'hôtel checks the table settings in the elegant Southpoint Ballroom, which accommodates up to 600 guests for banquets.

ular stop for hotel patrons and the after-work Southpoint business crowd alike. The contemporary, Florida-style lounge comes alive with dancing later in the evening, when a disc jockey spins the latest hits.

A poolside bar is open on weekends for guest convenience. The pool's multilevel deck is a popular spot for casual, outdoor dining, and buffets are often set up for business groups.

Adjacent to the large outdoor pool is a Grecian-style, heated indoor pool and whirlpool. For golf and tennis enthusiasts, playing privileges are available at nearby clubs. Inside, a well-stocked gift shop is open during daytime and evening hours for guest convenience.

The location of the hotel, at the Southpoint office park at J. Turner Butler Boulevard, is approximately midway between downtown Jacksonville and the beaches. "We believe we have a perfect location because we're in the midst of the most active business growth in the city and we're not far from downtown either," Brennan explains. "We get some tourists, but the bulk of our guests are business travelers."

The Marriott Corporation operates more than 175 hotels throughout the world, and the Jacksonville Marriott is a slightly smaller, scaled-down version of most of the other hotels in the Marriott group. States Brennan, "We have more amenities in this hotel than in any other 250-room hotel you'll find."

PATRONS

The following individuals, companies, and organizations have made a valuable commitment to the quality of this publication. Windsor Publications and the Jacksonville Chamber of Commerce gratefully acknowledge their participation in *Jacksonville and Florida's First Coast.*

Allied-Signal Aerospace Company*
Amelia Island Plantation*
Robert M. Angas Associates*
Anheuser-Busch, Inc.*
AT&T American Transtech*
Atlantic Marine, Inc.*
Auchter Company*
Baptist Medical Center*
Barnett Bank of Jacksonville, N.A.*
BFGoodrich Co.*
Blue Cross and Blue Shield of Florida*
Bradbury Suites Hotel*
Burger King®
    (Southern Industrial Corporation)*
Byron Harless, Reid & Associates*
Castleton Beverage Corp. (Bacardi)*
Commander Legler Werber Dawes Sadler
    & Howell*

Continental Cablevision of Jacksonville*
Coopers & Lybrand*
Walter Dickinson Inc.*
Excel Industries of Florida, Inc.*
First Union National Bank*
Florida Asphalt Contracting Inc.*
Florida National Bank*
Hidden Hills Golf and Country Club*
Huntley's Jiffy Stores, Inc.*
Independent Life*
Jacksonville Marriott*
Jacksonville University*
KBJ Architects Inc.*
Law Engineering*
McIver Urological Clinic*
Mathews, Osborne, McNatt & Cobb*
Maxwell House Coffee Company*
Mazda Motor of America, Inc.*
Memorial Medical Center*
Methodist Hospital*
Miller Electric Company*
Nassau County Committee of 100*
Paxson Electric Company*
Peat Marwick*
Peoples Gas System*
Prudential Insurance Co.*

Ring Power Corporation*
Rogers, Towers, Bailey, Jones & Gay*
St. Joe Paper Company*
St. Luke's Hospital*
St. Vincent's Medical Center*
Sally Industries, Inc.*
SCM Glidco Organics*
Scott-McRae Group*
Seminole Kraft Corporation*
Sheraton at St. Johns Place*
Smith & Hulsey*
Summerhomes Incorporated*
University Hospital*
Vistakon, Inc.*
WAIV-WOKV*
Watson Realty Corp., Realtors®*
WJKS-TV*
WJXT-TV*

* Corporate Profiles of *Jacksonville and Florida's First Coast.* The histories of these companies and organizations appear in "Part Two: First Coast Enterprises," beginning on page 205.

BIBLIOGRAPHY

Aikin, Edward N. *Flagler: Rockefeller Partner And Florida Baron.* Kent, Ohio: Kent State University Press, 1988.

Boyer, Richard, and David Savageau. *Places Rated Almanac.* Chicago: Rand McNally, 1981.

Boyer, Richard, and David Savageau. *Places Rated Almanac.* Chicago: Rand McNally, 1985.

Davis, T. Frederick. *History Of Jacksonville, Florida And Vicinity, 1513 To 1924.* St. Augustine, Fla.: The Record Co., 1925.

Graff, Mary B. *Mandarin On The St. Johns.* Gainesville, Fla.: University of Florida Press, 1953.

Gill, Joan E., and Beth R. Read, editors. *Born of the Sun: The Official Florida Bicentennial Commemorative Book.* Hollywood, Florida: Worth International Communications Corporation, 1976.

Hagstrom, Jerry, and Neal R. Peirce. *The Book Of America: Inside Fifty States Today.* New York: Warner Books, 1984.

Judge, Joseph. "Exploring Our Forgotten Century." *National Geographic* (March 1988).

Koehl, Elaine B. *The Ponte Vedra Club: The First Fifty-Five Years.* Ponte Vedra, Fla.: The Inn at Ponte Vedra, 1982.

Lanier, Sidney. *Florida: Its Scenery, Climate and History.* A Facsimile Reproduction of the 1875 Edition with Introduction and Index by Jerrell H. Shofner. Gainesville: University of Florida Press, 1973.

Laudonniere, Rene. *Three Voyages.* Translated by Charles E. Bennett. Gainesville, Fla.: University of Florida Press, 1975.

Martin, Richard A. *A Century of Service: St. Luke's Hospital, 1873-1973.* Jacksonville: St. Luke's Hospital Board of Directors, 1973.

Martin, Richard A., and Daniel L. Schafer. *Jacksonville's Ordeal By Fire: A Civil War History.* Jacksonville: Florida Publishing Co., 1984.

Morison, Samuel Eliot. *The Oxford History Of The American People.* New York: Oxford University Press, 1965.

Mueller, Edward A. *St. Johns River Steamboats.* Jacksonville: Edward A. Mueller, 1986.

Rogin, Michael Paul. *Fathers & Children: Andrew Jackson And The Subjugation Of The American Indian.* New York: Alfred A. Knopf, 1975.

Sandburg, Carl. *Abraham Lincoln: The Prairie Years And The War Years.* New York: Harcourt, Brace and Company.

Smith, Bradley. *The U.S.A.: A History In Art.* Garden City, N.Y.: Doubleday & Company, Inc., 1982.

Smith, Page. *The Shaping Of America: A People's History Of The Young Republic.* New York: McGraw Hill, 1980.

Top 25 Lists. Jacksonville: *The Jacksonville Business Journal,* 1986 and 1987.

Ward, James Robertson. *Old Hickory's Town: An Illustrated History Of Jacksonville.* Jacksonville: Old Hickory's Town Inc., 1985.

Additional Sources:
Jacksonville Chamber of Commerce Research Department
The Florida Times-Union
The *Jacksonville Journal*
Jacksonville Business Journal
Jacksonville Magazine
Jacksonville Today Magazine
North Florida Golf Journal
The *St. Augustine Record*

INDEX

Dear Char & Tim,

All the hassles of changing jobs, moving, etc. are worth it when you're able to make a few good friends – we're glad we met you!

Love,
Elaine & Phil

Dear Char & Tim,

Sometimes we think we have plenty of time to get to know people. Then, zap! The unexpected happens and they move before the good times really roll. I'm sorry we didn't have more time together, but I'm glad for what we did have. I wish you the best & know that lots of exciting experiences await you. Good luck & enjoy the cold weather.

Sally & Dave